Financial Development, Economic Crises and Emerging Market Economies

Recurrent crisis in emerging markets and advanced economies in the last few decades has cast doubt on the ability of financial liberalization to meet the aims of sustainable economic growth and development. The increasing importance of financial markets and financial efficiency principles over economic decisions and policies since the 1980s laid down the conditions of the development process of emerging market economies.

Drawing heavily on the tumultuous crises of the 1990s and 2000s, *Financial Development, Economic Crises and Emerging Market Economies* argues that those experiences can shed light on such a crucial issue and lead economic theory and policy to overcome the blindness of efficient free market doctrine to economic catastrophes. This book focuses on the weaknesses and irrelevance of financialized economic structures and discusses the implications of the ongoing global crisis with regard to the financial prerequisites of a sustainable growth and global stability.

Different critical perspectives and case studies presented in this book develop arguments against financialization and market fundamentalism, which are regarded as the main pitfalls in the process of growth and development. Chapters give sound support for alternative economic and financial policies that would be able to lead banking and financial systems to accompany collectively manageable economic development. This book will be of great interest to those who study political economy, development economics and monetary economics.

Faruk Ülgen is Associate Professor, Grenoble Faculty of Economics, Director of the Department of International Relations and Conventions, and Head of the Department of Economics of the Branch Campus of Valence of the University Grenoble Alpes, France.

Routledge Critical Studies in Finance and Stability

Edited by Jan Toporowski
School of Oriental and African Studies, University of London, UK

The 2007–2008 Banking Crash has induced a major and wide-ranging discussion on the subject of financial (in)stability and a need to re-evaluate theory and policy. The response of policy-makers to the crisis has been to refocus fiscal and monetary policy on financial stabilization and reconstruction. However, this has been done with only vague ideas of bank recapitalization and 'Keynesian' reflation aroused by the exigencies of the crisis, rather than the application of any systematic theory or theories of financial instability.

Routledge Critical Studies in Finance and Stability covers a range of issues in the area of finance including instability, systemic failure, financial macro-economics in the vein of Hyman P. Minsky, Ben Bernanke and Mark Gertler, central bank operations, financial regulation, developing countries and financial crises, new portfolio theory and New International Monetary and Financial Architecture.

For a full list of titles in this series, please visit www.routledge.com/series/RCSFS

Financial Development, Economic Crises and Emerging Market Economies

Edited by Faruk Ülgen

Routledge
Taylor & Francis Group

LONDON AND NEW YORK

First published 2017
by Routledge

2 Park Square, Milton Park, Abingdon, Oxfordshire OX14 4RN
711 Third Avenue, New York, NY 10017

Routledge is an imprint of the Taylor & Francis Group, an informa business

First issued in paperback 2018

British Library Cataloguing in Publication Data
A catalogue record for this book is available from the British Library.

Library of Congress Cataloging-in-Publication Data
Names: Ülgen, Faruk, 1963–editor.
Title: Financial development, economic crises and emerging market
economies / edited by Faruk Ülgen.
Description: 1 Edition. | New York: Routledge, 2016.
Identifiers: LCCN 2016014249 | ISBN 9781138123755 (hardback) |
ISBN 9781315648644 (ebook)
Subjects: LCSH: Finance—Developing countries. | Financial institutions—
Law and legislation. | Global Financial Crisis, 2008–2009.
Classification: LCC HG195.F56 2016 | DDC 332.109172/4—dc23
LC record available at https://lccn.loc.gov/2016014249

ISBN: 978-1-138-12375-5 (hbk)
ISBN: 978-1-138-61138-2 (pbk)

Typeset in Times New Roman
by Keystroke, Neville Lodge, Tettenhall, Wolverhampton

Contents

Figures

Tables

Contributors

Philip Arestis is Professor of Economics, Department of Land Economy, University of Cambridge, and University of the Basque Country (UPV/EHU), Spain.
pa267@cam.ac.uk

Joaquín Arriola is Associate Professor of Political Economy, University of the Basque Country (UPV/EHU), Spain.
joaquin.arriola@ehu.es

Ozan Bakis is Associate Professor of Economics, Bahçeşehir University Economic and Social Research Center (BETAM), Istanbul, Turkey.
ozanbakis@gmail.com

Paul Borghaerts is an independent historical researcher, the Netherlands.
pdata@borghaerts.nl

Aboubakar Sidiki Cisse is Professor of Economics and Head of the Department of Education Program at the Institute of Territorial Development, University of Bamako, Mali; and Professional in Charge of Regional Market, Department of Regional Market, Trade, Competition and Cooperation, Commission of West African Economic and Monetary Union (WAEMU), Ouagadougou, Burkina Faso.
c.aboubakar@gmail.com

Eugenia Correa is Professor of Economics, Universidad Nacional Autónoma de México (UNAM), Mexico.
eugenia.correa.vazquez@gmail.com

James K. Galbraith is Lloyd M. Bentsen Jr. Chair in Government/Business Relations and Professor of Government, Lyndon B. Johnson School of Public Affairs, University of Texas at Austin, USA.
galbraith@grandecom.net

Shazia Ghani is Team Lead, Prime Minister's Performance Delivery Unit, Prime Minister's Office, Islamabad, Pakistan.
shaziaghani@gmail.com

Alicia Girón is Professor of Economics, Universidad Nacional Autónoma de México (UNAM), Mexico.
alicia@unam.mx

Fatih Karanfil is Associate Professor of Economics, EconomiX–CNRS, Université Paris Ouest, Nanterre La Défense, France, and Galatasaray University Economic Research Center (GIAM), Istanbul, Turkey.
fkaranfil@u-paris10.fr

Merijn Knibbe is Professor of Economics, Van Hall Larenstein University of Applied Sciences, the Netherlands.
merijn.knibbe@hvhl.nl

Yan Liang is Associate Professor of Economics, Department of Economics, Willamette University, Salem, Oregon, USA.
liangy@willamette.edu

Nadezhda N. Pokrovskaia is Professor of International Management, Saint Petersburg State University of Economics (SPbSUE) and Vice-Director of the International School of Economics and Politics (ISEP), SPbSUE, Russia.
nnp@bk.ru

Sezgin Polat is Associate Professor of Economics, Galatasaray University, and Galatasaray University Economic Research Center (GIAM), Istanbul, Turkey.
sezginpolat@gmail.com

Sergio Rossi is Professor of Economics, University of Fribourg, Switzerland.
sergio.rossi@unifr.ch

Pierre Salama is Professor Emeritus, Université Paris 13, and Director of Research at Maison des Sciences de l'Homme (MSH), Paris, France, where he is co-responsible for the BRICS Research Seminar Series.
pierresalama@gmail.com

Malcolm Sawyer is Professor of Economics, Economics Division, Leeds University Business School, UK.
M.C.Sawyer@lubs.leeds.ac.uk

Faruk Ülgen is Associate Professor of Economics, Grenoble Faculty of Economics, Director of the Department of International Relations and Conventions, Head of the Department of Economics of the Branch Campus of Valence and member of the Centre de Recherche en Economie de Grenoble (CREG), University Grenoble Alpes, France.
faruk.ulgen@univ-grenoble-alpes.fr

Foreword

James K. Galbraith

What has been the role of the financial sector in the recent debacle of the world economy? Is it the fundamental driving force behind the collapse and the ensuing stagnation? Or is it merely a reflection of deeper realities, a window into the world of technological change, globalization, resource shortages, climate change and conflict? This type of question cannot be answered definitively by scientific method; it has some of the metaphysical characteristics of the mind–body problem or the question of the existence of God.

Finance is of course intertwined with and affected by deeper realities. Yet financial institutions are also themselves institutions. They have specific interactions with law and contract. They create and direct economic and political activity for good or ill. They absorb resources and they dominate the upper reaches of the personal income distribution. For all of these reasons, finance is worth far more attention from students of economic systems than typically it gets from the economics profession.

Indeed, a noted feature of the so-called mainstream approach to economic modelling is that banks play no role at all. In these models the entire economic system is represented as the interaction between producers and consumers, as well as between savers and investors. The institutions that clear the transactions and make the loans are depicted as passive artefacts rather than active players in this scheme of things. No doubt the "Masters of the Universe" would be surprised by this characterization, however convenient they might find it when the Senate Permanent Subcommittee on Investigations comes round.

The chapters that make up this book address themselves to the economics of financialization on its own terms. They provide a wide-ranging review of previous work by economists in the Minsky tradition, and a survey of views from around the world. A fascinating chapter details the experience of a part of sixteenth-century Holland, Friesland, where banks did not exist. Useful chapters on Turkey, Brazil, Russia and China round out the volume.

I recommend this work to those who believe – as I do – that the power of finance is excessive and dangerous.

James K. Galbraith
Austin, Texas
26 March 2016

Introduction

Financial development

The sword of Damocles hanging over the process of economic development

Faruk Ülgen

After several painful crises in emerging market economies (EMEs) and in some smaller advanced economies in the 1990s, it took a systemic crisis in the heart of global capitalism, the United States economy, for economists finally to recognize (although timidly) the need for questioning their belief in the spontaneous efficient working of free markets and then to ask, "What's going to save financialized market economies and put capitalist finance on a right path?" Old and forgotten critics came back, through Minsky-like analyses and renewed words, like institutional consistency and macro-prudential regulation, gave old debates new clothes. Indeed, 30 years after the publication of Carlos Diaz-Alejandro's article – "Goodbye financial repression, hello financial crash" – the balance sheet of financial reforms seems rather negative. Recurrent crises in major EMEs but also in most advanced economies in the last decades and the persistence of poverty all around the world cast doubt on the aptness of a financially liberalized environment to give economies relevant and consistent means and ways with regard to the prerequisites of sustainable economic growth and development.

The United Nations (UN) (2009) puts the emphasis on this fact in its *Rethinking Poverty. Report on the World Social Situation 2010* and states that trade liberalization, financial liberalization and privatization did not result in the expected positive outcomes in developing and emerging market economies. It is also noted that excessive reliance on markets and on the private sector carries high risks, especially with regard to the poverty reduction objective. The UN then argues, ten years after its 2000 Millennium Summit held in New York, that there is an "urgent need for a strategic shift away from the market fundamentalist thinking, policies and practices of recent decades towards more sustainable development and equity-oriented policies appropriate to national conditions and circumstances" (UN 2009: iv). Analyses offered in this UN report point out several critical insights on the assumed positive relationship between liberalization, openness, privatization and growth/development/welfare. Some of those pitfalls might be summarized as follows:

- Capital account liberalization does not result in any significant decline in the cost of finance. Instead, the cost of finance may behave perversely, rising sharply during economic downturns (forcing real interest rates to rise) and falling during booms (yielding low real interest rates) (UN 2009: 106).

- Financial deregulation undermines important social functions of finance and makes it less inclusive (UN 2009: 107).
- Financial deregulation destroys an important industrial policy instrument such that:

> Most late industrializing countries, at least since the twentieth century, have created well-regulated financial markets and often State controlled financial institutions designed to mobilize savings to support priority investments. They used directed credit policies and differential interest rates to support nascent industries with the potential to expand into export markets. They also created development banks with the mandate to provide long-term credit on attractive terms. These financial sector policies contributed significantly to rapid economic transformation and poverty declines in those countries.
>
> (UN 2009: 107)

- In the process of development, there is a crucial space for public economic policies, guided by strategies aiming at the collective good, especially in the financial area:

> Developing countries should therefore consider, selectively, the formulation of trade and industry policies to augment the development of new potentially viable production capacities and capabilities. Not only should financial policy in developing countries be concerned with ensuring financial stability, but it must also be counter-cyclical, developmental and inclusive. In many developing countries, this will require explicitly addressing the needs of food agriculture through rural banking and other inclusive finance initiatives. Governments should consider reintroducing specialized development banks, especially to promote employment-intensive small and medium-sized enterprises and agriculture. This may involve directed and subsidized credit as well as other proactive financial policy initiatives.
>
> (UN 2009: 111)

- Privatization is not the panacea for better and durable employment:

> Employment in State-owned enterprises may represent a better way of providing social security than social security payments themselves from the point of view of self-esteem, learning by doing and reciprocal obligations. Privatization must not ignore employment conditions and likely job losses, as they affect poverty, especially of the working poor. There should be adequate protection of employment conditions as well as active labour-market programmes in place. Similarly, provision of utilities must remain inclusive regardless of ownership. Public utilities,

if privatized, must stipulate mandatory adequate service provisions to disadvantaged groups and areas.

(UN 2009: 113)

The World Bank (2005: 163) also accepts that deregulation and privatization might have been pushed too far in some countries and some sectors.

• Economic and financial liberalization may result, even in the long term, in poverty and worsening of the conditions of life of populations (UN 2009: 102). On this last point, the World Bank notes that:

> The distributive effects of trade liberalization are diverse, and not always pro-poor. Trade reforms were expected to increase the incomes of the unskilled in countries with a comparative advantage in producing unskilled-intensive goods. Yet evidence from the 1990s suggests that even in instances where trade policy has reduced poverty, there are still distributive issues. One important policy lesson is that countries need to help workers affected move out of contracting (import-competing) sectors into expanding (exporting) sectors. This is an issue relevant to both developing and industrialized countries. . . . Global markets are the most hostile to the products produced by the world's poor – such as agricultural products and textiles and apparel. The problems of escalating tariffs, tariff peaks, and quota arrangements systematically deny the poor market access and skew the incentives against adding value in poor countries.
>
> (World Bank 2005: 132)

Indeed, there is a two-facet relationship between instabilities and wellbeing/welfare; the coin has two (interdependent) sides. Although instabilities due to financialized capitalism have aggravated poverty and inequalities, in a recent book, James Galbraith (2012) argues that inequality also triggers instability.

In a very comprehensive study on capital flows, financial development and economic welfare, a 2009 report of the Bank for International Settlements (BIS) concludes in a very precautionary way that:

> Overall, it is a combination of sound macroeconomic policies, prudent debt management, exchange rate flexibility, the effective management of the capital account, the accumulation of appropriate levels of reserves as self-insurance and the development of resilient domestic financial markets that provides the optimal response to the large and volatile capital flows to the EMEs. How these elements are best combined will depend on the country and on the period: there is no "one size fits all".
>
> (BIS 2009: 134)

Therefore, the United Nations (2009: 106) advocates: "In light of the disappointing experience, authorities should institute mechanisms to restrict large and sudden flows of short-term capital or 'hot money'". Moreover, Rodrik and Subramanian

(2008), among others, remark that the assertion of the positive effect of financial globalization and liberalization rests on the assumption that the growth and development process in developing/emerging economies is constrained by lack of savings that could be eased thanks to more foreign capital that would flow in after the liberal reforms. The authors maintain that this is a false problem since these countries are much more likely to suffer from low levels of investment that is due to low expectations of profitability and returns. From this perspective, increasing access to international capital markets and financial opening up would not have a significant positive effect on growth and development financing.

Obviously, the organization of financial systems – according to the assumption of free market efficiency held from the early 1980s in most advanced and emerging market economies – led to loosely regulated financial markets and allowed short-sighted speculative financial operations to gain ground and dominate over private economic decisions, development strategies and public policies. Numerous crises thereafter experienced in emerging and emerged economies gave rise to flourishing work on the links between financialization, growth and economic development. Several decades of observations and lessons can now be integrated into economic models to give more sophisticated and multivariable approaches to financial development with respect to growth and development issues. From three decades of recurrent crises all around the world, one could draw at least two conditions for a successful growth-enhancing financial evolution in a market-based and private-enterprise-dominated world economy: macroeconomic stability and consistent supervision. However, even after the 2007–2008 global crisis, economists do not agree on the meaning of those conditions.

On the one side, for liberal and equilibrium economists, good finance and supervision do mean market-friendly structures. For instance, the World Economic Forum (WEF) (2012: xiii) defines financial development "as the factors, policies, and institutions that lead to effective financial intermediation and markets, as well as deep and broad access to capital and financial services". In accordance with this definition, measures of financial development are captured across the seven pillars of the WEF *Financial Development Index*. The first pillar is "institutional environment" which encompasses financial sector liberalization, corporate governance, legal and regulatory issues and contract enforcement; the second is "business environment" which considers human capital, taxes, infrastructure and the costs of doing business; and the third is "financial stability" related to the risk of currency crises, systemic banking crises and sovereign debt crises.

On the other side, for institutionalists, post-Keynesian and Marxist economists, good finance and supervision must lie in collectively designed and managed public structures.

Drawing heavily on the tumultuous crises of the 1990s and 2000s, this book argues that those experiences can shed light on such a crucial issue and allow economic theory and policy to overcome the blindness of the efficient free market doctrine to economic catastrophes. It also points to new challenges to global stability in the wake of the reconfiguration of the international financial arena under the weight of major EMEs.

This book, then, maintains that the means (finance) became the aim (financial liberalization) and pushed economic development and citizens' wellbeing into the background. Such an evolution perverted economic systems and reduced the capacity of market economic decisions to bring sustainable and durable welfare to society. Furthermore, after several decades of worldwide financial liberalization, the relatively high resilience of rather interventionist and less financialized EMEs to the 2007–2008 crisis – compared with more financialized but recessionist advanced economies in the last decades – could allow us to draw some relevant implications about the required conditions and environment for a sustainable growth and development process in the world. The book then focuses on strong objective implications of the ongoing global crisis with regard to the financial prerequisites of a sustainable growth and with respect to global financial stability. The analysis of financial markets' development suggested in this book is a critical one. The standard assertion is that financial development rests on open and liberalized structures and can be defined in relation to the length, depth and liquidity of financial markets. Through an opposed stance, this book points to the weaknesses and irrelevance of such a theoretical and policy viewpoint by putting together theoretical analysis (from different critical perspectives) and case studies on different economies. Most chapters rely on approaches that develop arguments against financialization and market fundamentalism as representing the main pitfalls in the process of growth and development – especially in EMEs. Analytical developments presented, then, can be expected to give sound support for alternative economic and financial policies that would be able to lead banking and financial systems to accompany collectively manageable economic development.

The book gets started with a focus on core issues common to all economies in their respective development adventure, with regard to the relationship between financial liberalization, growth, crises and then development – lost in transition. In this vein, the first six chapters take a general conceptual stance in order to deal with the concerns related to the evolution of financial structures in market-based (advanced as well as emerging) economies regarding economic growth, systemic instability and development issues. Those chapters mainly elaborate the meaning of financial development, global financialization of economies, links between financial development and economic growth, and between financialization and instability, and offer some reform proposals. The following chapters (7–13) deal with some specific issues in different economies from a historical and theoretical perspective. These studies also examine the evolution of banking and financial systems and the rise of systemic instabilities.

With this aim, Philip Arestis, in Chapter 1, discusses the origins of the "great recession" with a specific emphasis on the distributional effects and financialization through a distinction between main factors and contributory factors. The main factors are distributional effects, financial liberalization and financial innovation. The contributory factors are international imbalances, monetary policy and the role of credit rating agencies. In discussing the origins of the current crisis, this chapter is very much aware of the limitations of current macroeconomics. Adopting a Minskian viewpoint, the chapter maintains that the "great recession" was caused by US financial liberalization attempts and the financial innovations that followed them. That was greatly helped by significant income redistribution effects from wages to profits of the financial sector. An interesting statistic on this score is also the pronounced above-average rise in the salaries of those employed in finance. Such an evolution is related to the process of deregulation that also led to further financial innovation. The analysis of the financial liberalization aspect of crises results in some economic policy implications, emphasizing recent experience with the great recession in order to point to alternative development policies.

In Chapter 2, Joaquín Arriola supplies an in-depth analysis of the origins of the new global financial and monetary configuration and identifies the main structural elements of a phase that is still not a coherent system associated with a new global productive dynamic. The emergence of a double financial and monetary circuit is analysed. On one side, there is the traditional system of international payments and credits, linked to the balance of payments flows (trade, investment, income). The hierarchy of this system is called into question by the financial and monetary initiatives of the BRICS (Brazil, Russia, India, China, South Africa). On the other side, there is a system of global financial euro-markets associated with the attempt by major financial players to break free from state regulations. The euro-markets have expanded without external control or regulation, and are the main source of financial innovation and at the same time of global economic instability. The analytical characterization of the liquidity generated by these euro-markets and their connection with the international and national economies is still incomplete, but the traits of a mutation in the nature of financial capitalism are clearly perceptible. This chapter delineates those traits and shows how emerging economies – more delinked from these global markets – perform in the medium term better than advanced economies.

Chapter 3, written by Faruk Ülgen, seeks to assess the relevance and the consistency of a liberal regulatory and institutional environment with the financial stability of market economies. Through a brief synthesis of the theoretical foundations of liberalization reforms, it studies the links between the process of financial development and the crises in emerging market economies with respect to the main lessons which could be drawn from the 2007–2008 crisis of global financialized capitalism. This ongoing crisis reveals that monetary and financial problems do not lie only in the economic fragilities that would be due to underdevelopment, but rather are due to the way in which liberalized economies work. From this perspective, this chapter maintains that financial instabilities are more the result of endogenous problems of financialized economic systems than the natural outcome of the difficulties of transition towards an efficient market economy of some emerging and developing economies.

In her analysis of financial markets' underdevelopment in some emerging market economies, Shazia Ghani seeks, in Chapter 4, to assess the underlying challenges as well as the suggested policy responses in the face of financial and economic development – long-lasting – issues. Although several EMEs remained resilient to the onslaught of the 2007 crisis, yet the state of underdeveloped financial markets and related infrastructures in majority of developing economies/ EMEs poses a serious challenge to the policy-makers. These challenges become manifold when unconventional policies pursued by the advanced economies in the post-2007 crisis are expected to be reversed in the near future. Several EMEs are already showing signs of instability and vulnerability in the form of interest rate and currency fluctuations, costs of borrowing and alarming debt levels (Turkey, South Africa, Chile, India, Indonesia, Argentina, Russia and Brazil – the fragile eight), accentuated by slower global growth, falling commodity prices and current account weaknesses. It is, therefore, judicious to analytically assess the connections between the policy choices of advanced economies and their spill-over impacts on EMEs, with a special focus on the unconventional policies in the post-crisis period that leave a narrow policy space for EMEs, while domestic financial infrastructure's development, an essential prerequisite of the develop-ment process, is not yet achieved. The focus is then put on the peculiar necessary conditions and required institutional and regulatory/supervisory frameworks to achieve stable, liquid and deeper financial markets in the EMEs.

Dealing with the same crucial issue in the evolution of capitalist economies, Malcolm Sawyer offers, in Chapter 5, a review of the recent literature on financial development and economic growth, and on financial liberalization and finan-cial crisis which indicates that the positive link between financial development and economic growth has been much reduced and perhaps broken. This then leads into a consideration of the growth of and structural changes in the financial system (which are included within the term financialization) over the past three decades and their impact on economic development (broadly conceived to go beyond economic growth). Therefore, Sawyer discusses alternative financial institutions and their role in the promotion of high-quality employment. In a number of respects, the promotion of alternative financial institutions alongside policies to constrain the operations of financial markets would amount to de-financialization.

The analytical developments above point to some proposals for radical systemic reform. From this perspective, Chapter 6 by Sergio Rossi states that the origin of the 2007–2008 financial crisis can be found in the structure of domestic payment systems, which are also used for international settlements, despite the purely accounting nature of bank money. This chapter deals with the essential principles of the necessary reform of the current international payment system and shows that only a supranational currency would guarantee national and international financial stability. Arguing first that the nature of bank money is purely scriptural, the analysis shows how the architecture of the payments system should be struc-turally reformed at the international level, to avoid problems that were the origin of the systemic financial crisis that burst out in 2007–2008 at a global level. In this regard, the emerging market economies may decide, individually or as a group, to shield themselves from the present non-system for international payments, setting up an international clearing institution in charge of issuing a supranational means of payment finality for their foreign trade. Such a system will contribute to financial stability, thereby supporting economic development in a sustainable way, and those benefits will increase employment levels across the world.

In order to give those analyses an empirical support in light of a specific past experience in terms of the monetary and financial evolution of a now-advanced economy, the Netherlands, Merijn Knibbe and Paul Borghaerts ask, in Chapter 7, a crucial question: why do banks exist? The authors show that even if the "textbook economics" states that the mission of banks is to match the supply of funds with the demand for funds, it seems that Frisians in the sixteenth to eighteenth centuries, a fully commercialized society, did not need this service. Therefore a new question arises: why not? In the entire province of Friesland, there were hardly three people calling themselves "banker", while the function of "pawn shop" was a privilege of the local orphanage of Leeuwarden. Financial functions like lending and saving were clearly part of the household economy and not of specialized institutions, as is also clear from the Frisian *"hypotheekboeken"* (mortgage books), a (voluntary) register of larger loans between households. This does change the question posed above. Banks do not exist because of intermediation required between borrowers and lenders – but because of another reason. With this aim, the *hypotheekboeken* are used, together with data from the occupational census and probate inventories, to investigate the nature of financial transactions in the Netherlands in the sixteenth to eighteenth centuries, and to ponder why this society – though very market-oriented but still a small-scale economy – did not see the need to use the services of banks. In the end, it is discussed what changed and why banks took over in order to understand the role of banks and the related financial system in economic development.

In the Chapter 8, Aboubakar Sidiki Cisse reminds us that financial development is defined as the accumulation and diversification of financial assets and institutions, improving efficiency and competition in the financial sector and increasing the access of the population to financial services. It is in this spirit that since the 1970s, financial liberalization as a means of achieving financial development has been advocated by the international financial institutions (the International Monetary Fund [IMF], the World Bank, etc.). However, the recurrence of financial instability in EMEs questions this dominant position on the relationship between financial liberalization, financial development and economic growth. The chapter then shows that if financial development has a positive impact on economic growth, the instability that may result reduces its impact on the real economy. Thus, there is a broader issue of macroeconomic stability in developing countries in general, and in the African countries of the franc zone in particular. This chapter then insists on a gradual and controlled financial liberalization in the countries of the franc zone. This is crucial to preventing the recurrent instability observed in those economies and to solving the problem of sustainable development over time.

Chapter 9 by Ozan Bakis, Fatih Karanfil and Sezgin Polat examines a specific case – the banking system behaviour in the Turkish economy – through a time-series analysis with respect to credit supply, employing both banking data and other financial variables over the period from 1990 to 2009. The chapter provides a vector error-correction (VEC) model to test for multivariate cointegration and Granger causality. More specifically, the chapter seeks to fill the gap on how the bank behaviour interacts with the financial structure given the conditions of macroeconomic policy. The results point to the existence of Granger causality between the credit–deposit ratio and maturity of time deposits which implies that depositor decisions on maturity change the composition of the balance sheet of banks leading to low credit creation. This implies that macroeconomic uncertainty and instability lead to a kind of credit contraction with the decrease of deposit maturity. The results also reveal that economic cycles are credit-driven in Turkey. The chapter then maintains that free bank/financial markets' decisions do not ensure sustained financing of the economy, and calls for specific monetary and financial policies to support economic growth and development.

In a similar critical vein, Eugenia Correa and Alicia Girón draw, in Chapter 10, on Minskian financial instability analysis to study the major characteristics of the credit expansion and its main consequences for Latin American countries. The banking sector in Latin America has operated in countries with weak economic and financial structures, especially in industrial and external sectors, prior to opening-up policies. Since the 1970s, local banks have confronted the competition of foreign financial flows and the growing demand for foreign currency. Dollarization has been the answer not only as an exchange rate policy, but also as a credit policy supported by government indebtedness and macroeconomic deflation. Other routes to local financial development were deployed when securitization and global finance arrived in Latin American countries, increasing the participation in local credit by the large foreign banks since the 1990s. In recent years, financial development has been closely linked with the main trends in global financial markets. The analysis of this chapter supports Minsky's proposal that securitization is the main force behind the transformation of global financial markets, resulting in financial crises and economic turmoil.

Chapter 11 by Pierre Salama takes the case of another large emerging market economy, Brazil, and studies the links between financialization and the labour market in Brazil, aiming to assess the real effects of financialization on economic growth and employment. In a world where financial development comes along with an increasing disparity of income, a greater casualization of jobs, an important social disaffiliation, and a tendency towards the stagnation of real wages, Brazil gets loose by its peculiarity. As in advanced economies, the share of dividends considerably increases in Brazil in the 2000s, but poverty falls, the disparities of income slightly decrease, wages increase, the ratio between formal employment and informal employment improves, unemployment decreases and deindustrialization becomes more marked. Such a situation is surprising, raising two questions: would there be a happy financialization in Brazil? And is there a relation between the financialization and the deindustrialization? The chapter shows, however, that the miracle of financialization is, most of the time, a mirage. From 2011, growth slows down strongly and the increase of real wages becomes more modest, leading to expectations of reversals to the detriment of workers. The apparently "happy" financialization (absence of negative effects on employment and wages) tends to mutate into a "dangerous" financialization similar to that in the advanced countries.

Nadezhda N. Pokrovskaia argues in Chapter 12 that the discussions on the role and functions of public regulation in the economic system directly or indirectly rest on issues related to the conditions of production of public goods and related external effects. Those issues are usually linked to the political debate on the limits of state intrusion into the natural spontaneous evolution and growth of market economies, assumed to work in an efficient way under perfect free competition and profit-seeking private agents' decisions. The chapter shows that the Russian experience points to some possible financial regulation alternatives during times of crisis. The chapter then analyses the pendulum of regulation preferences of the Russian social and economic model within the historical genesis of transitive chaos from the Soviet command planning towards the naïve liberal ideas. The Russian economy, facing a critical worldwide environment, moves back to sustainable middle-term strategic policy choices aiming at creating investment programmes and plans – even long-term projects and national industrial policies are included in the strategic papers (i.e. the National Energy Strategy) – and structural modernization of the economy (for instance, public financing directed at research and development [R&D] and stimulation of private innovations with a tax incentives policy).

In Chapter 13 (last, but not least), Yan Liang takes a Minskian approach to examine the role of shadow banks in credit expansion and the implications thereof for financial stability. Minsky's incisive analysis of "fringe banks" and an endogenous process of financial fragility is developed to shed light on China's situation. Liang documents how China has undergone two salient developments in its financial landscape since the global financial crisis erupted in 2007. First, there has been a rapid and massive growth of the shadow banking sector which has played an increasingly weighty role in credit creation. And second, debt levels, especially in the corporate sector, have risen significantly to reach an alarming level. Shadow banks have caused elevated financial risks at both the institutional and systemic levels. Liang argues that an imminent financial crisis is unlikely to occur due to the financial prowess of the traditional banks and the central government. However, it is also maintained that shadow lending and debt build-up are not inconsequential. The debt burden may push private enterprises to hold back investment and production, further slowing down the economy and, in turn, exacerbating the debt burden. Therefore, policy-makers must take shrewd and measured steps to regulate shadow banking, to carefully deleverage, to continue to rebalance the skewed demand structure, and to boost real economic growth.

The common lessons which could be drawn from these analyses might represent a simple but crucial result: the working of market-based capitalist economies does not rest on a socially optimal equilibrium-generating dynamic, but follows a somewhat adventurous and potentially hazardous uncertain evolutionary path. To reduce hazardous effects and augment the potential of success on such a path, even in an economy based on private property and individual interest, markets must be democratically and collectively organized and directed towards socially consistent objectives in order to give societies sustainable and durable development possibilities. The performance of financial systems should therefore be related to their contribution to societal-human development and not rely on short-term "return-on-investment" criteria. Of course, these things are probably easier said than done, but the first step, after several decades of ideological obsession with free market fundamentalism, might consist of taking stock of our mistakes and going ahead via objectively relevant alternatives. Our hope is that the analyses in this book might provide some positive contributions to such a human objective. We, the authors, thank the reader for her/his attention from this perspective.

References

Bank for International Settlements (BIS) (2009). *Capital Flows and Emerging Market Economies*. Committee on the Global Financial System. CGFS Paper No. 33, January 2009. Available at the permanent link: www.bis.org/publ/cgfs33.pdf (accessed on 15 March 2016).

Diaz-Alejandro, C. (1985), "Good-bye Financial Repression, Hello Financial Crash", *Journal of Development Economics*, 19(1–2): 1–24.

Galbraith, J. K. (2012). *Inequality and Instability: A Study of the World Economy Just Before the Great Crisis*. New York: Oxford University Press.

Rodrik, D. and Subramanian, A. (2008). "Why did financial globalization disappoint?" Available at www.iie.com/publications/papers/subramanian0308.pdf (accessed on 21 April 2012).

United Nations (UN) (2009). *Rethinking Poverty. Report on the World Social Situation 2010*. United Nations, Department of Economic and Social Affairs: New York.

World Bank (2005). *Economic Growth in the 1990s. Learning from a Decade of Reform*. The World Bank: Washington, DC.

World Economic Forum (WEF) (2012). *Financial Development Report*. World Economic Forum: Geneva, Switzerland.

1 Financial liberalization, crises and policy implications

Philip Arestis

Introduction

In recent contributions, Arestis and Karakitsos (2013, 2015) discuss the origins of the international financial crisis of 2007–2008 and the emergence of the 'great recession' by emphasizing the 'distributional effects' and 'financialization' as the main features of it. A distinction between main factors and contributory factors is made. The main factors contain three features: distributional effects, financial liberalization and financial innovation. The contributory factors contain three features: international imbalances, monetary policy and the role of credit rating agencies. In relation to the term 'financialization', it encapsulates the two features of the main factors, namely financial liberalization and financial innovation, since they define it for the purposes of their contribution as the process where financial leverage overrides capital (i.e. equity), and financial markets dominate over the rest of the markets in the economy. Financialization, as it has just been defined, is a broad sense of the term. In this broad sense it has been around for a long time, although the term itself, 'financialization', is of a recent origin. Kotz (2011) elaborates on this issue to show the difference in terms of financial dominance of the late nineteenth and early twentieth centuries and financialization as it is used currently. Financialization, in terms of its current usage, is defined by Epstein (2001: 1) as the term that "refers to the increasing importance of financial markets, financial motives, financial institutions, and financial elites in the operation of the economy and its governing institutions, both at the national and international levels".

In discussing the origins of the current crisis we are very much aware of the limitations of current macroeconomics. Indeed, we agree with Minsky (1982: 60), who argued that "from the perspective of the standard economic theory of Keynes's day and the presently dominant neoclassical theory, both financial crises and serious fluctuations of output and employment are anomalies: the theory offers no explanation of these phenomena" (see also Arestis 2009; Palley 2012). The 'great recession' was caused by US financial liberalization attempts and the financial innovations that followed them. That was greatly helped by significant income redistribution effects from wages to profits of the financial sector. An interesting statistic on this score is reported in Philippon and Reshef (2009) in the case of the United States. This is the pronounced above-average rise in the salaries of those employed in finance. Relative wages, the ratio of the wage bill in the financial sector to its full-time-equivalent employment share, enjoy a steep increase over the period from the mid-1980s to 2006. What explains this development is mainly financial deregulation in a causal way, followed by financial innovation. The deregulation impact accounts for 83 per cent of the change in wages. Indeed, wages in the financial sector are higher than in other sectors, even after controlling for education. A further interesting example in relation to financialization in the United States refers to the size of the financial sector as a percentage of Gross Domestic Product (GDP); it grew from 2.8 per cent in 1950 to 7.9 per cent in 2012. It is also the case that incomes in the US financial sector increased by 70 per cent relative to other sectors over the period from 1980 to 2012.[1] Similar but less pronounced financial shares are relevant in the UK, Canada, Germany and Japan, among others. In China, financial intermediary shares to GDP increased from 1.6 per cent in 1980 to 5.4 per cent in 2008 (Greenspan 2010: 15).

It is the case that ever since both developing and developed countries adopted the essentials of the financial liberalization thesis, banking crises have been unusually frequent and severe. The World Bank (1989) demonstrates the magnitude of the crises over the period – early 1980s – at least two-thirds of the International Monetary Fund (IMF) member countries experienced significant banking-sector crises. A further relevant observation is that beyond the financial costs of banking crises, not just for the local economies involved, they have exacerbated downturns in economic activity, thereby imposing substantial real economic costs (Honohan and Klingebiel 2000; see also Arestis 2004, 2005). In this chapter, we discuss further the financial liberalization aspect of crises, emphasizing two examples that led to crises (the South East Asian crisis and the August 2007 international financial crisis that led to the 'great recession'). We then turn our attention to, and discuss, the economic policy implications, emphasizing recent experience with the great recession. Finally, we summarize and conclude.

Financial liberalization

Theoretical aspects of financial liberalization

The financial sector of an economy provides real services, whereby financial instruments, markets and institutions arise to ameliorate market frictions: they can mitigate the effects of incomplete information and transaction costs. In fact, Levine (2004: 5) suggests that the financial system provides the following functions: to "produce information ex ante about possible investments and allocate capital; monitor investments and exert corporate governance after providing finance; facilitate the trading, diversification and management of risk; mobilize and pool savings; ease the exchange of goods and services". Also, Levine (2005) in his extensive review of the empirical literature concludes that:

> A growing body of empirical analyses, including firm-level studies, industry-level studies, individual country-studies, time-series studies, panel-investigations, and broad cross-country comparisons, demonstrate[s] a strong

positive link between the functioning of the financial system and long-run economic growth. While subject to ample qualifications and countervailing views noted throughout this article, the preponderance of evidence suggests that both financial intermediaries and markets matter for growth even when controlling for potential simultaneity bias. Furthermore, microeconomic-based evidence is consistent with the view that better developed financial systems ease external financing constraints facing firms, which illuminates one mechanism through which financial development influences economic growth. Theory and empirical evidence make it difficult to conclude that the financial system merely – and automatically – responds to economic activity, or that financial development is an inconsequential addendum to the process of economic growth.[2]

(Levine 2005: 921)

It is also true that more recently, further studies have accounted for other real sector variables in the relationship between finance and growth. Such variables include the pattern of countries' trade balance and changes in income distribution and poverty levels (see, for example, Beck 2012).[3]

Even so, there are studies that would argue for a weak relationship between finance and growth. Lucas (1988: 6) dismisses finance as an 'over-stressed' determinant of economic growth, while Robinson (1952) assumes a passive role for finance, with financial development simply following economic growth. At the other extreme, Miller (1998: 14) suggests that whether financial markets "contribute to economic growth is a proposition too obvious for serious discussion". The middle ground is covered by the idea that the relationship between finance and growth cannot be safely ignored without endangering our understanding of development and economic growth (Bagehot 1873; Schumpeter 1911; Gurley and Shaw 1955; Goldsmith 1969; McKinnon 1973; Shaw 1973). In this respect, the results of the study by Arestis *et al.* (2015) are relevant. Those authors conduct a meta-analysis of the existing empirical evidence on the effects of financial development on growth. They conclude that:

[O]ur meta-regression analysis shows that the type of data employed, and the different variables used to measure financial development in the literature can constitute sources of heterogeneity. Specifically, the usage of market-based proxies of financial development seems to result in lower correlations than the usage of either liquid liabilities or market-based variables. On the other hand, the estimated coefficients of bank-based measures and complex indices are found statistically insignificant in all specifications. This is robust evidence on the fact that the kind of financial variable used plays an important role. Additionally, panel data, which are frequently used from the late 1990s onwards, produce smaller correlations. The same seems to hold for time series. Furthermore, taking into [account] endogeneity and using a specific set of regressors seem to explain part of the heterogeneity. Overall, the meta-regression analysis produces evidence suggesting that the empirical literature on the finance–growth nexus is not free from publication bias. Beside this bias, however, the results suggest the existence of a statistically significant and economically meaningful positive genuine effect from financial development to economic growth.

(Arestis *et al.* 2015: 557–560)

It is also the case that other studies also question the link between finance and growth. The argument is that the finance–growth link has become weaker over time (Beck *et al.* 2013; see also Rousseau and Wachtel 2011), and the financial sector is "a drag on productivity growth" (Cecchetti and Kharroubi 2012: 14).

Interest in these matters emanates from the fact that a number of writers question the wisdom of financial repression (the practice of administering interest rates), arguing that it has detrimental effects on the real economy. On the whole, the financial liberalization literature portrays regulation and control over interest rates as suppressing savings, investment and thereby growth. More concretely, Goldsmith (1969) argued that the main problem with financial repression was its negative effect on the efficiency of capital. McKinnon (1973) and Shaw (1973) stressed two other problems: first, financial repression affects negatively the efficient allocation of savings to investment; and second, through its effect on the return to savings, it has a restraining influence on the equilibrium level of savings and investment. In this framework, therefore, investment suffers not only in quantity but also in quality terms, since bankers do not ration the available funds according to the marginal productivity of investment projects, but according to their own discretion. Under these conditions, the financial sector is likely to stagnate. The low return on bank deposits encourages savers to hold their savings in the form of unproductive assets such as land, rather than the potentially productive bank deposits. Similarly, high reserve requirements restrict the supply of bank lending even further while directed credit programmes distort the allocation of credit since political priorities are, in general, not determined by the marginal productivity of different types of capital.

The financial liberalization thesis argues for the removal of interest rate ceilings, reduction of reserve requirements and abolition of directed credit programmes. In short, liberalize financial markets and let the free market determine the allocation of credit. With the real rate of interest adjusting to its equilibrium level, low-yielding investment projects would be eliminated, so that the overall efficiency of investment would be enhanced. Also, as the real rate of interest increases, saving and the total real supply of credit increase, which induce a higher volume of investment. Economic growth would, therefore, be stimulated not only through the increased investment, but also due to an increase in the average productivity of capital. Moreover, the effects of lower reserve requirements reinforce the effects of higher saving on the supply of bank lending, while the abolition of directed credit programmes would lead to an even more efficient allocation of credit, thereby stimulating further the average productivity of capital. Again, however, we point out that these authors have failed to recognize that the core policy combinations of fixed exchange rates and external government debt are themselves inherently repressive, and that liberalizing in these circumstances, therefore, promotes instability.

Furthermore, there is literature that considers the negative effects of financial liberalization in that it creates financial instability and crisis with negative effects on economic growth, thereby creating cycles. The early experience of countries which went through financial liberalization has been reviewed in a number of studies (see, for example, Demetriades and Luintel 1996; Arestis and Demetriades 1997, 1998; Arestis 2004, 2005). Arestis and Stein (2005) pay attention to the linkages between financial liberalization and subsequent financial crisis, when they report on the relevant experience of a total of 53 countries, covering the period between 1980 and 1995, which resulted in financial and banking crises. They conclude that, "On the whole, financial Liberalization in those and other countries had a destabilizing effect on the economy and [was] abandoned" (2005: 384; see also Creel *et al.* 2014). Those experiences lead to the conclusion that what happened in the relevant economies was that financial liberalization typically unleashed a massive demand for credit by households and firms that was not offset by a comparable increase in the saving rate. Loan rates rose as households demanded more credit to finance purchases of consumer durables, and firms plunged into speculative investment in the knowledge that government bailouts would prevent bank failures. In terms of bank behaviour, banks increased deposit and lending rates to compensate for losses attributable to loan defaults. High real interest rates completely failed to increase savings or boost investment – they actually fell as a proportion of Gross National Product (GNP) over the period. The only type of savings that *did* increase was foreign savings, i.e. external debt. This, however, made the 'liberalized' economies more vulnerable to oscillations in the international economy, increasing the debt/asset ratio and thus service obligations, and promoting the debt crises experienced in the recent past. Financial liberalization thus managed to displace domestic for international markets. Long-term productive investment never materialized either. Instead, short-term specu-lative activities flourished whereby firms adopted risky financial strategies, thereby causing banking crises and economic collapse.

Despite, though, the early troublesome attempts at financial liberalization, and the increasing problems and scepticism surrounding the financial liberaliza-tion thesis over the years since its inauguration, it, nevertheless, had a relatively early impact on development policy. When events following the implement-ation of financial liberalization prescriptions did not confirm their theoretical premises, there occurred a revision of the main tenets of the thesis. Gradual financial liberalization is to be preferred. In this gradual process, a 'sequencing of financial liberalization' (for example, Edwards 1989; McKinnon 1991) is recommended. Employing credibility arguments, Calvo (1988) suggests a narrow focus of reforms with financial liberalization left as last. A further response by the proponents of the financial liberalization thesis has been to argue that where liberalization failed it was because of the existence of implicit or explicit deposit insurance coupled with inadequate banking supervision and macro-economic instability (for example, McKinnon 1988a, 1988b, 1991; World Bank

1989; Villanueva and Mirakhor 1990). These conditions were conducive to excessive risk-taking by the banks, a form of moral hazard, which can lead to 'too high' real interest rates, bankruptcies of firms and bank failures. This experience led to the introduction of new elements into the analysis of the financial liberalization thesis in the form of preconditions, which should have to be satisfied before reforms are contemplated and implemented. These include 'adequate banking supervision', aiming to ensure that banks have a well-diversified loan portfolio, 'macroeconomic stability', which refers to low and stable inflation, a sustainable fiscal deficit, and sequencing of financial reforms. It is also argued by the proponents that the authorities should move more aggressively on financial reform in good times and more slowly when borrowers' net worth is reduced by negative shocks, such as recessions and losses due to terms of trade (see also World Bank 1989). Caprio *et al.* (1994) reviewed the financial reforms in a number of primarily developing countries, with the experience of six countries studied at some depth and length. They concluded that managing the reform process rather than adopting a *laissez-faire* approach was important, and that sequencing along with the initial conditions in finance and macroeconomic stability were critical elements in successfully implementing financial reforms.

These *post hoc* theoretical revisions were thought sufficient to defend the original thesis of a disappointing empirical record. Despite all these modifications, however, there is no doubt that the proponents of the financial liberalization thesis do not even contemplate abandoning it. No amount of revision has changed the objective of the thesis, which is to pursue the *optimal* path to financial liberalization, free from any political, i.e. state, intervention. Sequencing does not salvage the financial liberalization thesis for the simple reason that it depends on the assumption that financial markets clear in a Walrasian manner while the goods markets do not. But in the presence of asymmetric information, financial markets too are marred by imperfections.

The relationship between financial liberalization and crises

The period of financial liberalization since the early 1970s has exacerbated the frequency and depth of crises. Laeven and Valencia (2012) record 346 financial crises in the period from 1970 to 2011, of which 99 were banking crises, 18 sovereign debt crises and 153 currency crises, 11 banking and debt, 28 banking and currency, 29 debt and currency, and 8 combined all three elements. A total of 25 banking crises are recorded for the period from 2007 to 2011. In what follows we concentrate on two of these crises, perhaps the most serious in terms of their impact, in an attempt to elaborate on the relationship between financial liberalization and crises. These crises, especially the recent international financial crisis of 2007–2008, have shed doubt on the previous findings of a positive impact of finance on growth.

The study by Arestis and Glickman (2002) is a good example that clarifies this relationship. It draws on the financial crisis in South East Asia (1997/1998) and focuses on the role of financial liberalization in the process. The analysis suggests that the threats to growth and employment emanating from the financial sector, which Minsky (1986) identified in the closed economy setting, are greatly intensified in open, liberalized, economies. Financial liberalization is demonstrated to be a key factor in this process. The gist of the argument is that

> financial liberalization produces an upward step-change in the intensity of the domestic drive towards financial innovation, as it sweeps away the rules and conventions which previously governed the way banks related to one another and their customers. It thereby speeds up the process by which debt ratios of commercial concerns and financial institutions rise, escalating financial fragility, and it hastens the day when banking and financial crises loom.
>
> (Arestis and Glickman 2002: 244–245)

Proponents of financial liberalization favour 'sequenced' programmes of 'free' market reforms as elaborated earlier in this chapter. But such reforms only serve to weaken the barrier of financial conservatism, which acts to contain pressures leading to fragility of the financial system. This, however, raises the feeling of invulnerability, weakening inhibitions against speculation and reinforcing the tendency towards euphoria (Minsky 1986).

In an open economy, this mood will spread rapidly beyond the confines of the country concerned. In the absence of capital controls, speculators will turn their attention to the domestic economy, especially when the higher interest rate differentials might be in their favour. Capital flows will offset any tendency for the domestic upswing to push interest rates higher. The exchange rate may be pegged without much difficulty, or allowed to appreciate. In either case, the external position is interpreted as evidence of 'economic' health, fuelling optimism further. Success is an endogenous factor driving financial innovation forward, and openness extends the scope of achievable success. Sooner or later the economy can be led to one of the following: a crisis that is domestic in origin but impacts on its external situation; a crisis that is external in origin but impacts on its domestic situation; a crisis that is a combination of these two factors. Under these conditions, the exchange rate becomes a source of further uncertainty. Speculators begin to doubt the ability of the state to support its currency, and they may very well move against the currency concerned, possibly on a massive scale as in the case of the South East Asian crisis. This analysis clearly suggests that financial liberalization should be expected to lead to crisis. The experience of countries with financial liberalization discussed above and in Arestis and Glickman (2002) clearly testifies to this real possibility. Consequently, Minsky's (1986) view that the instability of the financial system threatens high growth rates and low unemployment is validated by these experiences. Financial liberalization, as a key euphoria-inducing factor, "intensifies this threat by adding further major stresses to the financial infrastructure" (Arestis and Glickman 2002: 258).

Another relevant case and experience is the US financial liberalization experience prior to the international financial crisis of 2007–2008. Financial liberalization in the United States began in the 1970s. More precisely, it began in 1977, when the United States started to deregulate its financial system. There was the deregulation of commissions for stock trading in 1977 to begin with, and subsequently investment banks were allowed to introduce unsecured current accounts. Two Acts followed: the Depository Institutions Deregulation and Monetary Control Act of 1980, and the Garn–St Germain Act of 1982. Both deregulated interest rates gradually, thereby removing the placing of ceilings on retail-deposit interest rates, and loosened the restrictions that had segmented the financial sector. The repeal of the key regulation, the Glass–Steagall Act of 1933, in 1999 (promoted by the US financial sector, using as their main argument the Big Bang of 1986 in the UK) was the most important aspect of US financial liberalization for the purposes of the question in hand. The final step in the process was another major and relevant legislative phase, which was the repeal of the Shad–Johnson Jurisdictional Accord of 1982, which banned regulation of over-the-counter derivatives. That repeal went through the Commodity Futures Modernization Act (CFMA) of December 2000; it is also the case that "In the 2000s deregulation was followed by 'desupervision', as US regulatory authorities made calculated decisions not to investigate financial-sector practices" (Galbraith 2013: 32).

The US experience with financial liberalization and deregulation from around the mid-1970s set the financial sector free, thereby enabling the process of financialization to proceed and develop. The apotheosis of financial liberalization in the United States, however, took place in 1999 with the repeal of the 1933 Glass–Steagall Act. This Act was designed to avoid the experience of the 1920s and 1930s in terms of the conflict of interest between the commercial and the investment arms of large financial conglomerates (whereby the investment branch took high risk tolerance). The ultimate aim of the 1933 Glass–Steagall Act was to separate the activities of commercial banks and the risk-taking 'investment or merchant' banks along with strict regulation of the financial services industry. In effect, the Glass–Steagall Act of 1933 broke up the most powerful banks. The goal was to avoid a repetition of the speculative, leveraged excesses of the 1920s and 1930s. In fact, prior to the financial liberalization period, from around the late 1930s to the early 1970s, there had been direct controls on bank lending and exchange controls on international flows, which may very well have contained innovation and efficiency in the banking sector. But as Bordo *et al.* (2001) demonstrate, that period was free from serious banking crises. Haldane (2010: Chart 2) also shows that the 1933 Act was effective from the 1930s to the late 1980s when the US authorities began to relax it. The repeal of the Act in 1999 enabled investment banks to branch into new activities; and it allowed commercial banks to encroach on the investment banks' other traditional preserves. Insurance and other companies, like the American International Group (AIG), and hedge funds were also involved in the encroaching.

The repeal of the Glass–Steagall Act in 1999 allowed the merging of commercial with investment banking, and enabled financial institutions to use risk management in their attempt to dispose of their loan portfolio. This was also helped by "a greater willingness to supply credit to low-income households, the impetus for which came in significant measure from the government" (Rajan 2010: 40). House prices kept rising over the period from 1999 to 2007 with an unprecedented height to the US housing price bubble achieved between 2000 and 2006 primarily (Reinhart 2012: 17); this enabled households to borrow against home equity they had built up. Also, risk aversion fell sharply, thereby producing the mispricing of risk that led to the credit crisis in 2007–2008. This underpricing of risk came about by low risk spreads whereby the differentials between risky assets and safe assets declined substantially. It came about particularly over the long period from 2001 to 2005 of unusually low nominal, and very low real, interest rates. But even over the longer period of the late 1980s/early 1990s to 2007, macroeconomic risks were reduced substantially in view of the 'great moderation' or 'great stability', or even NICE (Non-Inflationary Consistently Expansionary) era of low and stable inflation and steady growth.

Those developments led to an important financial innovation. Financial institutions engineered a new activity, through the 'shadow banking' system, that relied on interlinked securities, the Collateralized Debt Obligations (CDOs), mainly emerging from and closely related to the subprime mortgage market. The sale of CDOs to international investors made the US housing bubble a global problem and provided the transmission mechanism for the contagion to the rest of the world. With the collapse of the subprime market, and thereby the banks and 'shadow banking' stopping their lending procedures as they did by August 2007, the wider financial system ground to a halt. It all spilled over into the real economy through the credit crunch and collapsing equity markets; and all that led to the freezing of the interbank lending market after August 2007. A significant recession emerged: the 'great recession' (see Arestis and Karakitsos 2013, 2015; and Arestis 2016, for further details on the emergence of the August 2007 financial crisis). A clear implication from the point of view of our discussion is that the financial system as an unconditionally growth-enhancing sector has been fatally tarnished (see also Beck 2012).

Policy implications

Clearly, financial liberalization is not free of problems, to say the least. It is indeed clear that the assumption that markets, left to themselves, are self-correcting, cannot be relied upon. Unregulated markets can and have produced crises. In particular, and as Keynes (1936: 100–101) argued, this tendency is exacerbated in the case of financial markets. Furthermore, the experience prior to August 2007, as discussed above and elsewhere (see for example, Arestis and Karakitsos 2013, 2015; Arestis 2016), clearly implied serious policy implications in terms of the then monetary policy experience. Clearly this is what has come to be known as inflation targeting, and its theoretical framework, under the auspices of the New Consensus Macroeconomics (see, for example, Arestis 2009, 2011). An important policy implication in terms of the inflation targeting policy is that such an approach to policy, whereby manipulation of the rate of interest to achieve price stability is the single objective of economic policy, and it is assumed that markets would then produce macroeconomic stability and growth, should be abandoned; and the evidence from the international financial crisis strongly supports this proposition (Arestis 2016). King (2009) suggests that "price stability does not guarantee stability of the economy as a whole" and "Inflation targeting is a necessary but not sufficient condition for stability in the economy as a whole" (King 2009: 5; see also Bean *et al*. 2010). The IMF (2009) is also very clear on this score:

> We must learn lessons from the events of the past two years. They cannot be final conclusions because the present crisis has some way to run. But two stand out. First, price stability does not guarantee stability of the economy as a whole. Second, the instruments used to pursue financial stability are in need of sharpening and refining.
>
> (IMF 2009: 5; see also Blanchard *et al*. 2010)

Black (2011) goes a step further when arguing that

> The global financial meltdown of 2008 . . . changed the tenor of the discussion and brought an increased awareness of the interconnectedness of the markets, the need for more effective regulation to deal with systemic risk, and the importance of a coordinated approach toward securities regulation.
>
> (Black 2011: 461)

The IMF (2010a) goes even a step further to suggest that financial stability in the form of macro-prudential policies is the way forward. Indeed, the same publication suggests that if the current low interest rates were to produce excessive risk-taking or bubbles, these should be addressed through macro-prudential policies and not through the interest rate policy measure. The IMF (2010b) suggests a macro-prudential approach to contain systemic effects of 'too-important-to-fail' institutions, including now non-bank institutions. Also, Bean *et al*. (2010: 32) suggest that macro-prudential policy is a better policy to prevent asset and credit bubbles than merely monetary policy; the latter "seems too weak an instrument reliably to moderate a credit/asset price boom without inflicting unacceptable collateral damage on activity". An important implication of this discussion is, then

> that governments must bear a responsibility not only for allowing the recession to develop but also for the measures needed to counteract it. Governments can and must act to control market failure in ways that the market left to itself cannot.
>
> (Gould 2013: 164)

It is true actually that only a micro-prudential approach was the basis of the regulatory framework prior to the 'great recession'. A number of writers have argued that the regulatory framework was problematic because of that deficiency (see Hansen *et al*. 2011, and a number of additional references therein).

A macro-prudential approach is thereby of enormous importance. Hansen *et al.* (2011) summarize the argument very well:

> A microprudential approach is one in which regulation is partial equilibrium in its conception and aimed at preventing the costly failure of individual financial institutions. By contrast, a 'macroprudential' approach recognizes the importance of general equilibrium effects, and seeks to safeguard the financial system as a whole. In the aftermath of the crisis there seems to be agreement among both academics and policymakers that financial regulation needs to move in a macroprudential direction.
>
> (Hansen *et al.* 2011: 3)

The difficulty with only a micro-prudential framework is that since it attempts to tackle problems with individual institutions, the overall result could very well be a serious damage to the economy as a whole. It is, thus, paramount for a macro-prudential approach to co-exist with a micro-prudential one. Indeed, "Strong supervision of individual institutions is essential both to ensure that macroprudential policymakers can draw on supervisory information in risk assessment and to ensure that the macroprudential policy stance adopted is effectively enforced across institutions" (IMF 2014: 5).

Clearly, macro-prudential policy acts more directly at the source of the problem. It is a 'system-wide oversight' approach, and as such, it "would broaden the mandate of regulators and supervisors to encompass consideration of potential systemic risks and weaknesses as well" (Bernanke 2005). In terms of the macro-prudential tools, Hansen *et al.* (2011) discuss six sets of such tools:

1. time-varying capital requirements;
2. higher-quality capital;
3. corrective action targeted at capital as opposed to capital ratios;
4. contingent capital;
5. regulation of debt maturity; and
6. regulating the shadow banking system.

They offer empirical evidence to conclude that macro-prudential regulation is of paramount importance. The danger is that "given the intensity of competition in financial services, they will also drive a larger share of intermediation into the shadow banking realm" (Hansen *et al.* 2011: 25). Regulating this system, long overdue in our view, along with the rest of the financial system, is the obvious conclusion, although this is "a complex task, and one that will require a variety of specific tools" (Hansen *et al.* 2011: 25). Still, such regulation is of vital importance, however complex such a task might be.

What is particularly interesting about the arguments in favour of macro-prudential policies, along with more intervention, is that the intellectual weight given to it all has come from a revival of interest in the contribution of Minsky (1986) and other critics of the *laissez-faire* doctrine. It is the case that this development has given strong intellectual weight to the macro-prudential approach. Still, though, a critique on this score is that the macro-prudential approach, as suggested currently, lacks theoretical foundations. Kregel (2014) makes the point that a theory of endogenous financial instability, which can explain the tendency of the financial system to generate crises as part of its 'normal' functioning (which is part of Minsky's Financial Instability Hypothesis [FIH]), is needed. Kregel suggests that

> There are two important features of Minsky's approach to financial regulation that distinguish it from the current approach. The first is the necessity of an underlying theory to provide the background for regulatory proposals. The second is the need to assess the impact of regulation in light of current economic conditions, ongoing changes in financial institutions, and likely monetary policy measures. Minsky's FIH provided the basis for what were the first proposals of what is now called 'macro' prudential regulation. In addition, he proposed a new examination structure to capture the elements of this dynamic approach to macroprudential regulation.
>
> (Kregel 2014: 4)

At the same time, though, monetary and macro-prudential and, more generally, financial stability policies should be coordinated. Financial stability policy measures should "include capital requirements and buffers, forward-looking loss provisioning, liquidity ratios, and prudent collateral valuation" (IMF 2010c: 3). Still, and in this view, price stability "should remain the primary objective of monetary policy" (IMF 2010c: 3); interestingly enough, though, the argument is not for price stability to be the single objective of economic policy. It is also suggested that

> changes to central bank liquidity operations and broad crisis management frameworks are needed to address moral hazard. Changes to enhance the flexibility of central bank operational frameworks will improve the resilience of the system. Institutions and markets that are potential recipients of liquidity support, in times of stress should be monitored and regulated.
>
> (IMF 2010c: 3)

So the focus seems to be on systemic financial stability. All these changes, the IMF argues, "should be done in a way that preserves central bank independence" (2010c: 4).

The conclusion from this discussion is then that financial stability and monetary policy should be the responsibilities of the central bank. This means of course that central banks would have an added objective – that of financial stability. Such an additional objective, though, raises the issue of how to incorporate financial stability in the loss function of the central bank in view of the fact that it is impossible to measure such a variable. Blinder (2010: 4) raises the issue and wonders "whether the right loss function is actually lexicographic, with financial stability logically prior to the other goals". This is a serious challenge for those central banks that use the New Consensus Macroeconomics modelling framework (see, for example, Arestis 2009, 2011). One might ask at this stage, as Strauss-Kahn, then IMF Managing Director, did in 2011:

> What about fiscal policy? Under the old paradigm, fiscal policy was definitely the *neglected child* of the policy family. Its role was limited to automatic stabilizers – letting budget deficits move up and down with the cycle – and discretionary policy was regarded with deep suspicion. But fiscal policy had a *Sleeping Beauty* moment during the crisis – with monetary policy running out of steam, and with the financial system on its knees, the forgotten tool arrived to prop up aggregate demand and save the world from an economic freefall. We need to rethink fiscal policy.
>
> (Strauss-Kahn 2011: para. 15)

Indeed, we have to rethink fiscal policy seriously and suggest that the time has come to assign a strong macroeconomic role to it (see Arestis 2012, 2015).

We agree that monetary and financial stability policies should be coordinated. But we go further and argue that it is vital to have full coordination of both policies with fiscal policy, along with discretion in applying them. Fiscal policy should be used both in the short term and in the long term to address demand issues. In this respect, relatively frequent adjustments to fiscal stance in the light of macroeconomic developments are necessary. Regional and industrial policies should be employed to create the required capacity. The perception of how one reaches such a conclusion relies heavily on the belief that the objectives of macroeconomic policy are sustainable (environmental and otherwise) along with equitable economic development and growth. Within this general focus, the main objective of macroeconomic policy is the achievement of full employment of the available labour force. Achieving such an objective would require, *inter alia*, the maintenance of a high level of aggregate demand consistent with full employment of labour. Also, the provision of sufficient productive capacity to enable the achievement of full employment, where sufficient is to be interpreted in terms of quantity, quality and geographical distribution. In this sense, industrial and regional policies are required to enhance supply. Public expenditure, particularly investment, can also be structured to ease supply constraints. It should also be argued that under these propositions the independence of central banks should be abandoned, for otherwise coordination as suggested above could not be pursued. In any case, central bank independence has had very little to do with the battle against inflation as recent experience has clearly demonstrated. It is also the case that central bank independence "is a major step away from democratic government", and "It can be relied upon always to put the interests of the financial establishment ahead of those operating in the rest of the economy" (Gould 2013: 112). These propositions are easily reinforced "when we come to assess the reaction of the so-called independent central banks to the global financial crisis" (Gould 2013: 112), as we have also demonstrated in this chapter.

We may summarize the argument that the main operation of any central bank should be directed towards financial stability. The events leading to the 'great recession' testify to this important requirement. Financial stability has not been addressed properly, and as such it requires further investigation. The focus of financial stability should be on proper control of the financial sector so that it becomes socially and economically useful to the economy as a whole and to the productive economy in particular. Banks should serve the needs of their customers rather than provide short-term gains for shareholders and huge profits for themselves. Indeed, as Gould (2013) argues:

> A central bank is essential to maintain a proper prudential supervision of banks and of the financial sector more generally – something that has, as has become apparent, been sadly missed from the scene in many western countries over recent years. A central bank should regulate and enable the banks to interact with other sectors in the economy in an efficient way that benefits the economy as a whole.

(Gould 2013: 113)

De-financialization thereby would help to achieve the objective of shrinking the financial sector. In this sense, the suggestion by Lawrence (2014) that de-financialization through measures such as targeting credit at the productive economy and a reassertion of the public interest in the financial system is very apt. We would further suggest that separating investment banking from commercial banking is the right step forward.

With the objective of financial stability, the central bank would become more like a Central Financial Agency (CFA). It would be responsible for policies which seek to influence the credit and lending policies of the full range of financial institutions. Our current contribution in this context is to argue the case for full coordination of both monetary and financial stability policies with fiscal policy; we would go one step further and suggest that discretion is as important in applying them.

Summary and conclusions

We have considered in this chapter the theoretical premise that has come to be known as the financial liberalization thesis. We have identified a number of theoretical propositions, which we have examined closely. We suggested that these critical issues of the thesis are marred by serious difficulties. We looked at the available evidence and found that it is not of much help to the thesis either. It is clear from this excursion in the literature that no convincing evidence has been provided in support of the propositions of the financial liberalization hypothesis. On the contrary, the available evidence can be interpreted as indicating that the theoretical propositions of the thesis are at best weak, and as such they ought to be abandoned. It is indeed the case that financial liberalization has caused crises, the most serious one being the international financial crisis of 2007–2008 and the subsequent 'great recession'. Policy implications emerge, which are very different from those of the financial liberalization thesis as discussed in this chapter.

Even so, and although a number of relevant proposals have been put forward (see, for example, Arestis and Karakitsos 2013), relevant solutions are still to be implemented and the banking reform remains a work in progress across the world. We may thereby conclude by suggesting that the pre-2007 *laissez-faire* approach is in need of substantial reforms. There is, however, a lesson from the failures of the various proposed reforms, which is that working within the pre-2007 paradigm, and yet suggesting policy proposals, is simply not good enough. In this sense we should recall Keynes's (1930) essay on "Economic Possibilities for our Grandchildren", where he warns precisely against the kind of developments to which we have just referred. As Gould (2013: 82) argues when referring to this essay, Keynes "presciently foresaw and warned against these essentially modern developments".

Notes

1 The relevant details referred to in the text are available at: www.investopedia.com/terms/f/financialization.asp
2 Beck (2012) provides a short summary of developments on the finance–growth relationship stretching back to Smith's (1937 [1776]) publication.
3 As noted above, 'distributional effects' was one of the main causes of the 2007–2008 international financial crisis. Distributional effects along with financial liberalization (especially the repeal of the US 1933 Glass–Steagall Act in 1999) produced the third main cause of the crisis, namely financial innovation (for further details, see Arestis 2016).

References

Arestis, P. (2004). "Washington Consensus and Financial Liberalization", *Journal of Post Keynesian Economics*, 26(2): 251–271.

Arestis, P. (2005). "Financial Liberalization and the Relationship between Finance and Growth", in P. Arestis and M. Sawyer (Eds), *Handbook of Alternative Monetary Economics*. Cheltenham, UK: Edward Elgar Publishing Limited, pp. 346–364.

Arestis, P. (2009). "New Consensus Macroeconomics and Keynesian Critique", in E. Hein, T. Niechoj and E. Stockhammer (Eds), *Macroeconomic Policies on Shaky Foundations: Whither Mainstream Economics?* Marburg, Germany: Metropolis-Verlag, pp. 165–186.

Arestis, P. (2011). "Keynesian Economics and the New Consensus in Macroeconomics", in E. Hein and E. Stockhammer (Eds), *A Modern Guide to Keynesian Macroeconomics and Economic Policies*. Cheltenham, UK: Edward Elgar Publishing Limited, pp. 88–111.

Arestis, P. (2012). "Fiscal Policy: A Strong Macroeconomic Role", *Review of Keynesian Economics*, 1(1): 93–108.

Arestis, P. (2015). "Coordination of Fiscal with Monetary and Financial Stability Policies Can Better Cure Unemployment", *Review of Keynesian Economics*, 3(2): 233–247.

Arestis, P. (2016). "Main and Contributory Causes of the Recent Financial Crisis and Economic Policy Implications", in P. Arestis and M. Sawyer (Eds), *Emerging Economies During and After the Great Recession*. Annual edn of *International Papers in Political Economy*. Houndmills, Basingstoke, UK: Palgrave Macmillan, pp. 1–16.

Arestis, P. and Demetriades, P. O. (1997). "Financial Development and Economic Growth: Assessing the Evidence", *Economic Journal*, 107(442): 783–799.

Arestis, P. and Demetriades, P. O. (1998). "Financial Liberalization: Myth or Reality?", in P. Arestis (Ed.), *Method, Theory and Policy in Keynes: Essays in Honour of Paul Davidson*, Vol. 3. Cheltenham, UK: Edward Elgar Publishing Limited, pp. 205–225.

Arestis, P. and Glickman, M. (2002). "Financial Crisis in Southeast Asia: Dispelling Illusion the Minskyan Way", *Cambridge Journal of Economics*, 26(2):, 237–260.

Arestis, P. and Stein, H. (2005). "An Institutional Perspective to Finance and Development as an Alternative to Financial Liberalization", *International Review of Applied Economics*, 19(4): 381–398.

Arestis, P. and Karakitsos, E. (2013). *Financial Stability in the Aftermath of the 'Great Recession'*. Houndmills, Basingstoke, UK: Palgrave Macmillan.

Arestis, P. and Karakitsos, E. (2015). "Causes of the 'Great Recession' and Economic Policy Implications", in P. Tridico and S. Fadda (Eds), *The Economic Crisis in Social and Institutional Context: Theories, Policies and Exit Strategies*. London: Routledge, pp. 26–41.

Arestis, P. with Chortareas, G. and Magkonis, G. (2015). "The Financial Development and Growth Nexus: A Meta-Analysis", *Journal of Economic Surveys*, 29(3): 549–565.

Bagehot, W. (1873). *Lombard Street: A Description of the Money Market*. London: John Murray.

Bean, C., Panstian, M., Penalver, A. and Taylor, T. (2010). "Monetary Policy After the Fall", paper presented at the Federal Reserve Bank of Kansas City Annual Conference, 28 August, Jackson Hole, Wyoming.

Beck, T. (2012). "The Role of Finance in Economic Development: Benefits, Risks, and Politics", in D. C. Mueller (Ed.), *The Oxford Book of Capitalism*. New York: Oxford University Press, pp. 161–203.

Beck, T., Degryseb, H. and Kneer, C. (2013). "Is More Finance Better? Disentangling Intermediation and Size Effects of Financial Systems", *Journal of Financial Stability*, 10: 50–64.

Bernanke, B. S. (2005). "The Global Saving Glut and the US Current Account Deficit", Sandridge Lecture, 10 March, Virginia Association of Economists, Richmond, Virginia.

Black, B. (2011). "Introduction: The Globalization of Securities Regulation – Competition or Coordination?", *University of Cincinnati Law Review*, 79(2): 461–470.

Blanchard, O., Dell'Ariccia, G. and Mauro, P. (2010). "Rethinking Macroeconomic Policy", IMF Staff Position Note SPN/10/03. Washington, DC: International Monetary Fund.

Blinder, A. S. (2010). "Commentary: Rethinking Monetary Policy in Light of the Crisis", paper presented at the Federal Reserve Bank of Kansas City Annual Economic Symposium, 28 August, Jackson Hole, Wyoming.

Bordo, M. D., Eichengreen, B., Klingebiel, D. and Martinez-Perio, M. S. (2001). "Is the Crisis Problem Going More Severe?", *Economic Policy*, 32: 51–82.

Calvo, G. A. (1988). "Servicing the Public Debt: The Role of Expectations", *American Economic Review*, 78(4): 647–661.

Caprio, G. Jr., Atiyas, I. and Hanson, J. A. (Eds) (1994). *Financial Reform: Theory and Experience*. Cambridge, UK: Cambridge University Press.

Cecchetti, S. G. and Kharroubi, E. (2012). "Reassessing the Impact of Finance on Growth", BIS Working Paper No. 381.

Creel, J., Hubert, P. and Labondance, F. (2014). "Financial Stability and Economic Performance", *Economic Modelling*, 48: 25–40.

Demetriades, P. O. and Luintel, K. B. (1996). "Financial Restraints in the South Korean Miracle", *Journal of Development Economics*, 64(2): 459–479.

Edwards, S. (1989). "On the Sequencing of Structural Reforms", *OECD Department of Economics and Statistics Working Papers*, No. 70. Paris: OECD Publishing.

Epstein, G. (2001). "Financialization, Rentier Interests, and Central Bank Policy", paper presented at the Department of Economics and Political Economy Research Institute (PERI) Conference on Financialization of the World Economy, 7–8 December. Available at: www.peri.umass.edu/fileadmin/pdf/financial/fin_Epstein.pdf (accessed 28 April 2015).

Galbraith, J. K. (2013). "New Thinking and a Strategic Policy Agenda", in H. Flassbeck, P. Davidson, J. K. Galbraith, R. Koo and J. Ghosh, *Economic Reform Now: A Global Manifesto to Rescue our Sinking Economies*. New York: Palgrave Macmillan, pp. 23–54.

Goldsmith, R. W. (1969). *Financial Structure and Development*. New Haven, CT: Yale University Press.

Gould, B. (2013). *Myths, Politicians & Money: The Truth behind Free Markets*. Houndmills, Basingstoke, UK: Palgrave Macmillan.

Greenspan, A. (2010). "The Crisis", *Brookings Papers on Economic Activity*, Spring: 201–246.

Gurley, J. G. and Shaw, E. S. (1955). "Financial Aspects of Economic Development", *American Economic Review*, 45(4): 515–538.

Haldane, A. G. (2010). "The $100 Billion Question", speech given at the Institute of Regulation & Risk North Asia (IRRNA), Hong Kong, 30 March 2010. Available at: www.bankofengland.co.uk/archive/Documents/historicpubs/news/2010/036.pdf (accessed 26 November 2012).

Hansen, S. G., Kashyap, A. K. and Stein, J. C. (2011). "A Macroprudential Approach to Financial Regulation", *Journal of Economic Perspectives*, 25(1): 3–28.

Honohan, P. and Klingebiel, D. (2000). "Controlling Fiscal Costs of Banking Crises", mimeo. Washington, DC: World Bank.

IMF (2009). *World Economic Outlook. Sustaining the Recovery*. Washington, DC: International Monetary Fund.

IMF (2010a). "Central Banking Lessons from the Crisis", Monetary and Capital Markets Department, 27 May. Washington, DC: International Monetary Fund.

IMF (2010b). *Global Financial Stability Report: Sovereigns, Funding, and Systemic Liquidity*. Washington, DC: International Monetary Fund.

IMF (2010c). "Shaping the New Financial System", IMF Staff Position Note, SPN/10/15, Monetary and Capital Markets Department, 3 October. Washington, DC: International Monetary Fund.

IMF (2014). *Staff Guidance Note on Macroprudential Policy*, 6 December. Washington, DC: International Monetary Fund.

Keynes, J. M. (1930). "Economic Possibilities for our Grandchildren", reprinted in J. M. Keynes (1963), *Essays in Persuasion*. New York: W. W. Norton & Company, pp. 358–373.

Keynes, J. M. (1936). *The General Theory of Employment, Interest and Money*. London: Macmillan.

King, M. (2009). Speech at the Mayor's Banquet for Bankers and Merchants of the City of London, The Mansion House, 17 June 2009. Available at: www.bankofengland.co.uk/archive/documents/historicpubs/speeches/2009/speech394.pdf (accessed 26 November 2012).

Kotz, D. M. (2011). "Financialization and Neoliberalism", in G. Teeple and S. McBride (Eds), *Relations of Global Power: Neoliberal Order and Disorder*. Toronto, ON: University of Toronto Press, pp. 1–18.

Kregel, J. (2014). "Minsky and Dynamic Macroprudential Regulation", Public Policy Brief No. 131, Jerome Levy Economics Institute of Bard College. Available at: www. levyinstitute.org/pubs/ppb_131.pdf (accessed 11 February 2015).

Laeven, L. and Valencia, F. (2012). "Systemic Banking Crises Database: An Update", IMF Working Paper WP/12/163. Washington, DC: International Monetary Fund.

Lawrence, M. (2014). *Definancialisation: A Democratic Reformation of Finance*. London: Institute for Public Policy Research.

Levine, R. (2004). "Finance and Growth: Theory and Evidence", NBER Working Paper No. 10766. Cambridge, MA: National Bureau of Economic Research.

Levine, R. (2005). "Finance and Growth: Theory and Evidence", in A. Philippe and N. Steven (Eds), *Handbook of Economic Growth*. London: Elsevier, pp. 865–934.

Lucas, R. E. (1988). "On the Mechanics of Economic Development", *Journal of Monetary Economics*, 22(1): 3–42.

McKinnon, R. I. (1973). *Money and Capital in Economic Development*. Washington, DC: Brookings Institution.

McKinnon, R. I. (1988a). "Financial Liberalization in Retrospect: Interest Rate Policies in LDCs", in G. Ranis and T. P. Schultz (Eds), *The State of Development Economics*. Oxford: Basil Blackwell, pp. 386–410.

McKinnon, R. I. (1988b). "Financial Liberalization and Economic Development: A Reassessment of Interest-Rate Policies in Asia and Latin America", Occasional Paper No. 6, International Centre for Economic Growth.

McKinnon, R. I. (1991). *The Order of Economic Liberalization: Financial Control in the Transition to a Market Economy*. Baltimore, MD: Johns Hopkins University Press.

Miller, M. H. (1998). "Financial Markets and Economic Growth", *Journal of Applied Corporate Finance*, 11(1): 8–14.

Minsky, H. P. (1982). *Can "It" Happen Again: Essays on Instability and Finance*. Armonk, NY: M.E. Sharpe.

Minsky, H. P. (1986). *Stabilizing an Unstable Economy*. New Haven, CT: Yale University Press.

Palley, T. I. (2012). *From Financial Crisis to Stagnation: The Destruction of Shared Prosperity and the Role of Economics*. Cambridge, UK: Cambridge University Press.

Philippon, T. and Reshef, A. (2009). "Wages and Human Capital in the U.S. Financial Industry: 1909–2006", NBER Working Paper No. 14644, January. Washington, DC: National Bureau of Economic Research.

Rajan, G. R. (2010). *Fault Lines: How Hidden Fractures Still Threaten the World Economy*. Princeton, NJ: Princeton University Press.

Reinhart, C. (2012). "A Series of Unfortunate Events: Common Sequencing Patterns in Financial Crises", NBER Working Paper No. 17941, March. Washington, DC: National Bureau of Economic Research.

Robinson, J. (1952). "The Generalisation of the General Theory", in J. Robinson, *The Rate of Interest and Other Essays*. London: Macmillan, pp. 67–97.

Rousseau, P. L. and Wachtel, P. (2011). "What Is Happening to the Impact of Financial Deepening on Economic Growth?", *Economic Inquiry*, 49(1): 276–288.

Schumpeter, J. (1911). *The Theory of Economic Development: An Inquiry into Profits, Capital, Credit, Interest and Business Cycle*. Cambridge, MA: Harvard University Press.

Shaw, E. S. (1973). *Financial Deepening in Economic Development*. New York: Oxford University Press.

Smith, A. (1937 [1776]). *An Inquiry into the Nature and Causes of the Wealth of Nations*. New York: Modern Library.

Strauss-Kahn, D. (2011). "'Global Challenges, Global Solutions' – An Address at George Washington University", 4 April. Washington, DC: International Monetary Fund. Available at: www.imf.org/external/np/speeches/2011/040411.htm (accessed 13 April 2011).

Villanueva, D. and Mirakhor, A. (1990). "Interest Rate Policies, Stabilisation and Bank Supervision in Developing Countries: Strategies for Financial Reform", IMF Working Paper WP/90/8.

World Bank (1989). *World Development Report*. Oxford: Oxford University Press.

2 Global financing
A bad medicine for developing countries

Joaquín Arriola

The context[1]

The long cycle of financial crisis – from the European Monetary System in 1993, the Mexican crisis in 1994, Southeast Asia in 1997, the Russian crisis of 1998 or the Nasdaq crisis in 2000, until the crisis in the interbank lending market in 2007 – has generated a rich academic and social debate, which has so far only been able to come to certain partial and tentative conclusions.

The global financial evolution expresses the existence of new structures and dynamics that require on one hand, to go beyond the identification of the financial sector as the "credit supplier" of the productive economy; and on the other, to insert the financial crisis into the new global monetary settings derived from the expansion of the Eurocurrencies as money for private financial payments at the international level.

Most studies, however, belong to an analytical perspective of *business as usual*, which at most takes note of the quantitative dimension of current global finances. Therefore, from a financial perspective, the cause of this evolution of recurrent crises until (for now) the final implosion in 2007, is generally ascribed to a long period of low interest rates ("easy money") and to the loopholes in the process of supervision and regulation of banking and financial activities (de Larosière *et al.* 2009). Depending on the circumstances, there is talk of a banking crisis, a stock market crisis, a credit crunch or housing boom crisis as a trigger factor.

From a macroeconomic perspective, there are two factors usually referred to: a system of international payments with a deficient financial architecture which encourages moral hazard (Eichengreen 1999) and facilitates the accumulation of huge imbalances in the current account – the impressive US deficit and its counterpart, the huge surpluses of China, Japan and Germany – and therefore a concentration of liquid reserves that travel the world in search of the highest possible financial return (Wolf 2008; Reinhart and Rogoff 2009).

Some more sophisticated analysis also points to the accumulation of liquidity in the hands of large corporations, following a long cycle of super-profits based on one side on a continual reduction in the share of wages in value added; and on the other, in the processes of centralization of capital implying foreclosures and the shutting down of companies, liquidity that would have moved financial markets massively (Aglietta and Rigot 2009; Rajan 2009).

Table 2.1 Average annual change in per capita productivity (GDP/population) at 2010 prices

	1961–1972	*1973–1982*	*1983–1995*	*1996–2008*	*2009–2015*
EU15	3.9	2.1	1.9	1.8	−0.1
USA	3.2	1.3	2.4	1.4	1.7
Japan	8.0	2.4	3.1	0.3	1.5

Source: EC: Directorate General ECFIN, AMECO database 05/15.

This is a process that the Organisation for Economic Co-operation and Development (OECD) (2008) recognizes as it points statistically to a long period of deterioration on the part of labour income (salaried and self-employed) in the Gross Domestic Product (GDP) of all major developed countries. In a 30-year period, labour in core countries lost ten points of share in GDP. This means that every year, capital gains get more surplus at a rate of around 3 billion US dollars (in 2010 prices), than the surplus that would be transformed into profits with the distribution shares of 30 years ago, not as a result of the development of the productive powers of capital, but thanks to a structural change in income distribution.

Anyway, what is not so commonly seen in the typical analysis is that the financial crisis is analysed from the long-term trends that manifest themselves in the form of a structural crisis of capitalism. The most important of those trends is the tendency to productivity stagnation, a long-term trend that can be traced back to the early 1970s.

The group of developed countries has been undergoing a long process of production slowdown, not only from the relatively high growth rates in the 1960s,

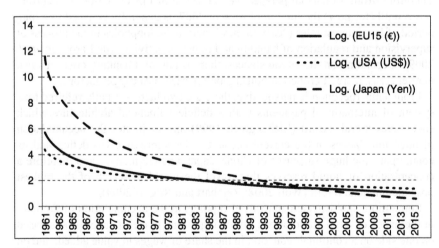

Figure 2.1 Annual change in per capita productivity (GDP/population) at 2010 prices (logarithmic trend).

Source: EC: Directorate General ECFIN, AMECO database 05/15.

but even from the great crisis of the first half of the 1970s, when the developed economies grew more than in the subsequent boom phase, up to the global stagnation since 2011.

These developments point to a depletion of the sources of growth of relative surplus value, a factor that helps to understand the enormous pressure that capital is applying in order to extract more absolute surplus labour through legal and political reforms intended to substantially reduce the participation of wage income (direct, indirect and deferred wages) in value added.

The great wave of technological changes of the early twenty-first century, based on immaterial production, spatial fragmentation of production processes, biotechnology or the communication network as a productive force, has not resulted in a new process of accelerating development of the productive forces of labour, which is only happening in the new spaces incorporated into the world market as production sites on the basis of the *Fordist* norms associated with chain production (China and Southeast Asia principally).

Unlike the two previous stages, this capitalism has not been able (yet) to conduct the energy transformation that accompanies any massive advance in the productive powers of labour. If coal replaced wood in the first Industrial Revolution, oil is the symbol of American technological supremacy in the Fordist era. However, faced with the depletion of fossil energy resources, capitalism has proved incapable of generating a leap to new energy technologies. One reason is that renewable energies are more efficient through a decentralized use of them, something incompatible with the highly centralized capitalist version of our day. Atomic energy goes back to the front page, as an alternative that meets capital requirements of centralized control, but faces a strong social rejection in many centres of the system.

The current crisis is much more than a financial crisis of global dimensions. It is the symptom of the exhaustion of the procedures set up by US capital in the late 1970s and early 1980s to continue to attract material resources and labour in the form of goods from all around the world, always on credit.

The dollar in financial globalization

Financial globalization can be interpreted as the result of the US decision to deal with its balance of payments problems without any real adjustment of its economy, and avoiding the pressures of central banks around the world, reluctant to continue charging its commercial debts with non-convertible paper dollars. Since the 1980s, in order to facilitate the management of global liquidity by the United States, successive decisions were taken to advance the deregulation of the financial system, eliminating the regulation and supervision of central banks over trans-border financial transactions. In fact, only the United States has the ability to regulate the inflow and outflow of financial capital in dollars or foreign currencies through adjustments in the central interest rate (usually the reference rate of 5 Year or 10 Year Treasury bonds). In the rest of the world, the interest rate primarily affects the investment rate, and in any case, the International Monetary

Fund (IMF) forced the developing countries subject to adjustment policies to use the interest rate as a means of stabilizing the exchange rate.

Liberalization of transactions and bank deposits has led to the replacement of the monetary authority of national governments and central banks by decisions derived exclusively from market signals. Only in the international financial market is market authority almost absolute. Only *"almost"* because – and it is no small issue – currencies remain national monies. While people and goods from one country have a national market, and if they want to leave the country they must go through the mechanisms of international trade, the currencies of the countries have a world market. There is no currencies inter-national trade, subject to national regulations like any other trade, but an overall and worldwide purchase and sale of currencies in a global and unified market.

The future global financial market evolution, its dynamics and contradictions, is the determinant condition of any possible globalized accumulation. The globalization process, conditioned by financial developments, requires an under-standing of the determinants of this financial environment, in order to achieve a more accurate perspective on the current process of structural changes.

The financial evolution analysis requires a little reminder about the condition of money in modern society.

Capital, money and banks

Money in pre-capitalist societies fulfilled the functions of a medium of exchange, a unit of account and expression of the value of goods and services sold for money. Its emergence and generalization facilitate personal division of labour, through workers' specialization. As commerce extends to more distant regions, the use of money facilitates spatial division of labour, through the productive specialization of regions placed through trade into economic relation.

Pre-capitalist societies, societies *with* markets, operated under the logic of production and the exchange of *equivalents*, according to the well-known formal expression of Marx: [M–C–M'] and [M = M'], where M represents money and C the commodities, goods and services sold for money.

During the thousands of years that money exerted functions as an intermediary between commodities – that is, general equivalent functions – even in the first stage of capitalism, money was always commodity-money; i.e. it had an intrinsic value. Even the surge of *fiat* money does not break that bond of money with a particular use-value; that is, as Marx analysed, fiat money was merely a subordinate representation of real money, which for him could only be a commodity-money.[2]

But in capitalist societies, money broadens its functions, leading events to change in nature. We are in the first society in history which is *a market* society; that is, where the market relations determine the whole set of social relationships. Social reproduction is done under the logic of *accumulation* and realization of value: [M–C–M'] and [M < M'].

Money appears as a precondition for production and exchange, even reaching the point of acquiring autonomy from commodities production in its social reproduction and the accumulation process [M → M']. Thus, money becomes *capital*, a driving force, the beginning and end of the process of production and exchange. And banks are constituted into a system, a hinge axis of the transformation processes of money into capital out of its money form, into the productive form, then the trade form, and finally recovering its money form as a bank deposit.

Generalization of the capitalist process involves the widespread use of money in the implementation of the process of exchanging money for means of production and labour force for the production of goods and services, and in the subsequent process of exchanging those goods for cash, a sign of validation by the market of the overall production decisions, while at the same time, the monetary form of the surplus in its social distribution process.

Money management in this process lies in the hands of special institutions, whose development largely determines the structural dynamics of money itself; the feasibility of a global financial-capital market depends in turn on the evolution of the banking system. V. Chick and S. Dow,[3] set five stages in the organic evolution of the banking system under capitalism:

1   A first phase in which bank commitments (liabilities) are still not means of payment, banks remaining as pure intermediaries between savers and investors. Deposits determine reserves, and these determine loans, so investment is limited by saving $[I = f(S)]$.
2   A second phase in which securities and bank deposits (bank money) are used as means of payment. At this stage, reserves become the restriction variable for investment $[I = f(R)]$. The banking system can lend an amount equal to a multiple of the increase observed in the volume of reserves, so that loans can grow at a rate higher than that of deposits, at least for a reasonable space of time. The lower the reserves multiplier is the more decentralized the system is, and the lower the market share of the bank in question. In the first two phases, the interest rate is set by the difference between the evolution of savings and credit demand.
3   In the third phase, interbank loans are institutionalized, increasing the coherence of the system and allowing an increase in the volume of bank credit creation over the constitution of reserves.
4   In the fourth phase, the coherence of the interbank system is rounded with the creation of a central monetary authority which agrees to assume the role of lender of last resort. Reserves remain exogenous as long as the monetary authorities (the central bank) are prepared to manipulate it, by legal restrictions (actions on the amount of credit) or through open market operations (actions on the price of credit). In any case, the supply of credit becomes more elastic when the banking system can expand credit without the danger of being short of reserves. At this stage, the supply of credit for investment is determined by demand $[L^o = L^D]$. Credit expansion goes beyond the needs of the productive economy, and development of financial markets occurs, claiming a growing share of the credit for their own interbank transactions. In downturns, this demand could restrict the volume of credit available for productive activities,

a *crowding out* effect more real than the credit demand by the public sector. With the creation of the interbank market, the interest rate depends almost exclusively on the changes in deposits.

5   In the fifth phase, interbank competition forces banks to meet all credit demands, covering the expansion of credit volume competing for deposits of other banks, and even attracting long-term savings funds from other financial corporations. Banking competition will be extended to obtaining loans share from other banks, and the end result will be a rate increase in the liabilities that will result in significant pressure on liquidity and the profit margins of banking business. At this stage, the ability of monetary authorities to control the volume of credit decreases, leading to a transformation of the availability of financial resources in a pure market activity, dependent on the cost of funds and the expectations of bankers. Reserves become endogenous and an increasing proportion of funding becomes autonomous with respect to the needs of the productive economy, and is intended for speculative uses, breaking the link between bank credit and financial assets trade with real economic activity production and the trade of goods and services. The interest rate is determined by the dynamism of the speculative finance itself.

In this evolution, it is important to remember that at some point, the banking system is able to *create credit regardless of savings*, with a structural development that exceeded the historical phase of savings–investment identity, so dear to neoclassical economics. When the evolution of the system reaches that point, bank money is money in the full sense of the term, and stops any direct link with a real merchant base (credit money replaces money as a general equivalent commodity of the productive system, becoming a unit of account *by convention*).

The globalization of finance

In fact, the fifth phase in the evolution of national banking systems does not reach its completion until the banking system breaks the last ties established by the existence of a central monetary authority. Financial globalization with the emergence of the Euro markets offers this possibility: the last phase of the evolution of national banking systems requires overcoming the national dimension thereof. The last phase thus becomes the *terminal phase* of national banking systems.

New technologies have contributed decisively to this development, eliminating the differences in time and space in the movement of financial capital: a dollar may now be in Hong Kong, and by pressing a key on a computer console, in the next second it will be *located* in New York, and with another push of the button in the next second it has been changed for 85 cents of a euro in Frankfurt, Germany.

Also important are the reasons inherent in the very nature of financial capital, the particular facilities of money circulation: there is no weight, no space, for you can transfer any amount of money just by some accounting entries, and with the new communication technologies, there is no time incorporated into the movement of money from one point of the planet to another.

The size factor is also important: the concentration and centralization of capital has reached a point where existing national markets, even the larger ones (Japan, United States, and so on) have been outgrown, given the amount of funds that can be mobilized by large financial agents (banks, pension funds, insurance companies and others).

In principle, banks (multinationals) provide support to the implementation of multinational capital in the [M–C–M'] 'circuit'. At the end of the nineteenth century, its international development accompanied the commercial and productive companies in their expansion to the colonies and the formation of empires on the one hand, and the increasing flow of exchanges in Europe and North America on the other.

By contrast, most of the funds handled by multinational banks today are applied to strictly financial operations in the capital markets, especially in the Eurocurrency markets, operations that involve only the big banks, buying currencies and granting international credit to each other.

The international capital market, where financial transactions are made, consists of a network of financial centres located throughout the world: London, New York, Tokyo, Paris, Frankfurt, Amsterdam, but also Singapore, Hong Kong, Panama, Luxembourg, Bahrain, the Bahamas and the Cayman Islands. The network of financial markets has contributed to increasing the autonomous nature of the financial flow, to multiply the amount of operations strictly internal to the financial framework, not linked to the actual production process, to amplify the increasingly fictitious character of capital movements (casino economy[4]). Multinational banks can make huge tax savings through the techniques of registration and transfer of profits abroad by means of financial free zones; financial institutions have designed the most sophisticated mechanisms to make sure that "money makes money".

Today, daily transactions on a global scale have reached a volume about twice that of the total foreign exchange reserves available to major industrialized countries. Global foreign exchange reserves reached in the first quarter of 2015 the equivalent of 11.5 billion US dollars, when the banks' consolidated foreign claims figure is more than double that (24.3 billion US dollars).

The Bretton Woods system crisis

The Bretton Woods system crisis is traditionally presented as the impossibility of the key currency – the dollar – to cope with the commitment to support all gold-convertible dollars deposited in central banks around the world, following a current balance of payments deficit higher than the federal gold reserves. The measures taken so far to solve the international payments system crisis have identified two phases in the international monetary system (Lelart 2011) marked by three key decisions at the political-economic level:

1a 1971: the dollar–gold unlinking – a *de jure* inconvertibility, then *de facto*, it manifested itself at least since 1967, with the French decision to abandon the gold pool and the subsequent dismantling of this dollar–gold price stabilization arrangement. This decision marks the end of the international monetary *system*, whose institutional continuity has two key elements: on the one hand, the IMF, an institution that no longer has a real role in stabilizing prices and solvency in international payments; and on the other hand, the dollar reserves held by central banks, which in the absence of a replacement system continue to be accumulated by surplus countries, but now without a material amount of value equivalent, the dollar reserves are at risk of great and sudden depreciation.

1b   1976: the suspension of adjustable fixed exchange rates and their replacement by a system of flexible exchange rates or market rates, which in practice meant the conversion of currencies in a commodity whose circulation determines the emergence of an international money *market*, which articulates itself to an expanding and convoluted international *financial* market.

2   1980–1981: the deregulation of international capital flows, or the creation of the global financial market. In this context of an absence of an organized international monetary system, the global credit or Eurocurrency market appears, meaning the creation of an unrestricted global liquidity space, without a clear development of the concomitant restricted national spaces of liquidity creation necessary to prevent *contagion* from the global market.

All measures taken in the different phases have the sole purpose of maintaining the dollar as the hegemonic currency, even after the end of the international monetary system in force from 1948 to 1971–1976.[5]

The structural situation in the US balance of payments reflects the evolution of the payments system and the US economic policy: in 1977, the period of current account structural deficits starts. But we must wait until 1983, so that the net balance of equity (foreign assets within the United States minus US assets abroad) starts to be positive, reflecting a policy of attracting foreign capital to offset the current account imbalance. As this deficit is increasing, the compensation policy is not sufficient to redress the balance of payments. It is from 1991 that positive balances are achieved, coinciding with the explosion of the Eurodollar markets.

The new system of financial globalization

From the 1980s, the fundamental role of the key currency is no longer as a means of international payment, but that of a monetary reserve of international value. The United States puts its economic policy in the service of maintaining this international role for its currency. To do this, in the absence of commercial hegemony, it develops a parallel system of an international movement of financial capital, the *Euro markets*, which will allow the dollar to be kept as the dominant currency, avoiding transferring to the currency the US trade and financial imbalances.

Thus, we see a period of dollar hegemony passing through three distinct phases or monetary settings:

1   1948–1971: under Bretton Woods rules, the international movement of goods is ultimately a barter trade: payments are made in metallic money, i.e.

in gold (backed dollars). This system can work as long as the United States guarantees sufficient reserves of gold and foreign currency equivalent to the value of accumulated dollars in central banks' reserves around the world. Therefore, in principle, the United States would be required to adjust the import/export prices (through the dollar-gold exchange rate or the wage rate), at the moment when the dollar accumulates into the reserves of the rest of the world and these become higher than the gold reserves in the United States.

2　1971–1985: however, when the structural conditions change, and the first current account deficits in the United States begin to appear, this country rejects the possibility of an adjustment of parities and prices and breaks the rules of the game: its politico-military dominance is a guarantee for the acceptance of a credit volume according to its needs for importing goods and services not supported by gold or foreign currencies reserves. The declaration of inconvertibility of the dollar automatically transforms dollar reserves in central banks around the world into debt against the US economy without material value and without guarantee other than their acceptability as banknotes of such securities. Thus, the international movement of goods and services continues for nearly a decade with creditors being devoid of the necessary strength either to enforce the credit execution – that is to say, accumulating dollars as credit titles – or to establish a new international payments system with international money provided with a real value guarantee.

3　1985 onwards: this pseudo-system of unlimited credit to *manufacturers of dollars* generates strong inflationary pressures; the accumulation of dollars is equivalent to an issue of domestic liquidity, and taking into consideration the discomfort of the central banks, the United States needs to design another system for the international settlement of debts. Financial deregulation that began in 1980 culminates in the middle of the decade with the spread of the *Euro markets*. The starting point for these lies in a transaction in which a value produced in a country ("rest of the world") is realized – sold – in another (United States), without involving any monetary payment between buyer and seller: an accounting transaction within the US banking system results in a payment from a bank account in the name of the importer to an account credited to the bank acting on behalf of the seller *inside the United States*: no international departure of credit money occurs, and therefore no increase in international liquidity. In exchange, the receiving bank obtains an *issuing permit* in a currency other than the US dollar: the opening and crediting of an account in the country of the seller or in a third country, in Eurodollars or in any other Eurocurrency. When a bank starts issuing Eurocurrencies they represent at the same time a bank asset.[6] Therefore, transactions in the era of financial globalization eliminate the presence of the monetary authority, and give a new role to banking institutions, which become guarantors of real transactions in exchange for an unrestricted right to issue (euro)money in a new global financial market.

Table 2.2 Stages in the evolution of the international monetary system

International monetary system phase	Bretton Woods 1948–1971	Bretton Woods Crisis 1971–1980	Financial Globalization 1980–2015 . . .
Payment means	commodity money (gold dollar)	national credit money (inconvertible dollar)	worldwide bank money (Eurocurrency)
Institutional Authority	IMF	Federal Reserve	none
Limit of the system	US balance of payments	US political and economic credibility	collapse of money creation-acceptance chain
System credibility	payments solvency	state credibility	bank credibility

The United States manage to pay for their imports not with exports, nor with debt issue, but by creating a new commodity, which may be called *global emissions of world credit permit*. The growing financialization of the world economy also translates into an increased ability on the part of the United States to cover its current account imbalance by attracting international liquidity. Thus, the United States still does not have to adjust its external imbalance, unlike the rest of the world, which ultimately can only pay for imports with exports. The asymmetry between the dollar and other national currencies in the Bretton Woods system was based on the commercial and production dominance by the US economy. The globalized financial non-monetary system is based on the political role of the United States in building the *confidence* that constitutes the basis of Euro markets' immaterial transactions.

Thanks to the global financial system, the United States can receive through international trade a massive transfer of wealth embodied in goods and services, keeping the money-capital which serves as payment money intact. Hence its interest in maintaining the dollar as reserve currency and especially as a money safe haven: in the case of other currencies appearing to play the same role, there would be no way to avoid the incorporation of the issuing country on the privileged side of international transactions, now occupied exclusively by the United States.

The counterpart to this procedure of central banking sidestepping in the process of international transactions settlement is the full autonomy of the launched global financial (banking) system, which amounts to the realization of the fifth phase in the evolution of the banking system previously outlined.

The limits of globalization: new monetary and financial rivalries

Euro markets' growth can only be controlled if a system of reserve requirements for operations in all countries is established. But this is tantamount to the establishment of an international monetary authority, the only way to regulate a system of reserves for banks worldwide. As reserve requirements are essential to allow control over the size of the money multiplier, Euro markets are only compatible with a monetary authority if this is international; that is, if monetary policy is transferred to a supranational global authority.[7] It therefore requires a new international monetary system to no longer have *free* Euro markets and change them into regulated markets.

We must consider that the currency market is not a market like any other for at least two reasons:

1   If the goods and services markets are a matter of private actors, and a state's presence can always be treated as any another producer, consumer or agent, the state (or the monetary authority) plays a specific role in the currency market, since *it can act unilaterally over its offer.*

2   Currency is not demanded for itself, unlike steel or hairdressing services. It is possible to build a utility function or a demand for currency; but they are always defined in terms of the rest of the economy. *Isolation of the currency market* derives from transaction demand. Therefore it is not possible to construct an equilibrium on the currency market and on the commodities markets unless these are isolated from each other. In the absence of state regulation, i.e. under free or pure market conditions, the existence of a creation and circulation of money does not result in any case in a hypothetical equilibrium price or emptying, as the absence of any notion of a coherent economic balance is the defining characteristic of a currency market short-circuited from the circulation of real values.

Moving into the international economy poses additional problems:[8] first, at an international level, *a single currency has two prices* at the same time:

•   one price in *time* (the interest rate);
•   another price in *space* (the exchange rate), its price in another currency.

The exchange rate of two currencies, the relative price of one currency in terms of another, introduces into the market of one of them the consequences of decisions taken by the state that owns the other currency.

The exchange rate may be set, but then it is necessary to act on the balance of payments to balance them, or act on reserves, an operation which cannot last for more than a short period. If the state does not do so, or fails to do so, we can still assume that markets are efficient: if n–1 national money markets are in equilibrium, then the nth market will also be in equilibrium. But there are conditions for this efficiency, which exceeds their performances in the national space: efficiency responds not only to empiricism, but to the logic of these markets. To the extent that an autonomous money market maintains communication channels with the real national economies, the result will be the inability to balance these same economies.

Theorems based on international monetary theory defined in the first half of the 1970s (under a fixed exchange rate, the approach is defined by the monetary theory of the balance of payments; and under a floating exchange rate regime, the monetary approach is defined by the determination of the exchange rate, and the theory of its dynamics) are invalidated under the new conditions of the new type of financial crisis; that is, an autonomous financial crisis detached from the productive dynamics. The economic crisis shows that what was defined as a theory was nothing more than a set of hypotheses or assumptions that, despite kicking against the real economies' dynamics, becomes in the 1980s the official ideology of international funding agencies.

Since the system of the gold-dollar standard began to show its limits, the European Union (EU) acted to isolate itself from the international monetary crisis more quickly and effectively than Japan. The creation of the European Monetary System is the regional monetary stabilization response to the decision by the United States/IMF to initiate a worldwide phase of market exchange rates deregulation. The decision to create a European currency is the EU response to the attempt to keep the dollar as an international currency in a context of commercial hegemony decay on its part.

Central banks' reserves have a strategic importance in shaping the world imperialist hierarchy. While monetary creation is a national phenomenon, countries whose national currency is part of central banks' reserves in the rest of the world gain a privileged position in the real exchanges: having an accepted currency worldwide amounts to the procurement of real and actual value (commodities) in exchange for credits. In addition, objects of specific use-value (imports) are obtained in exchange for mere signals of generic exchange value: foreign holders of such currencies can exchange them for goods exported from the country issuing the currency, or they can spend them in the issuer country in exchange for any non-tradable good or service. So, while countries without an international accepted currency are forced to produce exportable goods of equivalent value to that of the desired imports, the country producer of international currency can import presenting its entire production of exchange values as the potential counterparty value of such imports, making imports a lesser restriction in the general resources allocation, while they become a major constraint in countries without currency accepted as a sign of international payment. For the latter, the higher the structural dependence on imports, the harder the imports restriction is.

This asymmetry is reinforced if the currency of the issuing country acts as an international reserve of value; that is, if central banks take hold of it in their reserves over long periods of time.

Monetary stability is one of the conditions for a currency to be accepted as an international reserve of value; that is, for it to stabilize over time and space its function of a general equivalent of value. But the stability of a currency is twofold: as an international means of payment, stability is given by the relative value of the currency in terms of other national currencies (exchange rate or amount of exchange values of international circulation which it can be changed for). But as a reserve of value, the stability reference is the amount of value that can be purchased in the issuing country: low inflation and high interest rate will be the key signals to determine the degree of stability of a currency that acts as an international reserve of value.

In this sense we can interpret the reaction of the United States to the process of the creation of the European single currency: the policy of raising interest rates and maintaining an overvalued exchange rate is an important part of the strategy of the creators of the dollar to prevent the euro disputing the position which the dollar enjoys currently through its hegemony in the constitution of central banks' reserves around the world and in the creation of Eurocurrency issuing permits.

The periphery, apart

The existence of this double international financial circuit (foreign exchange and Eurocurrency circuits) results in an exponential growth of speculative financial transactions, particularly in the interbank market, with the set-off of an important growth in global financial liquidity. According to Bank for International Settlements (BIS) statistics, between 2000 and 2015, total bank credit (local and cross-border claims) more than doubled from 38.9 trillion US dollars in March 2000 to 98.2 trillion US dollars in March 2015, from 120 per cent of global GDP in 2000 to 130 per cent in 2015.

International credit for its part, stepped from 11.5 trillion US dollars in March 2000 to 40.8 trillion US dollars in March 2008. After the outbreak of the interbank crisis, it has remained around 33 trillion US dollars annually, constituting more than half interbank credit.

The circuit of the Eurocurrency: financial derivatives

The deregulated interbank market is the only one in which Say's Law holds (all supply creates its own demand) and it articulates with the derivatives market, forming a *casino economy*, in which bets/transactions are established in Eurocurrency and gains are removed in national foreign exchange. Therefore, from the productive economy point of view, the problem is not so much the volume of transactions in the Eurocurrency markets, but the marginal returns on this fictitious capital, very real returns reflecting a strong pressure on the real surplus of the world economy exerted by financial income.

Thus, the notional contracts in over-the-counter (OTC) derivative financial markets' products have grown from an outright amount to an outstanding value of 72 trillion US dollars in June 1998 to more than 630 trillion US dollars in December 2014,[9] with a market value that has risen from 2.6 trillion US dollars to 20.9 trillion US dollars. The financial crisis of 2007 slowed the pace of growth in the creation of derivative products, but did not reduce the size thereof, and there was only partly an adjustment in its economic value.

The massive accumulation of financial derivatives – in notional terms, from the 2007 crisis onwards, around 600–700 billion US dollars, approximately 10 to 12 times the value of world production – is practically a business between financial

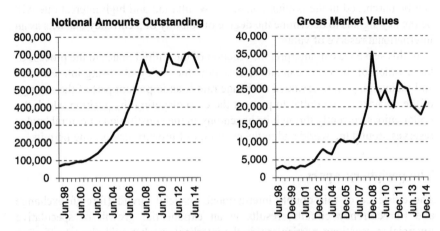

Figure 2.2 Over-the-counter (OTC) derivatives (billions of US dollars).

Source: *BIS Quarterly Review*, September 2015 and database.

agents. Non-financial corporations have increasingly reduced their weight in the OTC markets, and their weight in the foreign exchange, interest rates and equity-linked derivative contracts has been reduced from 12 per cent of the notional amount at the beginning of the twenty-first century to 4 per cent in 2013–2014. Of the 605 trillion US dollars representing the notional amount value of those OTC contracts in December 2014, only 24.5 trillion US dollars had non-financial corporations as a counterpart, with a gross market value equivalent to 1.5 trillion US dollars.

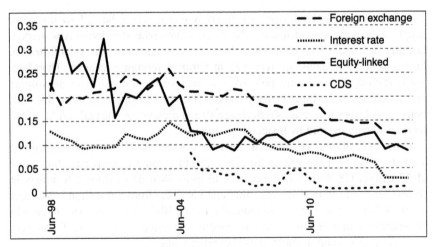

Figure 2.3 Non-financial institutions counterparties of OTC deals. Percentage of notional amounts outstanding.

Source: BIS semi-annual OTC derivatives statistics.

In any case, assuming – only in order to estimate the extent of the phenomenon – an average return of 0.5 per cent on the 20.9 trillion dollars gross market value of financial derivatives in unregulated markets, they represent a profit of more than 104 billion US dollars in December 2014, which would appear in the form of foreign exchange as financial rents to be realized only in exchange for real production surplus. Speculative gains in the Eurocurrency markets represent a pressure to increase the share of financial capital participation in the distribution of value added.

The international debt securities issues

In 1993, international debt securities issues for the first time exceeded 100 billion US dollars, around 0.4 per cent of global GDP, and gradually grew to 1.4 trillion US dollars in April 2015, 1.9 per cent of world GDP.

Issues from developing countries exert a countercyclical effect in relation to issues from developed countries: industrial crises in the early 1970s and early 1990s coincided with a rise in peripheral countries' issues of international debt

Table 2.3 Net issues of international debt securities (millions of US dollars)

	1980–1989	1990–1999	2000–2009	2010–2015Q2
All countries	865,190	3,680,870	14,091,529	3,441,697
Developed countries	695,759	2,468,569	12,371,549	1,006,615
Developing countries	15,970	456,777	455,591	984,653

Source: BIS securities statistics database.

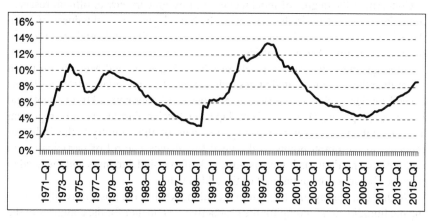

Figure 2.4 International debt securities issued from developing countries (% of total amounts outstanding).

Source: BIS, quarterly data.

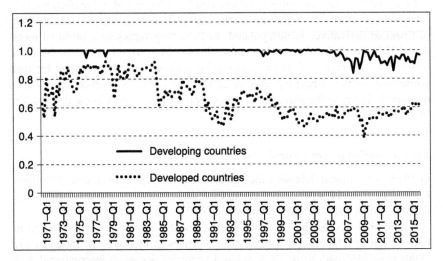

Figure 2.5 International debt securities issued in foreign currencies (% of total).

Source: BIS, quarterly data.

securities; this happened again after the 2007 crisis, when their weight equalled that of the central countries, which experienced a slowdown in net issues – a large part of the gross emissions are allocated to deleveraging – while on the contrary, on the periphery, international issues of debt securities underwent a significant growth.

A fundamental difference in peripheral international debt securities issues from the issues of core countries is that almost all those peripheral countries' issues are carried out in foreign currency.

Concerning the degree of indebtedness in foreign currency to official reserves in the largest countries in the periphery, the high degree of indebtedness of Latin American countries stands out, in clear contrast with the prudential management of reserves in most Asian countries.

Although the indebtedness levels of Chile, Argentina and Mexico are much lower than those of the United States (where securities in foreign currencies issues exceed foreign exchange reserves by 530 per cent), Germany (310 per cent) and France (313 per cent), issues from Japan in foreign currencies only represent 15 per cent of the foreign exchange reserves of this country;[10] the indicator reflected in the graph points to the need to enhance control of participation in international markets, as it increases the risk of over-indebtedness and the need to transfer abroad a substantial part of the added value.

Neither can we say that this international market has the possibility of increasing the liquidity and funding for the productive system, nor for the countries of the periphery. Eight out of every ten dollars of international debt securities issued by developed countries belong to the financial sector, and even if the financial sector in the case of developing countries only reaches half of these issues, in recent

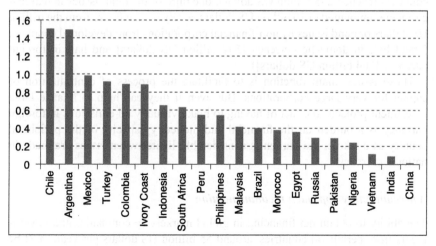

Figure 2.6 International issues of debt securities in foreign currencies on a residential basis (amounts outstanding) as a percentage of foreign reserves (2015).

Source: BIS, quarterly data. Debt securities statistics database.

years there is a clear increase in financial corporations' weight in total emissions, coinciding with the increased importance of the peripheral countries' issues.

Between 2010 and the second quarter of 2015, net issues of international debt securities in foreign currencies by non-financial corporations from developing

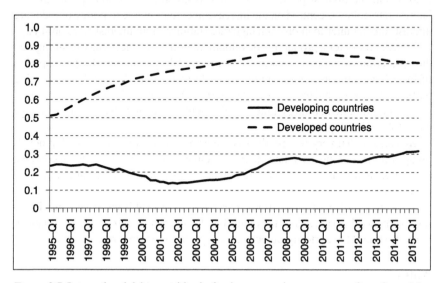

Figure 2.7 International debt securities in foreign currencies: percentage from financial corporations (amounts outstanding).

Source: BIS, quarterly data. Debt securities statistics database.

countries reached 298 billion US dollars, one third of the total. Issues in national currencies amounted to 30 billion US dollars, a very distant figure from the trillion US dollars of bond issues by non-financial corporations from developed countries (about half in domestic currency [552 billion US dollars] and half in foreign currency [504 billion US dollars]).

Those issues' main function is to facilitate the process of centralization of capital for very large corporations. But even if they can help to finance large investment projects, the fact of having to make virtually all emissions in foreign currency is a burden on the financial and monetary capacity of the peripheral country as a whole; the burden is considerably lighter when issues are made in national currency.

A precautionary approach recommendation

The ability to obtain net financing in global markets by companies and governments from peripheral countries, around 55 billion US dollars per year, must be carefully managed, with rigorous assessment criteria of exchange risks and the potential profitability of the investments pursued. Thus, the consideration of risks and their implicit translation into international financing cost would advise against nearly all issues on the international markets, except for those investment projects that imply a particularly high volume of funds and require an international credit union.

The main source of pressure for the stabilization of exchange rates derives largely from foreign currency funding by local agents. But if the policy objective is to obtain the highest possible rates of investment, it is a prerequisite that an interest rate policy is centred on the increase in credit volume (a policy of reducing interest rates), rather than on exchange rate stability (high interest rates policy).

To make room for a productive development policy, it is necessary to strengthen the regulation of national banking systems, legally preventing the participation of local financial corporations in the OTC derivatives markets and discouraging participation in organized derivatives markets by higher risk coverage requirements and more demanding capital requirements for entities that want to manage a portfolio of such products.

We can say that very few productive investments would be unfunded in developing countries, if they renounce their participation in global markets. In contrast, foreign exchange and exchange rate management would gain important degrees of freedom.

Since the problem of international currency has not yet been solved, the deflating of financial currency markets and the elimination of Eurocurrency financial markets should be a priority objective for a global economic restructuring.

Notes

1   A longer version of this chapter was presented in June 2009 at the second *Convegno Crisi e Alternative. I nodi della Transizione: Forze produttive, rapporti di produzione e scienza* in Pisa (Italy) with the title: *La Crisi: non solo economica e finanziaria.*

I want to thank Denise O'Flynn for her help to convert a text written in Spanglish into a readable document in English.

2 "Das Papiergeld ist Goldzeichen oder Geldzeichen", in Marx (1979: 142; see also 138–160).

3 Chick (1986: 111–126); Chick and Dow (1988: 219–250).

4

> Speculators may do no harm as bubbles on a steady stream of enterprise. But the position is serious when enterprise becomes the bubble on a whirlpool of speculation. When the capital development of a country becomes a by-product of the activities of a casino, the job is likely to be ill-done.
>
> (Keynes 1936: chapter 12)

5 A presentation of the key currency concept and its historical evolution, with different conclusions to those presented here, in Aglietta (1986).

6 The trigger mechanism of this process is well described in Krugman and Obstfeld (1994: 780ss), even if they do not go beyond the mechanical description of the process. Surprisingly, in subsequent editions of this well-known handbook, the explanation of the process of Eurocurrency creation is suppressed. See also Gill (1983: 157ss).

7 The loss of control over short-term monetary aggregates by central banks is explained by the presence of the Euro markets, and this explains in turn why inflation control is only achieved currently by acting firmly over those variables generating money demand, particularly wages.

8 The ideas in the following paragraphs are widely developed in the work of G. Destanne de Bernis. See Byé and de Bernis (1987: 320–406).

9 In the same period, derivatives contracts on regulated markets went from a notional amount outstanding of 13.4 trillion US dollars to 57.6 trillion US dollars, following a peak of 86.5 trillion US dollars in June 2007.

10 International issuances of debt securities in foreign currency are calculated on the basis of residence of the issuer, involving an amount greater than if estimated on the basis of the nationality of the issuer, in which case issues from US agents represent 242 per cent of US foreign exchange reserves, the German issuers 147 per cent, 128 per cent for French and 175 per cent for the Japanese issuers! – a clear signal of how Japanese multinational corporations' financial policy prefers to burden foreign reserves with a risk of an issuer default, rather than the Japanese national reserves. Argentine agents have issued at April 2015 the equivalent of 148 per cent of this country's reserves, Chilean corporations 128 per cent and China's agents 11 per cent. From the point of view of a possible impact on reserves safety, the appropriate criterion is the residence of the issuer.

References

Aglietta, M. (1986). *La fin des devises clés*. Paris: La Découverte.

Aglietta, M. and Rigot, S. (2009). *Crise et rénovation de la finance*. Paris: Odile Jacob.

Byé, M. andt de Bernis, G. D. (1987). *Relations économiques internationales*. Paris: Dalloz.

Chick, V. (1986). "The evolution of the banking system and the theory of saving, investment and interest", *Économies et Sociétés (Cahiers de l'ISMEA, Série Monnaie et Production)* 3: 111–126.

Chick, V. and Dow, S. (1988). "A postkeynesian perspective on the relation between banking and regional development", in P. Arestis (Ed.), *Post-Keynesian Monetary Economics: New Approaches to Financial Modelling*. Aldershot, UK: Edward Elgar, pp. 219–250.

de Larosière, J., Balcerowicz, L., Issing, O., Masera, R., McCarthy, C., Nyberg, L., Pérez, J. and Ruding, O. (2009). *Rapport du Groupe de haut niveau sur la surveillance* [réalisé sur demande du Président de la Commission européenne José Manuel Barroso en octobre 2008, et remis le 25 février 2009]. Available at: http://ec.europa.eu/internal_ market/finances/docs/de_larosiere_report_fr.pdf (accessed 18 October 2015).

Eichengreen, B. (1999). *Toward a New International Financial Architecture: A Practical Post-Asia Agenda.* Washington, DC: Institute for International Economics.

Gill, L. (1983). *Économie mondiale et impérialisme.* Montréal, QC.: Boréal Express.

Keynes, J. M. (1936). *The General Theory of Employment, Interest, and Money.* London: Macmillan.

Krugman, P. and Obstfeld, M. (1994). *International Economics, Theory and Policy,* 3rd edn. New York: HarperCollins Publishers.

Lelart, M. (2011). *Le système monétaire international.* Paris: Repères/La Découverte.

Marx, K. (1979). *Das Kapital,* Marx–Engels Werke Vol. 23. Berlin: Dietz Verlag.

OECD (2008). *Growing Unequal? Income Distribution and Poverty in OECD Countries.* Paris: Organisation for Economic Co-operation and Development.

Rajan, R. (2009). *Fault Lines: How Hidden Fractures Still Threaten the World Economy.* Princeton, NJ: Princeton University Press.

Reinhart, C. M. and Rogoff, K. S. (2009). *This Time Is Different: Eight Centuries of Financial Folly.* Princeton, NJ: Princeton University Press.

Wolf, M. (2008). *Fixing Global Finance.* Baltimore, MD: Johns Hopkins University Press.

3 Financial development, instability and some confused equations

Faruk Ülgen

Introduction

Luigi Zingales stated in 2003:

> In his survey, Levine emphasizes how much we have learned in the past decade about the relation between finance and growth. Here, I have stressed how much we still need to know before this relation can be confidently used for policy purposes. In this area, the next decade promises to be as exciting as the past one.
>
> (Zingales 2003: 47)

Indeed, the first 15 years of the new millennium were really "exciting" since most economies could not grow in a sustainable way; unemployment and poverty did not decrease, recurrent and often systemic financial crises (amongst other types of crises) did severely hurt numerous economies, and instabilities and imbalances did govern major economic and political decisions, preventing billions of people from expecting a better future.

From the late 1970s onwards, a conventional wisdom related to the quadriptych "stabilization-privatization-liberalization-opening" set in through dissemination of the free market efficiency doctrine in academic and political discourses. Supported by the "Financial Repression" literature[1] and the so-called "Washington Consensus",[2] the International Monetary Fund (IMF) then worked to convince developing and emerging market economies (EMEs) to open their capital accounts and liberalize banking and financial systems, as it was argued that privatized finance (and trade, as well) would result in higher growth by improving the efficiency of resource allocation and increasing investment and employment. This new consensus became the dominant economic paradigm and political doctrine of the liberal era. In the "Foreword" to the World Bank 2005 Report, Gobind Nankani notes that:

> The Washington Consensus was not the only point of view among economists. But it was the dominant view, making it difficult for others to be heard, and it provided the framework for many of the reforms implemented during the 1990s by a wide spectrum of countries around the world.
>
> (World Bank 2005: vi–vii)

Since the 1980s, many advanced and emerging market economies liberalized their banking systems, opened their capital accounts and financial markets up to international transactions and sought to receive more international resources to fund their growth process. Another aim of such reforms was to modernize domestic productive and financial structures and to reduce the so-called institutional weaknesses that economies were supposed to suffer from, thanks to competitive pressures that would come from the entry of (more efficient) foreign enterprises. This was assumed to achieve strengthened and stable economic and financial conditions. However, the "goodbye to financial repression" was accompanied by "hello financial crises" through macroeconomic volatility and recurrent instabilities, as had already been stated by Diaz-Alejandro (1985).

Crises faced by EMEs since the beginning of the 1980s are usually described as crises of transition from underdeveloped financial systems towards open and liberalized market economies. The arguments put forward to support such an assertion, both in academic work and in the work of international institutions (such as the IMF and the World Bank [WB]), rest on well-defined theoretical foundations that mainly assume the efficiency of free/open market mechanisms to improve the working of economies according to some results of the models of financial repression of the 1960s–1970s.[3] Financial liberalization is then regarded as a prerequisite for financial development, and the development of financial systems as a prerogative for a successful international integration. This vision maintains that financial development and economic growth are positively correlated. It then asserts that capital account liberalization does directly stimulate growth as it should improve the economy's financing mechanisms through the intensification of competition and the import of efficient financial services.

However, the recurrence of financial crises in EMEs casts doubt on the relevance of such assertions. Particularly, the consistency of the extent and the speed of the process of financial liberalization and of opening up with regard to the characteristics (needs, capacities, capabilities, etc.) of EMEs are questionable. It is then worth reconsidering these questions and statements in light of the global 2007–2008 economic crisis. Indeed, the characteristics of this ongoing crisis, mainly related to the functioning of developed financial markets, call for a review of analytical models that support monetary and financial reforms implemented in EMEs (and in advanced economies as well).

In face of the ambiguous results of four decades of liberalization, the purpose of this chapter is to call into question the relevance of liberal finance and the related regulatory institutional environment to ensure durable and consistent economic growth. With this aim, the chapter also examines the lessons that could be drawn from the 2007–2008 crisis in order to put into a broader perspective the concern about instability of market-based financialized capitalist economies, beyond the specific cases observed in the process of transition in EMEs.

The chapter is then organized as follows: the first section sets out the conceptual foundations of financial liberalization reforms and points to the specific definition of financial development which is usually regarded as a process of liberalization and opening up. The second section deals with the logical links that could be established between the process of the aforementioned type of financial development and the subsequent crises in EMEs and in advanced economies. The last section draws some lessons from the 2007–2008 crisis for EMEs and argues that monetary and financial crises have their origin not only in the economic weaknesses of EMEs and developing economies, but rather in the "normal" functioning of liberalized economies. From this point of view, financial instability lies more in endogenous problems of financialized economies than in concerns related to underdevelopment. The last section concludes by advocating some alternative regulatory principles that could get capitalist finance and the development process on the right track and make them move forward without systemic crises.

Financial development: from liberalization to (in)efficiency

Banking, financial and exchange crises that the EMEs have been experiencing since the 1970s, often related to macroeconomic difficulties (for instance, external imbalances), are usually regarded as transition crises of underdeveloped financial systems. The focus is on the structural weaknesses that would make these economies unable to cope with the requirements of a successful financial integration.

The theoretical foundations of this interpretation lie mainly in two types of argument. The first argument is normative and can be identified by the structure of competitive equilibrium models that are used as the main analytical reference. The second is a positive argument which rests on the models of financial repression of the 1960s and 1970s. The development of these arguments results in statements about the relationship between financial development and economic growth. The characterization of financial development is then of paramount importance to establish a "roadmap" for the reforms that should be carried out in those EMEs that look for general macroeconomic consolidation and improvement of the conditions of financing for economic development. As Zingales (2003) asks:

> What does cause financial development (or lack thereof)? This question is important from the perspective of both theory and policy. From a theoretical point of view, as stated earlier, only by understanding the real causes of financial development can we devise the appropriate instruments to identify the causal relation between finance and growth. From a policy perspective, this is probably the most important question. It is of little use to know that a relation between finance and growth exists if policymakers do not know how to promote financial development.
>
> (Zingales 2003: 50–51)

Theoretical foundations

The theoretical foundations of approaches that advocate the opening and liberalization of financial systems with the aim of reaching a sustainable path of economic growth are to be found in what Schumpeter called the real approach. Indeed,

Schumpeter (1963) points to a distinction between two opposite approaches in economic analysis, real and monetary, to understand the working of capitalist economies. In real analysis, money enters the picture only as a technical device that does not affect the economic process.[4]

Without giving a comprehensive account of different theoretical models, it should be noted that in this "real vision", based on the model of competitive equilibrium, the financing of the economy occurs in financial markets that could reallocate loanable funds between agents who have financing capacity and agents in need of funding. When financial markets can operate in a flexible and free way, equalization of savings and investment through the interest rate would result in the efficient allocation of financial resources towards optimal uses. Financial markets are then regarded as any other market (a market of nuts or beans!) and their operating rules should not differ from those guiding the markets of other goods and services. After all, the economics profession asserts that the market of beans or the labour market (without any distinction) could operate effectively at an equilibrium if they were free of any state intervention. The same assertion could then hold for financial markets. In this context, two main arguments are advanced to explain the monetary and financial difficulties in market economies:

1   The first (normative and general) argument is about the development of markets: the solution-objective for underdeveloped markets would be the establishment of mechanisms of open markets (competitive equilibrium models).
2   The second (more specific) argument is the assertion that underdevelopment would be due to the ill-fitting financial system with regard to the first assertion (models of financial repression of the 1960s and 1970s, followed by researches on financial integration).

These two arguments implicitly bring forth the idea that an efficient financial market is a market that should not be hindered by public intervention. Indeed, liberalization is regarded as the prerequisite of financial integration and financial development. This causal assertion was claimed both through international organizations' stabilization programmes in the 1980s and the theoretical research conducted by liberal economists.[5]

As Fry (1997) claims:

> Since there is no question that financial repression inhibits growth, the debate should concentrate on the tricky problems of moving from the state of financial repression to a state of financial liberalisation. So far, the economics profession has failed to produce adequate blueprints for this crucial transition.
> (Fry 1997: 768–769)

Therefore, a first assertion states that financial development does first require financial liberalization, and financial development (measured as the level of activity of financial markets) is assumed to depend on the opening of capital accounts

(Chinn and Ito 2005). The second assertion is that financial development and economic growth are positively correlated. Bekaert *et al.* (2005) argue that capital account liberalization stimulates economic growth. Similarly, Klein and Olivei (1999) note that capital account liberalization, assumed to lead to financial development, could speed up economic growth since it would increase competition and promote imports of financial services.[6]

The definition of financial development rests on these arguments and assertions. Havrylyshyn and Wolf (1999) assert that in a broad sense, transition implies:

- liberalizing economic activity, prices and market operations;
- developing market-oriented instruments for macroeconomic stabilization;
- achieving effective enterprise management and economic efficiency which would require privatization;
- imposing hard budget constraints which would provide incentives to improve efficiency; and
- establishing an institutional and legal framework in order to secure property rights, the rule of law, and transparent market-entry regulations.

The authors then maintain, through an analysis over the 1990s, that "Another key determinant of progress is *the degree of reform or market liberalization.*"[7]

Development of financial markets

Most researchers maintain that financial development stimulates economic growth by improving efficiency of market allocation mechanisms and then increases the rate of accumulation of productive capital. Those works notice that the legal environment, openness and economic development are the major determinants of a sound financial structure (Levine 2005). In this vein, Cournède *et al.* (2015) give a comprehensive account of the possible positive transmission channels from finance to growth. The development of financial services is expected to stimulate economic growth by encouraging savings to be directed towards illiquid but productive investments instead of unproductive but liquid investments.[8] In a world with risky financial investments, economic agents may be reluctant to engage in illiquid assets at short-run. This would provoke more stringent conditions for the financing of entrepreneurial activities. Therefore developed financial intermediation structures would allow lenders to minimize information and checking costs about borrowers since developed intermediation could match investment portfolios with the characteristics of productive activities better than individual lenders – who are ill-informed about the characteristics of projects – could do (Thakor and Boot 2008).[9]

Financial intermediaries, especially banks, are then specialized in the production of specific information in credit markets, in stock exchange markets as well as in the production of financial assets. They are involved in the channelling of savings into productive investment by reducing the problems of moral hazard (imperfect information of individual lenders about the behaviour of borrowers) and adverse selection (incomplete information of individual lenders about the nature and characteristics of the projects to be financed). Through better management of risks on financial investments, the amount of funds that banks and other intermediaries can collect in markets and put at the disposal of borrowers would be increased.

Financial intermediation models, then, establish close links between financial development and financial liberalization. They maintain that liberalized financial markets lead to increased competition which should create incentives for banks to improve their activities through numerous innovations (Pagano 1993). Following this line, Rajan and Zingales (2000) argue that the degree of openness of an economy does determine the level of development of its financial system, as it is assumed to increase competition in the financial sector. Bekaert *et al.* (2011) assert that financial openness improves total factor productivity and enhances economic growth. Similarly, it is argued that financial openness to international competition constitutes a factor of development of financial markets insofar as the protection of investors would be further guaranteed by foreign institutions (assumed to be more efficient and innovative compared with domestic institutions) (see Ülgen [2013c] for a synthesis of these arguments).

From an eclectic perspective but still from a general equilibrium view, Dorrucci *et al.* (2009) give the following definition of financial development:

> A domestic financial market is developed when it consists of complete markets where: (i) an equilibrium price is determined for every asset in every state of the world; (ii) assets are available that protect against adverse shocks and (iii) other important features supplement completeness, such as transparency reducing asymmetric information problems, competition and the rule of law.
>
> (Dorrucci *et al.* 2009: 18)

This approach is also that of Mendoza *et al.* (2007: 2): "Financial development is defined by the extent to which financial contracts are enforceable",[10] and that of Hartmann *et al.* (2007) who put the emphasis on financial innovations that would improve the efficiency of markets.

One may then define financial development through three criteria: the depth, the breadth, and the liquidity of financial markets:

1   Market depth means that financial markets include diversified products and instruments, letting agents undertake different strategies and investments and cover the related risks. Deep markets are assumed to rely on financial innovations that would give agents a wide range of new products, new processes and new ways of organizing transactions.
2   Market breadth means that the size and organization of financial markets make possible large amounts of transactions operated by a large number of agents. Market breadth is assumed to rest on market openness (no entry and exit – economic and/or legal – barriers) that implicitly calls for competitive market-friendly regulatory reforms.

3   Market liquidity refers to the capacity and capability of markets to permit large amounts of transactions without any quantitative restriction. It is partly related to monetary and financial policies that should reinforce the role of financial markets in the economy without restrictive public regulation. Usually it is assumed that in a deep and large market, large sales would not affect prices much, and in a liquid market, quick selling would not reduce prices much. Thus developed financial markets are sizeable relative to the size of the economy. They can then provide the economy with various financial means (credit and other financial services).

In this vein, Dorrucci *et al.* (2009) set some indicators of *domestic financial development* (*DFD*), based on the concept of complete financial markets allowing a national economy to effectively channel loanable funds (savings) towards investments. This capacity is assessed through three dimensions:

1   institutions and rules;
2   diversification (depth), size (breadth) and openness (no barriers) of markets;
3   liquidity of the financial system (operational performance), efficiency of banks (ability to perform financing relations within the economy) and the participation of the whole private economy in comparison with the public sector financial activity.

In the same vein, Calderón and Kubota (2009) present an analysis of financial depth and openness over the period from 1947 to 2007 for a large sample of countries, and conclude that financial globalization may have clear benefits for financial development in the longer term even if it may create some short-run tensions. Financial globalization is usually understood as "the integration of a country's local financial system with international financial markets and institutions. This integration typically requires that governments liberalize the domestic financial sector and the capital account" (Schmukler 2004: 39).

However, those works do not deal with the issue of financial instability and eschew the analysis of the complexity of current financial crises and the role of financial innovations in financial instability. Now, recurrent crises in EMEs and the scope of the 2007–2008 crisis which started in developed financial markets cast doubt about the positive links that one could assume between financial development/financial liberalization and economic growth/development.

Financial development: emerging economies and the ongoing crisis

The Washington Consensus, asserting the optimality of market mechanisms and the need to reduce restrictive public regulations in markets, generated in the 1980s and 1990s a huge wave of financial liberalization all around the world.[11] Following this line, the structural transformations in major EMEs were mainly based on liberalization and openness. The banking and financial sector has been one of the first areas where these changes have occurred.

However, transformations have resulted in ambiguous outcomes that cast doubt on the relevance of reforms both with regard to their speed and the areas in which they have been implemented.

At the same time, the 2007–2008 crisis in advanced economies moved the discussion from some weaknesses specific to EMEs towards the systemic nature of instabilities related to the liberal context.

Problems of transition in EMEs

There is a long-lasting debate about the effects of financial liberalization on market economies and especially on EMEs. Opposed views argue, on the one hand, that financial liberalization would have positive effects on growth and macroeconomic stability at the long-run while it might have a harmful impact at the short-run (Kaminsky and Schmukler 2003). On the other hand, it is argued that the positive effects of financial liberalization are mainly short-run outcomes, and at the long-run, it usually generates destabilizing evolution in EMEs. Fratzscher and Bussiere (2004: 29) note that: "economic growth immediately after liberalisation is often driven by an investment boom and a surge in portfolio and debt inflows, which then become detrimental to economic growth in the medium- to long-run".

Monetary and financial reforms indeed provoke profound modifications in EMEs. The transformations of productive structures, much more opened to the effects of international disequilibria, make the previous financial relations less viable. Banks do not appear to be capable of quickly modifying their long-term domestic commitments whilst they should be dealing with new global challenges. The transition is also followed by a wave of privatizations of banking institutions and public enterprises. This reform is considered as a first fundamental stage in the transformation process, but it does not always result in an improvement of previous structures. The new environment reveals itself to be very fragile because of the lack of experience and means to fight against international competition from transnational firms.

Transformations also generate wide financial innovations (of product, process; or commercial) that suddenly involve banks in new practices and pressures in domestic debt and mortgage markets. The increasing power of short-term financial flows in markets affects the commitments of banks by urging them to favour investments of portfolio at the expense of long-term investments. This phenomenon aggravates an already difficult situation in EMEs, mainly due to the very loose/weak implication of banks in the financing of the productive economy, and results in serious problems of inefficiency of the system of credit.

In the analysis of these difficulties and the mechanisms that are required for a successful transition, two visions are opposed: the shock therapy and the gradual approach.[12] The shock therapy approach (Lipton and Sachs 1990; Istvan and Bonin 1992; Rapaczynski 1996) argues that the expected modifications are, in most cases, the results of market mechanisms. In a Hayekian vein, it is asserted that efficient and consistent economic structures should emerge from free market mechanisms. This approach maintains that "stabilization-liberalization-privatization" is the relevant way to allow institutions to consistently evolve without needing restrictive interventions and a visible hand of government (Schröder 2000).

However, spontaneous development of market institutions seems to be very complex and difficult, in particular when it is related to the banking and financial system. One may also note a strong resistance of local structures and inadequacy of methods used during the hasty implementation of reforms. This leads to some questions about the efficiency of the shock therapy approach (Furubotn 2000). Also, in most EMEs, the transformation process has to deal with the problems of high inflation, corporate and bank failures and financial crises that reduce the consistency of reforms.

With regard to these results, the gradual approach considers that the emergence of a consistent institutional and economic structure depends on conscious and voluntary collective actions (Kregel *et al.* 1992). It relies on the idea that the State and non-market structures have to pioneer structural transformations. It is also argued that economic behaviour depends on the path of evolution of the entire society and is shaped through historical and institutional time. Changes in various economies do not all have the same shape or require the same methods and speeds (North 2000).

The State and institutions appear to be decisive in the process of modification of existing structures (Hare 2001), not only as supervisors, but also and especially as coordinators. The invisible hand of markets has to be replaced by a visible hand of institutions that has to assess and verify the weaknesses and needs of the national economy and then the subsequent limits of reforms. In this gradualist approach, the attention is directed towards the failures of deregulated markets (Lavigne 2000). Contrary to the assertions of the shock therapy approach which considers that the presence of the State leads to no transparent parallel structures of power and corruption (Sachs *et al.* 1999), gradualists think that the corruption develops between the public decision-makers and market agents because of the weaknesses of institutions which are loosely reframed in favour of private market mechanisms. These weaknesses would generate the phenomenon of "State capture" (Hellman *et al.* 2000). In such situations, market mechanisms prove to be powerless to allow agents to undertake productive activities and then fuel economic growth. Public authorities should intervene with the aim of developing an adequate regulatory structure to shape the behaviour of private actors with regard to the capacities and weaknesses of domestic structures.

Edwards (2008: 22) points to some evidence which suggests that sequencing does matter since "'financial liberalization first' strategies increase the degree of vulnerability to crises. This is particularly the case if these strategies are pursued with pegged exchange rates and if they result in large current account imbalances". Edwards (2008: 22) also states that "The evidence on the effects of financial openness on growth and overall economic performance, however, is not that clear cut." In the emergence of efficient and well-structured markets, financial stability is a prerequisite for economic growth. This stability is supposed to depend, among other factors, on the degree of development of the banking and financial system. Baxter (2011) argues that financial development can heighten the risks of regulatory capture, while Berg and Ostry (2011) and Cournède *et al.* (2015) document how financial development can exacerbate income inequality. Sahay *et al.* (2015: 15) show that "too much finance increases the frequency of booms and busts and leaves countries ultimately worse off and with lower real GDP growth". The authors maintain, through a comprehensive analysis based on panel-estimation over the period from 1980 to 2013, that the positive relationship between financial development, growth and stability is dependent on numerous variables and is not linear and continuous. At some point, according to the structural characteristics of each economy ("one size does not fit all"), the costs of financial development (as a process of opening up and liberalization) outweigh the benefits, and also, too fast a pace leads to instability. The same results are also documented by Gambacorta *et al.* (2014: 29) who state that financial development (increases in bank and market activities) is "associated with higher growth, but only up to a certain point". The authors also point to the specific role played by banks – especially in less developed countries: "banks provide services which differ from those offered by financial markets and . . . such services prove to be particularly beneficial for less developed countries" (Gambacorta *et al.* 2014: 32). Broner and Ventura (2015) maintain that an economy at an early stage of development should adopt a discriminatory financial system which could keep domestic financial markets out of enforcement problems affecting foreign debts and the "capital flight" effect. Furthermore, the authors document how both advanced economies and EMEs experience higher economic activity before a banking crisis, but the decline in output once the crisis has hit the economy is larger for advanced countries, with a slower recovery. This suggests a positive relationship between the degree of development and sophistication of the financial sector and the severity of banking and financial crises. Such results could revive the debate between the liberal market-based finance approach and a more interventionist bank-based finance view, and provide further arguments in favour of the traditional banking systems in the process of development, but also in regard to concerns about the systemic stability of economic development.

Those results also offer a vanguard analysis to understand the evolution of financial fragilities in advanced economies in the 2000s, insofar as they embarked in an extremely hasty deregulation and liberalization process which seems to have reduced the efficiency of the mechanisms of prudential supervision on financial markets.

Evolution of (de)regulated finance

From the beginning of the wave of opening and liberalization of banking and financial markets in the 1980s, policy-makers adopted, both in EMEs and advanced economies, practices corresponding to the recommendations of liberal approaches that transformed regulatory structures into more market-related private and decentralized rating and self-assessment mechanisms.

As a matter of logic, from the hypothesis of complete and efficient financial markets, problems of illiquidity and insolvency were only regarded as individual-risk-related concerns. It was supposed that free markets had self-regulatory mech-anisms resting on market prices which would produce relevant information to effectively direct the behaviour of decentralized actors through (socially) optimal strategies. Private self-regulation mechanisms were assumed to work more efficiently than any other alternative public regulation systems (Ülgen 2015). To guarantee such an efficiency, liberal approaches maintain that the relevant legal environment must consist in setting up good (market-friendly) institutions to let individuals freely undertake any activity that they expect to be profitable. Then the institutional framework consistent with free markets should lie in a set of incentives based on transparency, disclosure and accountability of relevant information about the products and financial accounts. In this way, the market discipline would incite economic agents to higher responsibility with regard to the risky engagements they would take, since market transparency (the perfect information hypothesis of standard neoclassical models) could allow all participants to prevent the cheating strategies of dishonest individuals. In this vein, Barth *et al.* (2006) assert that repressive regulations resting on strong restrictive regulation of banking activities would not result in more stable financial systems. Therefore, micro-prudential and self-regulation mechanisms that aim at assessing what risks financial institutions could take at their individual level replaced macro-prudential supervision schemas which were mainly resting on public authorities' supervision.

This regulatory approach was assumed to increase competition in financial markets since banks were expected to engage in innovations in order to face new competitors or to use new opportunities. More competition should increase the efficiency of markets and reduce intermediation costs (Blondal *et al.* 2008). However, the OECD (2011) notes that pre-crisis financial deregulation allowed banks to change their business models in response to competition in a way that has proven negative for financial stability. More accurately, the OECD indicates in its report that:

> Competition and stability can co-exist in the financial sector: Competition helps make the financial sector more efficient and ensure that rescue and stimulus packages benefit final consumers. The results of the empirical studies linking competition and stability are ambiguous, however. Structural and non-structural measures of competition are found to be both positively and negatively associated with financial stability, depending on the country and the sample analysed and the measure of financial stability used. In the final analysis, the design of financial regulation matters at least as much as market structure for the stability of the banking sector.[13]
>
> (OECD 2011: 29)

Financial liberalization does indeed provoke structural transformations of financial systems and crowds out traditional long-run and personal (non-market) relations between banks and enterprises. The part of the traditional banking system which consists in financing the current production or in offering a bridge between the present investment and the forthcoming entrepreneurial innovations is reduced in favour of transactional banking (financial investment funds management) which inflates the role of off-balance-sheet activities, particularly through securitization. Contrary to classical banking activity, transactional banking relies on arbitraging operations that use various and complex financial assets created or innovated by banks. Banks develop specific products independently of the activities of industrial companies. The process of securitization thus grows in importance in the activities of financial markets and contributes to the orientation of the risks towards a parallel banking system (shadow banking) through loans with high leveraging, without access to the mechanisms of deposit insurance and thus not submitted to regulatory constraints on bank capital.

Numerous systemic consequences then come into the picture. Financial innovations increase the elasticity of the supply of finance, the flexibility of funds and the negotiability of debt instruments issued by enterprises (Ülgen 2013c). Financial innovations (through securitization, swaps and other off-balance-sheet commitments) allow lenders and borrowers to match various types of products and services available with various types of needs through wider diversification of related risks. Also, the use of lines of credit and related bank guarantees increases the marketability of debt instruments issued by non-banks.

It is worth noting that at the same time, systemic financial fragilities increase insofar as product and process innovations are directed towards less controlled transactions. Various and high risks are quickly transferred to various investors (including banks themselves) who are looking for high short-term returns through financial assets, whatever their composition and content. This market expansion is accompanied by the increasing access of a large number of agents (including low-income households) to new products, thanks to various possibilities to individually manage portfolio fluctuations at the microeconomic level.

However, these changes, expected to increase the allocative efficiency of markets, are accompanied by blindness and cognitive dissonance phenomena (Ülgen 2014, 2015). In a euphoric environment, stakeholders believe in their own fanciful anticipation and tend to manipulate their own belief in selecting information that could confirm their desired beliefs (Akerlof 2005). Indeed, with financial expansion, commitments become more flexible. This fuels expectations to realize substantial speculative gains while agents believe that they could easily cope with a reversal in the trend without much difficulty. Al-Darwish *et al.* (2011) notice that in liberalized and innovative financial markets, complex interconnections are created among different institutions. These connections contribute to the development of financial markets and give the impression of a greater efficiency in the use of loanable funds, but at the same time they contain the seeds of a contagion at systemic level, a contagion that is out of the reach of individuals and financial institutions.

Implications for financial stability

It appears that financial crises are not only related to the process of transition of some developing or emerging economies. Although liberal programmes were presented as a panacea for economic development, the consequences of liberalization are system-wide and affect all economies. The lessons that could be drawn from the results of more than 30 years of financial liberalization point to the weaknesses of loosely regulated markets. Also, the assertion that financial development is a positive economic and social evolution must be called into question, since it seems to lead sooner or later to increasing systemic instabilities. This obviously results in a clear need to review the foundations and aims of sustainable development-oriented monetary and financial policies.

Some confused equations

Obviously, what did not work in developed financial markets cannot be suitable for the development process of EMEs which are plagued by persistent structural weaknesses and urgent needs. From this point of view, it is unwise to rely on the belief that open and liberalized markets would have the ability to provide the "good" functioning of economies leading in the medium/long term to sustainable and self-adjusting growth. Furthermore, recent studies show that global financial integration does not obviously serve EMEs by reducing the costs of their access to capital markets and by allowing them to engage in long-term development investments through sustainable and stable debt relations. Calderón and Kubota (2009) mention, for instance, that

> The growing globalization of financial markets has led to some important changes in the patterns of saving and investment across the world: emerging market economies driven by emerging Asian and oil exporting countries have become net suppliers of savings while the United States is an absorber of global savings.
>
> (Calderón and Kubota 2009: 2)

Such an evolution fuelled the accumulation of imbalances and – without improving the conditions of international financing of the development process – involved some EMEs within the global speculative operations on the one hand. And, on the other hand, it pushed the surplus countries to conserve thousands of billions of dollars of idle foreign exchange reserves that kept mounting,[14] while official development assistance evolved on a cyclic path, decreasing until 2013 in real terms as a result, mainly, of fiscal austerity in many donor countries and the lasting global crisis of 2007–2008, and stabilizing again for the years 2014–2015 (United Nations 2015).

The evolution of financial systems rests, on the whole, on a new (speculative) accumulation rule which weighs on growth and development. This regime is no longer based on the financing of job-creating and wealth-improving productive activities for economic and welfare growth, but on the profitability of speculative positions throughout securitization transactions on the creation and transformation of various forms of debt. Such an evolution is supported by new speculative bubbles that continuously emerge thanks to high returns in financial markets (Ülgen, 2013d). Crises usually generated by this kind of accumulation regime in capitalist development require serious questioning of the regulatory mechanisms in force, especially during the last three decades.

There are mainly two types of interpretation of financial difficulties in liberalized economies, notwithstanding the recurrence and intensity of the last decades' crises and the systemic nature of the 2007–2008 worldwide turmoil. The first one focuses on the weaknesses of emerging institutional structures to explain the lack of direct positive link between growth and financial development in EMEs. The second interpretation relates the difficulties mainly to the endogenous instabilities generated by liberalized financial markets.

In the first category, Daniel and Jones (2007) present a review of the literature and emphasize that financial liberalization often leads to financial crises. When the banking system is assumed to be well structured, liberalization could result in growth, but it is usually followed by an increase of risks. Regulatory measures that imply higher levels of capitalization of banks or relate the liberalization process to the development of the banking system could then reduce the probability of crises, but would at the same time slow economic growth down. It is also argued that capital account liberalization does not necessarily lead to economic development. In fact, Rodrik and Subramanian (2008) show that in most EMEs, a drop in US interest rates does not imply much easier financing of domestic investment by further external savings. It seems that financial openness is beneficial to EMEs if they implement strong institutional infrastructure reforms. Otherwise, the authors argue that domestic investment will be low and inelastic to interest rate differentials, and the liberalization and opening will only encourage domestic consumption with increasing external funding that would replace domestic savings.

From this perspective, Prasad *et al.* (2006) point to the paradox of financial openness and growth and document how there is a negative correlation between capital inflows and growth (and, respectively, a positive correlation between current account balance and growth) in EMEs. There are two reasons for this evolution: (i) low domestic financial development (DFD) restricts the scope of opportunities for investment and consumption with profitable funding; and (ii) the absorption of foreign capital may involve an overvaluation of the exchange rate, which is detrimental to growth. The authors argue that the liberalization of capital movements in economies which are not financially developed may negatively affect the DFD process. More accurately this would be due to the fact that:

1   Governments may be tempted to make use of external debt and not seek to develop domestic capital markets.
2   Domestic investors may have weak incentives to work for necessary reforms in the national financial system as they have the opportunity to move their savings toward international markets.

In line with these statements that focus more on foreign direct investments (FDIs), Obstfeld (2009) acknowledges the difficulties in establishing direct and obvious links between financial development and growth. However, he argues that financial globalization might be beneficial to EMEs if they create institutions able to make their economies more attractive to international finance.

The second category of research focuses on the negative consequences of financial liberalization for the economies. These works usually point to the concerns raised by Hyman Minsky through his analysis of the US economy after World War II. Minsky (1986) maintains that securitization, initially developed in US mortgage markets, helped saving banks to continue to increase their debt-transformation activities, despite the rise of market risks and the decline in their ability to cope with sudden reversals through the use of their own capital. Minsky regards financial instability as an endogenous and crucial phenomenon. He then maintains that the destructive power of financial markets and instabilities calls for the development of a macro-prudential framework consistent with the aim of enhancing the financing conditions of productive long-term economic activities. Indeed, in a weakly regulated environment, increasing financial fragilities will sooner or later involve the productive sphere in systemic financial crises. Hence, economic recovery depends on relevant supervision and control mechanisms that are more consistent with the financing needs of the development process. In the same vein, Coval *et al.* (2009) also show the links between the activity of securitization of banks and the onset of financial instability. Stiglitz *et al.* (2006) point out that financial liberalization increases systemic weaknesses as it does reduce the scope of regulatory mechanisms. From a Post-Keynesian perspective, Raines and Leathers (2011) underline how the evolution of financial markets causes the deterioration of financing conditions of entrepreneurial activities in favour of more financialized but fragile economic systems. Furthermore, in liberalized market economies, there is no automatic bridge between micro-prudential behaviour and macroeconomic stability. This bridge which rests on public organization and macro-prudential supervision of markets was broken down from the 1980s through financial liberalization policies. Private actors can therefore imagine, innovate and implement new products and processes in order to make further gains, but also to cover their own positions against risks without worrying about the systemic consequences of their individually rational strategies. Actually, they are not able to assess the likely effects of macroeconomic imbalances on their individual position. Macroeconomic stability is not in their individual field of action, while their individual behaviour affects macroeconomic stability through complex interlinkages created by financial markets' evolution. Moreover, macroeconomic imbalances increase the potential effects that a sudden reversal of market expectations could have on individual situations, regardless of the state of solvency of micro decision units.

Considering the numerous problems that developing countries suffered in the last decades, such as financial fragilities, greater propensity to crisis and negative deflationary and developmental effects, Ghosh (2005) asserts that there is a strong case for developing countries to ensure that their own financial systems are adequately regulated with respect to their own specific requirements. Ghosh (2005) then maintains that:

> the real solution for such problems is to encourage greater openness about the direction of finance and to increase public accountability of such financial transactions, rather than leave socially important decisions of resource allocation to the workings of private financial markets that are neither accountable nor transparent and that, in any case, are prone to various types of market failure.

> (Ghosh 2005: 17)

In the wake of the 2007–2008 crisis, several works shed light on the systemic weaknesses provoked by financial liberalization (Stiglitz *et al.* 2006; Jenkinson *et al.* 2008) and insist on desirable financial regulatory reforms with the aim of reaching greater stability of market economies (Brunnermeier *et al.* 2009; Galati and Moessner 2011). The common result that emerges from these works is the need to review the principles on which the organization of financial markets should be based. It is argued that the after-crisis interventions of authorities are very costly, and often ineffective as well in the case of EMEs (1990s to 2000s), compared to advanced economies (e.g. the current crisis) (Frenkel and Rapetti 2009).

Major lasting issues after four decades of assertions

The links between the recurrent crises in EMEs, the magnitude of the current crisis in financialized economies and the functioning of monetary and financial markets surely raise the question of the relevance of financial liberalization policies. At the same time, the right direction that EMEs should take for their economic and financial development process remains a long-lasting matter of debate. Recurrent crises reveal that maintaining the objective of financial development as defined by standard liberal models means the preservation of a permanent crisis-prone environment that regularly leads to systemic catastrophes. The recent experiences suggest that the assumed links between financial liberalization/openness and economic growth/development have to be questioned. Although they do not call into question the relevance of global financial liberalization, the comprehensive historical study of Rousseau and Sylla (2003) and the findings of Gambacorta *et al.* (2014) point to the crucial role of stable financing mechanisms in the process of emergence, especially when the banking system and public support are well directed through the long-term financial needs of economies. In the same prudent vein, Čihák *et al.* (2013: 19) state: "This paper illustrates that financial sectors come in different shapes and sizes, and they differ widely in terms of their performance. The paper also emphasizes a need for humility, and for further research".[15]

Estrada *et al.* (2010) put the emphasis on the necessary strengthening of prudential regulation and supervision systems to accompany financial integration of markets at a global level, and to prevent economies from suffering instabilities. More interesting is that the authors maintain that the primary role of financial development in growth is to shift away from mobilizing savings towards improving the efficiency of investment to contribute to higher productivity. One might surmise that, from a developmental perspective, the efficiency of investment should be related to the reinforcement of socially sustainable and welfare-producing activities supported by durable funding practices through stable and enhanced banking systems.

On the one hand, the last decades' experiences show that there is no direct link between a financially liberalized environment and sustainable growth. On the other hand, the likely effects of market-based financial development to improve the conditions for financing productive activities are not obviously positive. The supposed efficiency of free market mechanisms lies more in ideological assertions than in logically framed market-economy models and in observed objective results. Indeed, the links between finance and growth do not appear in the form of a positive direct link, but rather through speculative gains which fuel bubbles that create the illusion of growth which is continuously belied by financial crises. The case of EMEs – like Argentina, Brazil, Mexico and Turkey, amongst others – in the period from the 1980s to the 2000s, and that of the US economy and many European economies in the last decade appear to be a painful illustration.

One can rather draw from those experiences a negative conclusion about the relevance of financial liberalization policies that were mainly based on the doctrinal belief in self-regulating market forces, and then were not able to offer structured and sustainable development strategies. By definition, those policies relate any development strategy to the liberalization and openness of markets which are expected to generate positive development dynamics. It should be noted, however, that development is a process that must rest on a long-term sustainable objective-based programme. These objectives must be structural objectives (choice of development strategy, improvement in income distribution, a socially and environmentally sustainable productive system, structural approach to development, etc.). Along this line, two recurrent concerns threaten the EMEs' development process in the short term and require special attention:

1 What could be the advantages of regional trade agreements as coordination devices to cope with the dependence of EMEs on exports, particularly in the current situation where global demand remains sluggish and the problem of external imbalances rises again and creates the "mad waltz of FDIs" in EMEs?
2 What could be the relevance of regional monetary/financial agreements to deal with capital outflows? At the moment, FDIs take an opportunistic position on public and private debts in EMEs (until things improve in advanced economies). But with persistent difficulties in European markets, the accumulation of global imbalances may have a very strong impact on EMEs' access to international financial markets.

However, these issues may only be considered if a crucial question is asked and dealt with in advance: according to what objective, could (or should) regional coordination mechanisms (trade agreements, monetary/financial unions, etc., such as Mercosur or the Andean FTA) develop? If the main orientation is to replicate the choices that have hitherto guided financial reforms in the EMEs, the question would only find standard answers that have been repeated for decades and resulted in the crises of the previous decades. It seems that we need to revisit the concept of development both in the financial domain and in the social field. Stabilization policies must also be discussed and designed through a less partisan framework on market economies and in a more constructive way aiming at enhancing societal wellbeing in the world.

Conclusion

In a very "humble" report – but with only a relative *mea culpa* – the World Bank (2005) confesses that

> the growth benefits of the financial and nonfinancial reforms in the 1990s were less than expected. Financial crises raised questions of whether financial liberalization was the wrong model, what had gone wrong, and the appropriate direction of future financial sector policy.

> (World Bank 2005: 207)

In a very optimistic way, Rodrik (2006) thinks that this report

> warns us to be skeptical of top-down, comprehensive, universal solutions—no matter how well intentioned they may be. And it reminds us that the requisite economic analysis—hard as it is, in the absence of specific blueprints—has to be done case by case.

> (Rodrik 2006: 986)

In the wake of the 2007–2008 worldwide turmoil, Čihák *et al.* (2013) reiterate the same *mea culpa* and state that:

> Interestingly, there is not much of a difference between the reported measures of financial stability in different groups of countries . . . For example, the reported z-scores in developed economies and developing economies appear identical . . . This is in line with the global financial crisis experience: financial instability occurred both in developed economies and in developing economies. The distinguishing factors were other things, such as [the] quality of the regulatory and institutional framework, rather than the level of development.

> (Čihák *et al.* 2013: 13)

Indeed, in the wake of the (Alas! still ongoing) 2007–2008 financial – and then worldwide economic – crisis, assertions on the links between financial development/ financial liberalization and economic growth/development became a bit humble and tried to take into account, at least in public debates, some salient problems of the liberal ideology with regard to the long-lasting problems that market-based capitalist (advanced as well as emerging and developing) economies suffer in a recurrent way and under the weight of economic and financial crises of the last decades. Although the blind belief about the virtues of free market mechanisms remains dominant in academic and political discourses, some "dissent analyses" have come to be regarded as relevant studies in the understanding of the dysfunctioning of financial markets and self-regulated financial systems.

This chapter sought to give a brief account of the ambivalence towards the approaches and policies that involved market economies in a generalized financial liberalization process, and that resulted from the 1980s in recurrent systemic crises that outweighed the possible positive outcomes of globalization and intensified international economic and financial relations. The statistical and theoretical findings lead us to argue that even though financial and trade openness might provide participant economies with further growth and quantitative and qualitative development potential, the design, organization and management of the globalization process – especially in the financial area which is at the core of market-based capitalist economies – must be undertaken, supported and supervised through appropriate mechanisms which seek the public good. This does not mean that public authorities should govern every social activity within society, but it points to necessary public organization of the heart of our modern economies, the financial system, and required extra-market regulation. The fable of the invisible hand – the dream of a new, free society in the eighteenth and nineteenth centuries – that became an ideological weapon since the 1970s must be left in favour of more courageous societally consistent organizations and policies. As Fontana and Sawyer (2014) state:

> The monetary and financial systems should be re-structured to be consistent with sustainable growth and low unemployment. The major aims of this re-structuring would be to underpin financial stability, and more importantly to focus the financial sector on the allocation of funds into environmentally friendly investment.
>
> (Fontana and Sawyer 2014: 2)

The only way of preventing global imbalances and fighting worldwide poverty-generating systemic crises is to go beyond dominant ideologies and to frame constructive and consistent alternatives. The fear of new ways cannot lead to a bright future.

Notes

1 For instance, see the seminal works of McKinnon (1973), Shaw (1973) and Fry (1988, 1997), to quote but a few.
2 See Williamson (1990, 2000) and Naim (1999).
3 Balassa (1989) offers a comprehensive and insightful account of the main arguments of those seminal works of McKinnon (1973), Shaw (1973) and Fry (1988, 1997) that

have been advocating, since the 1960s and 1970s, domestic financial markets' liberalization and then capital account opening. Such structural changes would lift repression on bank and financial markets (and then on interest rates) and increase the extent of financial intermediation which would raise the rate of economic growth (improving the process of the allocation of capital towards efficient uses). However, Balassa concludes that

> excessively high interest rates will have unfavorable economic effects. Such a situation can be avoided if the liberalization of the banking system takes place under appropriate conditions, including monetary stability and the government supervision of the banks. This would further the goal of establishing equilibrium interest rates. Domestic financial liberalization may eventually be followed by the liberalization of the capital account. But, this would have to be preceded by trade liberalization in order to avoid unnecessary resource shifts.
>
> (Balassa 1989: 22)

4 This is the well-known money-veil image (roughly speaking, that is, the classical theory and Walrasian and neoclassical real equilibrium models) which would add nothing more to real phenomena. Contrary to this position, the "monetary approach" puts money at the heart of the analytical structure such that money is not added to a real economic structure which would already be at an equilibrium. Money and monetary relations would be, on the contrary, the *modus operandi* of economic relations. The monetary analysis is then defined as a theory of the economic process in terms of expenditure flows mainly financed by bank credit (i.e. the creation and circulation of entrepreneurial debts through the banking system). For a more precise analysis of this schema in a Keynesian perspective (Keynes 1939), see, among others, Cartelier (2007, 2013) and Ülgen (2013a).

5 For a presentation of the foundations and the scope of those approaches in economic policies, see references and related analysis in Ülgen (2013b).

6 It is worth noting that Arestis *et al.* (2015), pursuing a meta-analysis that covers a large number of the most representative empirical studies and estimations that are published as journal articles or working papers, point to the existence of *publication bias* in the finance-growth literature such that researchers and journal editors have a predisposition in favour of a particular theoretical and/or quantitative result that could provoke a kind of cognitive dissonance, preventing alternative works from relativizing the validity of assertions that advocate financial liberalization to strengthen the assumed links between finance, financial integration and growth.

7 My italics.

8 Although beyond the scope of this chapter, it is worth noting that this assertion has been proved to be wrong, as in the 2000s, highly "developed" financial markets in advanced economies served to direct resources towards unproductive liquid speculative investments instead of productive long-term and job-creating engagements and this resulted in a systemic catastrophe in 2007–2008.

9 A very interesting implication of such an analysis would be to argue that efficient markets are markets that should rest on a developed and enlarged intermediation process which could reduce the costs of direct (decentralized and individually guided) market mechanisms. But this is a frankly opposed conclusion to the dominant vision which asserts that financial development would lead to direct (disintermediated) financing mechanisms which could reduce costs of financing and augment the efficiency of financial markets.

10 However, Mendoza *et al.* (2007) argue that international financial integration (openness of domestic markets) can lead to large and persistent global imbalances if there is a financial heterogeneity among countries (such that they differ in the degree of domestic financial development).

11 See Serra and Stiglitz (2008) for a comprehensive account of the rules of this consensus and its implementation all around the world. See also Williamson (2005) and Rodrik (2006) for a clarification of a confused debate around the so-called Washington Consensus (which marked several decades of reforms in the EMEs and generated impassioned theoretical and political opposition among scholars and policy-makers) and also on the evolution of the position of major institutions like the World Bank vis-à-vis the liberalization reforms and their consequences for the development process.

12 Naim (1999) shows how much this starkly polarized debate was (and still is) an impassioned and ideology-related opposition between economists and policy-makers:

> Since the beginning, advocates of the Washington Consensus have been greatly divided about the pace and sequence of the reforms. Profound differences quickly emerged about the need or desirability of what came to be known as the application of a "shock therapy" [or alternatively "the big bang"] approach to policy reforms. This approach implied the implementation of as many reforms as quickly as possible. Others argued for a slower, more sequenced pace. This is not a debate just between experts in Washington and others elsewhere. It also rages among insiders. This is illustrated by Strobe Talbott's now famous remark during a 1993 trip to Moscow when he told an anxious Russian media that "what Russia needs is less shock and more therapy". The statement, warmly welcomed by many, was, however, clearly at odds with the line espoused by his colleagues at the US Treasury and by the IMF and World Bank with the active backing of the US government. That debate of course continues today and is far from resolved, with both sides declaring victory using the same facts to back their cases.
>
> (Naim 1999: section 1, para. 9)

13 However, the OECD staff believe that the problem is not the working of markets or the competition:

> The current crisis resulted from failures in financial market regulation, not failure of the market itself or of competition. . . . Competition and stability can co-exist in the financial sector. In fact, more competitive market structures can promote stability by reducing the number of banks that are "too big to fail".
>
> (OECD 2009: 7)

14 Sun (2015) reports that

> The money supply of the G4 (the United States, the United Kingdom, Euro Area, and Japan) – a proxy for global liquidity – rose from US$ 18 trillion in 2003 to US$ 35 trillion in 2014. Foreign exchange reserves – a proxy for official liquidity – increased four-fold from US$ 3.2 trillion in 2003 to over US$ 12 trillion in 2014. International debt security issuance by emerging market[s] – a proxy for private liquidity – increased four-fold from US$ 638 billion in 2003 to US$ 2.6 trillion in 2014. The external loans and deposits to emerging markets – another proxy for private liquidity – increased four-fold from US$ 734 billion in 2003 to US$ 3.1 trillion in 2014.
>
> (Sun 2015: 5)

15 For a similar analysis, see also Rodrik (2006).

References

Akerlof, G. A. (2005). *Explorations in Pragmatic Economics*, Selected Papers of G. A. Akerlof and Co-Authors. New York: Oxford University Press.

Al-Darwish, A., Hafeman, M., Impavido, G., Kemp, M. and O'Malley, P. (2011). "Possible Unintended Consequences of Basel III and Solvency II", IMF Working Paper WP/11/187.

Arestis, P., Chortareas, G. and Magkonis, G. (2015). "The Financial Development and Growth Nexus: A Meta-Analysis", *Journal of Economic Surveys*, 29(3): 549–565.

Balassa, B. (1989). "Financial Liberalization in Developing Countries", Policy, Planning, and Research Working Paper WPS 55, September. Washington, DC: World Bank.

Barth, J. R., Caprio, G. Jr. and Levine, R. (2006). *Rethinking Bank Regulation*. Cambridge, UK: Cambridge University Press.

Baxter, L. G. (2011). "'Capture' in Financial Regulation: Can we Channel it Toward the Common Good?", *Cornell Journal of Law and Public Policy*, 21(1): 175–200.

Bekaert, G., Harvey, C. R. and Lundblad, C. (2005). "Does Financial Liberalization Spur Growth?", *Journal of Financial Economics*, 77(1): 3–55.

Bekaert, G., Harvey, C. R. and Lundblad, C. (2011). "Financial Openness and Productivity", *World Development*, 39(1): 1–19.

Berg, A. G. and Ostry, J. D. (2011). "Inequality and Unsustainable Growth: Two Sides of the Same Coin?", IMF Staff Discussion Note, April 8, SDN/11/08.

Blondal, S., de Serres, A., Kobayakawa, S., Slok, T. and Vartia, L. (2008). "Regulation of Financial Systems and Economic Growth", in *Competition in the Financial Sector*, G20 Workshop Proceedings, 15–17 February, Bali, Indonesia, pp. 275–309. Available at: http://17g20.pa.go.kr/Documents/Proceeding_G20_WS_on_Competition_in_the_Fin_Sector.pdf (accessed on 9 September 2014).

Broner, F. A. and Ventura, J. (2015). "Rethinking the Effects of Financial Globalization", Universitat Pompeu Fabra, Department of Economics, Barcelona. Available at: http://crei.cat/people/broner/refglo.pdf (accessed 14 February 2016).

Brunnermeier, M., Crockett, A., Goodhart, Ch., Persaud, A. D. and Shin, H. (2009). *The Fundamental Principles of Financial Regulation*. Geneva Reports on the World Economy 11, Preliminary Conference Draft. Geneva, Switzerland: International Center for Monetary and Banking Studies (ICMB).

Calderón, C. and Kubota, M. (2009). "Does Financial Openness Lead to Deeper Domestic Financial Markets?", Policy Research Working Paper No. 4973. Washington, DC: World Bank.

Cartelier, J. (2007). "The Hypostasis of Money: An Economic Point of View", *Cambridge Journal of Economics*, 31(2): 217–233.

Cartelier, J. (2013). "Beyond Modern Academic Theory of Money", in F. Ülgen (Ed.), *New Contributions to Monetary Analysis. The Foundations of an Alternative Economic Paradigm*. London: Routledge, pp. 155–171.

Chinn, M. D. and Ito, H. (2005). "What Matters for Financial Development? Capital Controls, Institutions, and Interactions", NBER Working Paper No. 11370.

Čihák, M., Demirgüç-Kunt, A., Feyen, E. and Levine, R. (2013). "Financial Development in 205 Economies, 1960 to 2010", *The Journal of Financial Perspectives*, 1(2): 1–19.

Cournède, B., Denk, O. and Hoeller, P. (2015). "Finance and Inclusive Growth", *OECD Economic Policy Paper Series*, No. 14, June. Paris: OECD Publishing.

Coval, J., Jurek, J. and Stafford, E. (2009). "The Economics of Structured Finance", *Journal of Economic Perspectives*, 23(1): 3–25.

Daniel, B. C. and Jones, J. B. (2007). "Financial Liberalization and Banking Crises in Emerging Economies", *Journal of International Economics*, 72(1): 202–221.

Diaz-Alejandro, C. (1985). "Good-bye Financial Repression, Hello Financial Crash", *Journal of Development Economics*, 19(1–2): 1–24.

Dorrucci, E., Meyer-Cirkel, A. and Santabárbara, D. (2009). "Domestic Financial Development in Emerging Economies. Evidence and Implications", European Central Bank Occasional Paper No. 102.

Edwards, S. (2008). "Sequencing of Reforms, Financial Globalization, and Macroeconomic Vulnerability", NBER Working Paper No. 14384, October.

Estrada, G., Park, G. and Ramayandi, A. (2010). "Financial Development and Economic Growth in Developing Asia", Asian Development Bank Working Paper No. 223, November.

Fontana, G. and Sawyer, M. (2014). "The Macroeconomics and Financial System Requirements for a Sustainable Future", FESSUD Working Paper No. 53, August.

Fratzscher, M. and Bussiere, M. (2004). "Financial Openness and Growth: Short-Run Gain, Long-Run Pain?", ECB Working Paper No. 348.

Frenkel, R. and Rapetti, M. (2009). "A Developing Country View of the Current Global Crisis: What Should Not Be Forgotten and What Should Be Done", *Cambridge Journal of Economics*, 33(4): 685–702.

Fry, M. J. (1988). *Money, Interest, and Banking in Economic Development*. Baltimore, MD: The Johns Hopkins University Press.

Fry, M. J. (1997). "In Favour of Financial Liberalisation", *The Economic Journal*, 107(442): 754–770.

Furubotn, E. G. (2000). "Legal Reforms in Russia: Visible Steps, Obvious Gaps, and an Invisible Hand?", *Journal of Institutional and Theoretical Economics*, 156(1): 120–124.

Galati, G. and Moessner, R. (2011). "Macroprudential Policy: A Literature Review", BIS Working Paper No. 337.

Gambacorta, L., Yang, J. and Tsatsaronis, K. (2014). "Financial Structure and Growth", *BIS Quarterly Review*, March: 21–35.

Ghosh, J. (2005). "The Economic and Social Effects of Financial Liberalization: A Primer for Developing Countries", United Nations DESA Working Paper No. 4, October.

Hare, G. (2001). "Institutional Change and Economic Performance in the Transition Economies", paper prepared for the United Nations Economic Commission for Europe (UNECE) Spring Seminar, Geneva, 7 May.

Hartmann, P., Heider, F., Papaioannou, E. and Lo Duca, M. (2007). "The Role of Financial Markets and Innovation in Productivity and Growth in Europe", ECB Occasional Paper No. 72.

Havrylyshyn, O. and Wolf, T. (1999). "Determinants of Growth in Transition Countries", *Finance & Development*, IMF quarterly magazine, June, 36(2). Available at : www.imf.org/external/pubs/ft/fandd/1999/06/havrylys.htm (accessed 7 May 2015).

Hellman, J., Jones, J. and Kaufmann, D. (2000). "Beyond the 'Grabbing Hand' of Government in Transition: Facing Up to 'State Capture' by the Corporate Sector", *Transition: The Newsletter about Reforming Economies*, 11: 8–12.

Istvan, A. and Bonin, J. (1992). "The 'Big Bang' versus 'Slow but Steady': A Comparison of the Hungarian and Polish Transformations", CEPR Discussion Paper No. 626. London: Centre for Economic Policy Research.

Jenkinson, N., Peñalver, A. and Vause, N. (2008). "Financial Innovation: What Have we Learnt?", *Bank of England Quarterly Bulletin*, Q3: 330–338. Kaminsky, G. L. and Schmukler S. L. (2003). "Short-Run Pain, Long-Run Gain: The Effects of Financial Liberalization", NBER Working Paper No. 9787, June.

Keynes, J. M. (1939). "The Process of Capital Formation", *Economic Journal*, 49(195): 569–574.

Klein, M. and Olivei, G. (1999). "Capital Account Liberalization, Financial Depth and Economic Growth", NBER Working Paper No. 7384.

Kregel, J., Matzner, E. and Grabher, G. (1992). *The Market Shock*. Vienna: Agenda Group.

Lavigne, M. (2000). "Ten Years of Transition: A Review Article", *Communist and Post-Communist Studies*, 33(4): 475–483.

Levine, R. (2005). "Finance and Growth: Theory and Evidence", in P.Aghion and S. N. Durlauf (Eds), *Handbook of Economic Growth*. Amsterdam: Elsevier B.V., pp. 865–934.

Lipton, D. and Sachs, J. (1990). "Creating a Market Economy: The Case of Poland", *Brookings Papers on Economic Activity*, 1: 75–147.

McKinnon, R. I. (1973). *Money & Capital in Economic Development*. Washington, DC: The Brookings Institution.

Mendoza, E. G., Quadrini, V. and Rios-Rull, J.-V. (2007). "Financial Integration, Financial Deepness and Global Imbalances", NBER Working Paper No. 12909.

Minsky, H. P. (1986). *Stabilizing an Unstable Economy*. New Haven, CT and London: Yale University Press.

Naim, M. (1999). "Fads and Fashion in Economic Reforms: Washington Consensus or Washington Confusion?", working draft of a paper prepared for the IMF Conference on Second Generation Reforms, IMF Institute and the Fiscal Affairs Department, Washington, DC, 8–9 November. Available at : www.imf.org/external/pubs/ft/seminar/1999/reforms/Naim.HTM (accessed 21 February 2010).

North, D. C. (2000). "Big-Bang Transformations of Economic Systems. An Introductory Note", *Journal of Institutional and Theoretical Economics*, 156(1): 3–8.

Obstfeld, M. (2009). "International Finance and Growth in Developing Countries: What Have we Learned?", NBER Working Paper No. 14691.

OECD (2009). *Competition and Financial Markets. Key Findings*. Available at: www.oecd.org/daf/competition/43067294.pdf (accessed 14 December 2014).

OECD (2011). *Bank Competition and Financial Stability*. Paris: OECD Publishing.

Pagano, M. (1993). "Financial Markets and Growth. An Overview", *European Economic Review*, 37(2–3): 613–622.

Prasad, E., Rajan, R. and Subramanian, A. (2006). "Foreign Capital and Economic Growth", Research department, IMF. Available at: www.imf.org/External/NP/seminars/eng/2006/growth/as.pdf (accessed 21 April 2012).

Raines, J. P. and Leathers, C. G. (2011). "Behavioral Finance and Post Keynesian-Institutionalist Theories of Financial Markets", *Journal of Post Keynesian Economics*, 33(4): 539–553.

Rajan, R. G. and Zingales, L. (2000). "The Great Reversals: The Politics of Financial Development in the 20th Century", *OECD Economics Department Working Papers*, No. 256, October. Paris: OECD Publishing.

Rapaczynski, A. (1996). "The Roles of the State and the Market in Establishing Property Rights", *Journal of Economic Perspectives*, 10(2): 87–103.

Rodrik, D. (2006). "Goodbye Washington Consensus, Hello Washington Confusion? A Review of the World Bank's Economic Growth in the 1990s: Learning from a Decade of Reform", *Journal of Economic Literature*, 44(4): 973–987.

Rodrik, D. and Subramanian, A. (2008). "Why Did Financial Globalization Disappoint?", mimeo, Peterson Institute of International Economics.

Rousseau, P. L. and Sylla, R. (2003). "Financial Systems, Economic Growth, and Globalization", in M. D. Bordo, A. M. Taylor and J. G. Williamson (Eds), *Globalization in Historical Perspective*. Chicago, IL: University of Chicago Press, pp. 373–415.

Sachs, J., Woo, W. T. and Yang, X. (1999). "Economic Reforms and Constitutional Transition", Working Paper, Centre for International Development, Harvard University, Cambridge, MA.

Sahay, R. Čihák, M., N'Diaye, P., Barajas, A., Bi, R., Ayala, D., Gao, Y., Kyobe, A., Nguyen, L., Saborowski, C., Svirydzenka, K., and Yousefi, S. R. (2015). "Rethinking Financial Deepening: Stability and Growth in Emerging Markets", IMF Staff Discussion Note SDN/15/08.

Serra, N. and Stiglitz, J. E. (Eds) (2008). *The Washington Consensus Reconsidered. Towards a New Global Governance*. Initiative for Policy Dialogue Series C. New York: Oxford University Press.

Schmukler, S. L. (2004). "Financial Globalization: Gain and Pain for Developing Countries", *Federal Reserve Bank of Atlanta Economic Review*, Second Quarter: 39–66.

Schröder, R. (2000). "Lessons from the Past: Legal Transformations in Germany of the 19th Century", *Journal of Institutional and Theoretical Economics*, 156: 180–206.

Schumpeter, J. A. (1963). *History of Economic Analysis*. London: George Allen & Unwin Ltd.

Shaw, E. S. (1973). *Financial Deepening in Economic Development*. New York: Oxford University Press.

Stiglitz, J. E., Ocampo, J. A., Spiegel, S., French-Davis, R. and Nayyar, D. (2006). *Stability with Growth. Macroeconomics, Liberalization, and Development*. Initiative for Policy Dialogue Series. Oxford: Oxford University Press.

Sun, T. (2015). "The Impact of Global Liquidity on Financial Landscapes and Risks in the ASEAN-5 Countries", IMF Working Paper WP/15/211.

Thakor, A. and Boot, A. (Eds) (2008). *Handbook of Financial Intermediation and Banking*. Amsterdam: Elsevier.

Ülgen, F. (2013a). "Coordination in Economy. An Essay on Money", in F. Ülgen (Ed.), *New Contributions to Monetary Analysis: The Foundations of an Alternative Economic Paradigm*. London: Routledge, pp. 172–187.

Ülgen, F. (2013b). "Le développement des marchés financiers et les crises: Quelles leçons pour les économies émergentes?", *Investigación Económica, Revista de la Facultad de Economía de la PUCE*, 5, Enero [January]: 281–310.

Ülgen, F. (2013c). "Is the Financial Innovation Destruction Creative? A Schumpeterian Reappraisal", *Journal of Innovation Economics*, 11: 231–249.

Ülgen, F. (2013d). "Institutions and Liberalized Finance: Is Financial Stability of Capitalism a Pipedream?", *Journal of Economic Issues*, 47(2): 495–504.

Ülgen, F. (2014). "Financialized Capitalism and the Irrelevance of Self-Regulation: A Minskyian Analysis of Systemic Viability", paper prepared for the 12th International Post Keynesian Conference, University of Missouri–Kansas City, 25–28 September.

Ülgen, F. (2015). "Financial Liberalism and New Institutional Environment: The 2007–08 Financial Crisis as a (De)regulatory Deadlock", in P. O'Sullivan, N. F. B. Allington and M. Esposito (Eds), *The Philosophy, Politics and Economics of Finance in the 21st century. From Hubris to Disgrace*. London: Routledge, pp. 370–391.

United Nations (2015). *World Economic Situation and Prospects 2015*. New York: United Nations.

Williamson, J. (1990). "What Washington Means by Policy Reform", in J. Williamson (Ed.), *Latin American Adjustment: How Much Has Happened?* Washington, DC: Institute for International Economics, pp. 5–38.

Williamson, J. (2000). "What Should the Bank Think About the Washington Consensus?", *The World Bank Research Observer*, 15(2): 251–264.

Williamson, J. (2005). "The Strange History of the Washington Consensus", *Journal of Post Keynesian Economics*, 27(2): 195–206.

World Bank (2005). *Economic Growth in the 1990s: Learning from a Decade of Reform*. Washington, DC: World Bank.

Zingales, L. (2003). "The Weak Links", Commentary, *Federal Reserve Bank of Saint Louis Review*, July/August: 47–52.

4 Underdeveloped financial markets' infrastructure of emerging market economies

Assessment of underlying challenges and suggested policy responses

Shazia Ghani

Introduction[1]

Although several emerging market economies (EMEs) remained resilient to the onslaught of the Global Financial Crisis (GFC) of 2007 due to varied reasons, yet the underdevelopment of financial markets and related infrastructures (supervisory and regulatory frameworks particularly) in the majority of developing economies/EMEs poses a serious challenge to policy makers. Nonetheless, these challenges become manifold when unconventional policies pursued by the advanced economies in the post-GFC 2007 period are expected to be reversed in the months ahead.[2] Several EMEs[3] (e.g. Turkey, South Africa, India, Indonesia, Argentina, Russia and Chile) showed signs of financial instability and macroeconomic vulnerability in the form of interest rate and currency fluctuations and increased costs of borrowing, leading to alarming debt levels. Financial instability of these EMES has been further accentuated by slower global growth, falling commodity prices and current account weaknesses. With this background, the introduction of unconventional monetary policies (such as Quantitative Easing [QE], see Annex A) by the US Federal Reserve and its eventual exit from such policies have sparked a vigorous and ongoing debate among academics and policy makers about the spillover effects of these policies on EMEs.[4] With this context, this chapter reviews the debate and assesses the evidence of spillovers from QE by focusing on the trends of capital flows to EMEs as being the main channel of impact. It is believed that QE and its anticipated reversal (*known as taper talk*) fostered risk taking and unusual capital movement to EMEs, contributing to excessively loose financial conditions and exchange rate fluctuations in these countries. It is worth mentioning that this is not the first time that the economic policies of advanced economies have unleashed the forces of instability in EMEs. Since the late 1970s, most of the EMEs have been victims of policies of advanced economies, and the increased financial globalization[5] coupled with financial innovations and technological advancements over the last two decades have made these economies quite vulnerable even to the smallest shocks from advanced economies.

In the above context, the chapter is divided into three sections: the first section concisely gives a critical review of how the liberalized and integrated financial markets have always posed challenges for EMEs since the 1990s when most of the EMEs initiated programmes of capital account and financial market liberalization and deregulation, ultimately resulting in a financial, banking and currency crisis. The second section analytically assesses the connections between the policy choices of advanced economies and their spillover impact on EMEs in an environment of increased integration and financial liberalization. Debate in this section cites the most relevant and latest literature on the impact of quantitative easing and taper talk on EMEs generally, and discusses the cases of Turkey and India to elaborate why some EMEs are more vulnerable as compared to others. The third section focuses on the specific necessary conditions and required institutional and regulatory/supervisory frameworks to achieve stable, liquid and deeper financial markets in the EMEs. Discussion in this section also states that interconnected global financial markets/systems leave a narrow policy space for EMEs, while domestic financial markets and infrastructures are not developed enough to fulfil the required financing/funding needs of EMEs. It also brings to the fore the point that relevant supervisory/regulatory frameworks supported by macroprudential policies can go a long way to manage the external shocks. The last section concludes the debate.

Financial liberalization and financial crisis in EMEs

Finance and economic growth have a well-established theoretical and empirically tested relationship. Advocated by Bagehot (1873) long ago, modern researchers and policy makers also have asserted that when real activities expand in an economy, the finance grows too to respond to the increased demand for its services. In the words of Robinson (1952: 86), "*where enterprise leads, finance follows*". McKinnon (1973) and Shaw (1973) have argued that impediments to financial development are likely to hamper growth by preventing financial intermediation and the channelling of resources into the most productive activities. Succinctly summarized by Levine (2005), finance influences economic growth by producing information, allocating capital to productive uses, monitoring investments and exerting corporate control; furthermore, it facilitates trading leading to diversification and management of risk. Thus financial development is not only instrumental to economic growth, but also increases the capacity of an economy to absorb internal/external shocks and achieve much desired financial and economic stability. With this backdrop, several EMEs started financial liberalization (deregulation policies and opening up) in the late 1980s (Latin America) and 1990s (Asia) and received a huge and unprecedented amount of capital inflows. However, the path of financial liberalization and deregulation proved to be quite protracted because the majority of EMEs become vulnerable both economically and financially due to destabilizing and fragile outcomes of international integration (Lane *et al.* 1999). It is argued that financial liberalization policies were implemented in haste and without considering a properly sketched-out sequence or order. Therefore, the necessity of an appropriate and well-sequenced financial liberalization programme embedded in the proper legal structure and regularity apparatus cannot be overemphasized (Hallwood and MacDonald 2000).

A surge in capital flows to EMEs has been the most visible trend in the post-liberalization period. Credit-starved EMEs become the heaven of investors in search of good yields, and recipient countries introduced unprecedented policy measures to attract these inflows. However, the historical experiences of most EMEs have established that such capital flows always carry the risk of reversal (*sudden stops*) which ultimately lead the EMEs into currency and financial crisis (Volz 2012). The banking and currency crisis in EMEs during the 1980s and 1990s was so devastating and costly that some economists openly questioned whether the capital account needed to be opened at all (Rodrik 1998). Capital account liberalization has the probability of multiplying the speed and magnitude of international spillovers which ultimately result in increased financial vulnerabilities of individual institutions and national economies.

In the post-GFC 2007 era, several EMEs received huge capital inflows due to the lower growth and almost zero interest rates of the advanced countries, particularly the lower interest rates in the United States. However, the risks of excessive liquidity outflow from EMEs increased greatly in the anticipation of an increase in interest rates by the United States when the domestic financial markets of most EMEs are underdeveloped, illiquid and shallow. With this context, our discussion in the subsequent pages briefly presents the dynamics of crises and instabilities in EMEs and highlights the risks of reversal when the United States "normalizes" its policy decisions and increases the interest rates.

Specific dynamics of financial crisis in EMEs

The dynamics of a financial crisis and its trigger in EMEs are altogether different from those of advanced economies (AEs). Sachs (1995: 2) has argued that developing countries fall into international financial crisis for a variety of reasons which include irresponsible fiscal policy, mismanagement of exchange rates, financial liberalization and a weak domestic banking system. It is pertinent here to review very briefly some fundamental causes of various episodes of financial crisis within EMEs. First, it is mismanagement of financial liberalization in EMEs. Generally, EMEs have experienced financial crisis when these countries liberalize their financial systems by eliminating restrictions on financial institutions and financial markets (Mishkin 2008). However, 'hot money' inflows into local financial markets/systems without adequate institutional structure (particularly a weak regulatory framework) increase the likelihood of instability and crisis. The Mexican Currency Crisis of 1994, the Asian Currency Crisis of 1997 and the Turkish Financial Crisis in 2000 and 2001 are some noteworthy examples to quote here. Second, the presence of severe fiscal imbalances is another important factor. Reckless public budget financing and spending trends also lead EMEs into financial vulnerabilities and crisis. The financial crisis in Argentina in 2001–2002 is a very relevant example. Other instances of such crises are Chile in

1983 and 1986, Russia in 1998 and Ecuador in 1999. Certainly, in the environment of increased integration of EMEs to the global financial system (coupled with a surge in financial innovation and technology), any small change in the policy path can lead to crisis or instability; therefore, it is recommended that certain institutional arrangements like enhanced supervisory and regulatory capacities and appropriate legal standards must be put in place to maintain stability before a country decides to go for capital account liberalization (McKinnon 1993; Kawai and Takagi 2008). With this context, the next section analytically assesses the connections between the policy choices of advanced economies and their spillover impact on EMEs.

Interconnectedness, US monetary policy and capital flows

A surge in the capital flows into EMEs is one of the most visible aspects of the policies of financial liberalization and deregulation over the last three decades. Emerging market economies collectively received about 4.5 trillion US dollars of gross capital inflow between 2009 and the end of the first quarter of 2015 and this volume roughly represents one half of global capital flows (IMF 2015). However, large capital flows into the EMEs in the presence of weak domestic financial infrastructures and lack of the requisite supervisory/regulatory institutions has exacerbated the financial and macroeconomic vulnerabilities of the EMEs. Financial liberalization and the opening up of domestic markets has always posed a challenge for EMEs, resulting in credit booms and busts and sudden stops (see Diaz-Alejandro 1985; Calvo *et al.* 1993; Fernandez-Arias and Montiel 1995). The Asian Currency Crisis of 1997 is the most apt example to describe this phenomenon, and since then, a more sceptical view of the destabilizing impact of capital flows on EMEs due to financial liberalization and deregulation of domestic financial markets got the attention of policy makers. During the 1990s, EMEs witnessed how debt inflows created the economic shocks and financial vulnerabilities leading towards a full-blown banking and financial crisis (for detailed analysis, see Rodrik 1998, 2000; Prasad and Rajan 2008; Obstfeld 2009; Jeanne *et al.* 2012).[6]

Interlinkages between US monetary policy decisions (particularly those related to interest rates) and capital flows are as old as the forces of globalization and financial innovation. The literature is abundant with evidence that low US real interest rates affected the emerging economies' capital flows in the late 1970s, the early 1990s, and the early 2000s, and the phenomenon has strong correlations with various episodes of financial and economic crisis in EMEs (Calvo *et al.* 1993). It has been witnessed in the past that the decision of Volcker (then Federal Reserve Chairman) on monetary tightening during 1980–1982 worsened the Latin American Debt Crisis. Similarly, the Mexican Currency Crisis was amplified due to the Federal Reserve's monetary policy decisions of 1994. The Asian Currency Crisis was the result of massive capital inflows into EMEs; besides other factors, the lower US interest rates played a key role in the movement of hot capital from the international markets to the attractive Asian markets. The GFC of 2007 was the result of *great moderation*, where lower US interest rates played a major role in the development of a housing bubble which, when busted, sent shock waves to all connected international markets. Portes (2009) and Reinhart and Rogoff (2011) have discussed at length how current account deficits coupled with net capital inflows contributed to the GFC of 2007. Thus, it was not surprising that when the US Federal Reserve hinted about "*taper talk*" in May 2013,[7] the capital flows to emerging markets reversed again (Powell 2013) and stock markets jolted throughout the globe.

It is important to highlight that US interest rates are not the only reason for international capital movements and their destabilizing impacts on EMEs; however, it is one of the most significant reasons and the one with potentially the most direct impact. Capital flows into emerging markets are influenced by both global developments (i.e. the changes in the interest rate environment in advanced economies, particularly the United States) and domestic factors (deregulation of domestic financial markets and abolition of capital controls, etc.). Changes in the Federal Reserve's interest rates can impact the EMEs through two channels: first, any rise in interest rates would lead to capital outflows from the EMEs as international investors would prefer higher yields. Second, the majority of the EMEs' foreign debts are dollar denominated; thus, any increase in the US interest rates would lead to an increased cost of repayments for EMEs. According to the World Bank's latest estimates, global factors including the US interest rates explained about 60 per cent of the increase in capital flows into developing countries between 2009 and 2013 (World Bank 2015).

Impact of the so-called 'taper talk'

On 22 May 2013, the then Federal Reserve Chairman, Ben Bernanke, for the first time ever, talked about the possible reversal in quantitative easing by ending the Federal Reserve's assets purchase programme. This announcement resulted in a sharp decline in the financial markets of EMEs (Aizenman *et al.* 2014). Since then, there have been various bouts of uncertainty and researchers and policy makers have focused on the correlation between the US interest rates and the capital flows, and have identified the factors associated with the vulnerabilities of these flows (Alfaro *et al.* 2008; Caballero 2011; Gelos *et al.* 2011; Forbes and Warnock 2012; Bruno and Shin 2013). According to Fratzscher *et al.* (2012), the first round of quantitative easing resulted in lower interest rates in the global markets, while second-round quantitative easing was instrumental in channelling capital from the United States to EMEs. Furthermore, the impact of so-called *taper talk* on EMEs was not uniform or similar, and policy makers have attributed the eventual magnitude of its impact to various macroeconomic and financial markets' fundamentals. Eichengreen and Gupta (2014) have emphasized that the volume of capital flows in the pre-quantitative easing era and the size of local financial markets are the two main determinants of the impact. The EMEs that suffered more in terms of exchange rate fluctuations were those which received more capital inflows and had larger and liquid markets. According to a recent

World Bank report, any abrupt unwinding of central bank policies of advanced economies can cause a contraction of 80 per cent in the capital flows, causing serious economic and financial damages in terms of squeezed GDP (by 0.6 per cent), ultimately leading EMEs to severe financial crises (World Bank 2015). Debate in the next section focuses on who were the most effected by the taper talk, and what were the factors behind this vulnerability and fragility.

Why are some EMEs more vulnerable?

Although taper talk would have real impact on EMEs, the intensity of the impact should ultimately depend on their macroeconomic fundamentals, the degree of development of their domestic financial markets, and the quality of institutional infrastructure. According to Annunziata (2013), EMEs with larger funding needs, poorer fundamentals and weaker policies have been hit harder. Investors focused their attention particularly on countries which have larger external financing needs and big macroeconomic imbalances like Brazil, India, Indonesia, Turkey, and South Africa (Mishra *et al.* 2014). Similarly, Murray (2013) has asserted that underlying weak macroeconomic fundamentals and the EMEs' own financial vulnerabilities are the strongest determinant of the impact of policy change.

Summarily, poor macroeconomic fundamentals and less developed financial markets' infrastructure being the two key amplifiers of any event of financial crisis in EMEs, these are discussed in the following sections.

Poor macroeconomic fundamentals

Vulnerabilities in their own macroeconomic situation have always posed a risk for the liberalized financial markets of the EMEs. This was witnessed during the Latin American Debt Crisis of 1982 when deteriorated export (earning) and debt liabilities of the corporate sector (Kalemli-Özcan *et al.* 2012) amplified the crisis throughout the region. Similarly, during the Mexican Currency Crisis of 1994, the Asian Currency Crisis of 1997, the Russian Debt Crisis of 1998 and the Turkish Financial Crisis of 2001, weaknesses in the macroeconomic fundamentals were at the base of financial vulnerabilities, even though exchange rates were flexible in some cases. Thus, in the environment of weak macroeconomic fundamentals (i.e. slow growth, deteriorating commodity prices and shrinking exports, budgetary deficits, etc.) any *sudden stop* or policy reversal pertaining to the external sector (and specifically capital inflows) results in the loss of value of domestic currency, and foreign denominated debt levels increase enormously. Hence, it was not surprising to observe that the EMEs with big current account deficits and high inflation were the ones hardest hit in June 2013 and then between July and September 2015.

Underdeveloped financial markets' infrastructure

Emerging market economies have made substantial progress over the years to deepen their domestic financial markets by introducing financial and regulatory reforms and 'beefing up' supervisory frameworks in the light of lessons learned from past episodes of crisis. However, unfinished reform agendas and lower quality of institutional set-ups with weaker legal/enforcement regimes are serious issues and demand immediate attention. Until EMEs put their own house in order, they will always be prone to policy changes or sudden stops of capital movements. Illiquid financial markets and unfinished reform agendas combined with structural challenges cause investors' confidence to fluctuate immediately and significantly lead towards capital outflows.

Finance theory has emphasized the role of institutions in the financial development of a country and posits that international differences in financial development are to a great extent explained by the differences in the quality of the institutions (La Porta *et al.* 1997, 1998, 2000; Beck and Levine 2003). There is abundant literature on how the degree of financial markets' development, their liquidity and quality of supervisory (legal) institutions go a long way in the long-run economic development of a country. Levine *et al.* (1999) have discussed in detail the extent to which the legal and regulatory environment affects the domestic financial development of a country. It is the depth of markets and quality of institutional arrangements that impact the borrowing costs of EMEs in international markets. Certainly, investors and savers are always attracted to those destinations where legal systems enforce private property rights and support private contractual arrangements. Thus, the willingness of economic agents to participate in financial markets and the ensuing cross-country differences depend on the following three factors: (i) contract, company, bankruptcy and securities laws, credibility and transparency of accounting rules; (ii) the emphasis of legal systems on private property rights; and (iii) the efficiency of contract enforcement (Dorrucci *et al.* 2009: 14).[8]

Most EMEs started financial reforms during the late 1990s, and since then have had to greatly improve their domestic legal/regulatory frameworks in the light of lessons learnt from their own experience of financial crisis. As a result, some Asian EMEs performed well in the first round of the GFC 2007, but due to incomplete reforms and un-addressed regulatory challenges, the task of achieving stable and diversified financial markets seems very complex. In this environment, the post-GFC 2007 policies of the Federal Reserve have particularly emphasized that the imperative of developed financial markets is still very strong, calling for strengthening of domestic banking and widening of financial and regulatory systems. Emerging market economies need to reframe and redesign their supervisory/legal frameworks to address their domestic markets' capacity constraints in ever-evolving international policy regimes.

Let us now highlight some relevant examples from EMEs to investigate further the factors discussed above. Certainly, lack of sound financial markets' infrastructures and supervisory institutions amplifies the initial impact of shock. This subsection also underlines the particular policy responses introduced by various EMEs to combat the influence of taper talk. We know that Brazil, Colombia, India, Indonesia, Malaysia, Mexico, Peru, Poland, Russia, South Africa, Thailand and Turkey were the most hard hit economies during May to August 2013, and then most of these were again jolted in July to September 2015. However, the majority of these economies are not off the curve on policy response due to their previous experiences of crisis. Indeed, this was not the first time that policy spill-overs have exposed these EMEs and led their domestic financial conditions to deteriorate. Keeping in view the limited space, we will discuss only Turkey and India. Both EMEs have external imbalances (due to large funding needs and the factor of political instability) and a deteriorated macroeconomic situation; their financial vulnerabilities have increased manifold. India is one of the largest recipients of capital inflows, but its own structural rigidities pose a challenge to its financial stability.

Turkish economic history is replete with various episodes of boom and bust as the country has experienced several financial and currency crises since it initiated a market-based liberalization reforms programme. The first notable example is the foreign debt crisis of 1979. It was followed by a *"stabilization and liberalization programme"* in 1980 when Turkey introduced policies to liberalize its trade and finance and subsequently opened its capital account in 1989 (Uygur 2010). During the liberalized regime, the first crisis occurred in 1994 under a managed float exchange rate regime, and the second crisis occurred in November 2002 when the country was under an exchange rate based stabilization programme. Last, but not least, was the 2007 GFC when the post-crisis monetary policy decisions of the Federal Reserve played havoc with Turkey due to its own deteriorated macroeconomic conditions and political instability, coupled with the country's dependence on short-term foreign investments. It was not surprising at all when the Turkish lira lost about 30 per cent of its value and the central bank increased interest rates in January 2014 by 4.25 per cent (Orhangazi and Gökçer 2015). The initial impact was so damaging that the foreign exchange reserves of the country dropped by 12 billion US dollars in a month in an anticipation of capital outflows.

Fundamentally, the Turkish economy's dependence on external financing and its corporate sector's large open foreign exchange positions are the main reasons for financial vulnerability and risks. Summarily, three reasons explain the combined impact of boom in portfolio investments and external debt on the Turkish economy. First, the increase of the current account deficit; second, the unprecedented accumulation of external debt by the private sector; and third – and the most common – is the surge in capital flows fuelled by a credit boom (Choi 2013).

India qualifies as our second example. The Indian currency suffered bouts of depreciation immediately when Bernanke hinted about slowing down the asset purchase programme in May 2013. India is one of the biggest recipients of capital inflows and attracted 470 billion US dollars between 2009 and 2012 (IMF 2015). This very huge influx of capital is indeed one very basic reason for India's vulnerability in the anticipation of normalization of US monetary policy. The Indian rupee lost its value by 25 per cent between the end of May and the end of August 2013, and its bond spread increased and its stock market declined sharply. The two main reasons for this impact are: first, India is the largest recipient of capital inflows in the post-GFC 2007 period, which has naturally put the country in a disadvantageous position as investors flew out in search of high yields in any event of instability. Second, its own macroeconomic vulnerabilities in the years prior to taper talk have made it susceptible to capital outflows (Basu *et al*. 2014). A deeper analysis of fundamentals shows that India has paid the price of weaknesses in its domestic economic environment and supply-side constraints. Similarly, other EMEs like Russia, Indonesia and Brazil have suffered much due to their own macroeconomic weaknesses and underdeveloped financial markets. In this scenario, what are the ideal policies required to prevent instability and to achieve a more stable financial system of markets? This is not an easy question to answer.

Policy implications for EMEs: requisite institutional and regulatory frameworks

The appropriate policy mix to maintain stability depends upon country-specific macroeconomic conditions, the level of financial development and the quality of the financial infrastructure. Therefore, 'one size fits all' policy advice is not desirable; EMEs and advanced economies need altogether dissimilar policy advice and tools. The post-GFC 2007 narrative was that EMEs had weathered the onslaught of crisis and had emerged resilient. It was also discussed that due to the lessons learned from past episodes of crisis, they had put their own house in order and accumulated large foreign exchange reserves that would work as a cushion/buffer in the event of any instability. However, quantitative easing policies and their anticipated reversal show that EMEs need to do more on the institutional and policy fronts.

Short-term options/policy choices

Only short-term measures can be sought when economies are in the midst of a crisis, however, authorities need to focus on the medium- to long-term horizons once instability is contained. In the response to taper talk instabilities, most of the EMEs used foreign exchange reserves to stabilize their markets and support domestic currencies. The central banks of EMEs, being the key institutions, provided much required liquidity to stabilize the economy-wide specific sectors. Table 4.1 provides a summary of various policy measures that EMEs deployed during the period from May to August 2013.

Medium- to long-term options: institutional dimension of the financial markets

Once the initial consolidation is achieved, the authorities acquire some policy space that enables them to focus on the medium- to long-term horizons of the markets. Nevertheless, policy makers are fully aware that foreign exchange interventions and liquidity provisions have their limitations and cannot be exercised forever. Though these are advocated as an immediate option and we have seen that EMEs have used these measures in the short run, still EMEs' policy makers

Table 4.1 Policy tools deployed by selected emerging economies

	Monetary Policy		FX Intervention	Liquidity Provision	Fiscal Policy	Macroprudential Policy	CFMs*
	Tight	Loose			Tight	Tight	Removal
Brazil	•		•	•			•
India	•		•	•		•	•
Indonesia	•		•	•		•	•
Russia	•		•				
South Africa	•						
Thailand		•					
Turkey	•		•	•		•	

Source: IMF (2014: 22).
* Capital flow management measures.

need to focus on medium- to long-term options too. Properly conceived and sketched policy frameworks that have the capacity to limit vulnerabilities may include monetary policy, fiscal policy, macroprudential policy, capital flow management measures (CFMs) and foreign exchange intervention.

Capital inflows can be a boon or bane depending upon the macroeconomic and institutional frameworks of an economy. Therefore, besides the short-term measures cited in the previous subsection, much more attention needs to be paid to how financial and capital markets operate in these economies. The authorities of EMEs are not only responsible for unfreezing the markets in times of crunch, but are required to streamline the legal and supervisory/regulatory framework in which EMEs' financial markets operate. A lack of legal and regulatory protections or controls increased the risk taking in one particular sector enormously, leading to instability of the whole macro economy. Sufficient legal and regulatory apparatus with the right institutions in place greatly encourages financial intermediation by enhancing the depths of financial markets in EMEs. Rojas-Suarez (2014) has very succinctly dealt with the subject, giving a detailed account of EMEs' illiquid and underdeveloped capital markets and has identified the required conditions and grouped these into four pillars:

1   macroeconomic stability;
2   sound banking systems;
3   high institutional quality; and
4   an adequate regulatory and supervisory framework to achieve strong and stable markets.

Accordingly, the four pillars are interdependent, yet they are complementary and equally important. Further, for the stability of domestic financial markets, a macroprudential policy framework is the key and our next subsection dwells on the subject in detail. The speedy integration of EMEs into the world economy – as compared to the advanced economies – caused them to experience an influx of huge capital inflows relative to the size of their financial markets which increased the vulnerability of these economies to internal and external shocks. Some lessons are not new, but are indeed reinforced by the 2007 GFC (Rojas-Suarez 2014). Thus, coherent and credible macroeconomic policy frameworks can not only improve the growth prospects of EMEs, but also ensure their resistance whenever there is external shock in the form of international policy spillover.

Capital markets' development

Underdevelopment and illiquidity are the two main features of EMEs' capital markets. As we have discussed in the previous pages, reliable and stable access to finance/funding is a prerequisite to economic growth and stability. Though risky, the EMEs' funding needs have always led them to attract maximum foreign capital inflows. Nevertheless, the current international environment has once again emphasized that EMEs need to develop their own capital markets (which are quite small as compared to the size and potential of advanced economies) to have an effective and efficient source to meet their funding needs.

Financial reforms initiated by the advanced and emerging economies over the last three decades have allowed the private banks to lend more by providing diversified products. Therefore, development of a local currency debt market would provide EMEs with much-needed funding with more reliability and would maintain financial stability too. Having a stable and reliable capital market will minimize the uncertainties of policy normalization of the advanced economies.

Although EMEs' capital markets have been growing since 2005 (the corporate bonds market in Brazil, Russia and India grew at a compounded annual rate of over 20 per cent between 2005 and 2014), yet use of capital markets as a percentage of GDP (contributing 39 per cent of global output, but accounting for only 15 per cent of global corporate bond value) falls behind the advanced economies (World Economic Forum 2015). Further, although the corporate bond market values have grown, yet the concentration of issuance is more in the domestic market as compared to the international one.

Achieving a sound capital market is not an easy task and requires strong macroeconomic fundamentals as macroeconomic weakness results in high premiums by limiting the entrants into markets. Similarly, higher inflation erodes the returns of investors and obscures the market trends. Rojas-Suarez (2014) has discussed at length the four necessary conditions for having more liquidity: macroeconomic stability, a sound banking system, high institutional quality and an adequate regulatory and supervisory framework. Similarly, the World Economic Forum report (2015) has extensively dealt with the issue of capital market development in EMEs and has highlighted some preconditions too. These are, first, a stable macroeconomic environment encompassing monetary stability, flexible exchange and policy rates, fiscal soundness and financial and political stability. Second, capital account liberalization is another important requisite to signal to investors that the government believes in market-oriented policies. However, designing a balanced and well- sequenced capital account liberalization is a very challenging task. Emerging market economies must adopt a more gradual approach, putting in place transparent and well-documented legal frameworks that chalk out guidelines for foreign investors. Third, it is necessary to have a fundamental rule of law and a strong institutional framework. Fourth, the existence of a sound banking system is crucial, as a deep capital market and sound banking systems are complements to each other. Empirical studies have established that only those economies which have quite developed financial institutions have benefited from capital account liberalization and financial markets' integration (Chinn and Ito 2008). Several researchers have endorsed the view that adequate and well-enforced contracts, insolvency procedures, adequate accounting rules and standards, consistent auditing and disclosure practices, efficient risk management capacities of individual financial institutions and an efficient and smooth payment system, and a comprehensive regulatory framework altogether are the core institutional infrastructure requirements for the success of a liberalized financial system (Eichengreen and Mussa 1999). However, even if all the preconditions discussed above are achieved, still the uncertainties of global capital markets will lead investors to flee in search of safe assets. According to Rojas-Suarez (2014):

> In the current international financial architecture, there are only few safe assets and, besides gold and silver, they are all government securities issued by countries that also issue hard currencies (highly liquid, internationally traded currencies). Currently, US Treasuries can be said to be the most liquid securities in the world. The experience during the global financial crisis showed that equity and bond instruments in emerging markets lost liquidity and prices collapsed. When deep external shocks occur, corporates will find themselves with fewer and more expensive sources of funding even if local capital markets appeared to be highly liquid before the shock.
>
> (Rojas-Suarez 2014: 20)

Thus it is recognized that country-specific structural constraints must be taken into account and policy makers of EMEs should consider their country contexts and put in place necessary institutional arrangements.

Strong institutional frameworks

Long-term policy measures are the key to address the financial vulnerabilities (irrespective of the immediate or particular source of shock or instability) of EMEs. And the same will eventually shield and sustain their position in an integrated world economy. Many EMEs face institutional constraints for effective policy responses and skilful handling of external inflows and exchange rate depreciations. Hyman Minsky long ago emphasized the importance of institutions to stabilize the capitalistic economies and referred to these as circuit breakers (against financial euphoria), designed to counteract the dynamics of the crisis and govern the mechanism behind such crisis (limited space here does not warrant a detailed discussion of his work). According to Minsky, it is the capital development of an economy and the structure of its financial institutions that determine its growth trajectory. Further, he has endorsed institutions (the big bank and the big government) to function to ensure stability by halting the speed of euphoria, and emphasized the stabilization function of the institutions by preventing "It" (i.e. the instability) from happening (Minsky 1992: 12). Over the years, various bouts of instability and crisis have time and again emphasized that liberalized financial markets of EMEs need strong institutions. For EMEs, it is a continuous effort to 'beef up' the institutional and regulatory environment to face any kind of external or internal shocks.

Adequate regulatory and supervisory apparatus

Several EMEs in Asia and Latin America have greatly strengthened their regulatory and supervisory frameworks due to lessons learnt from their own financial history. This improvement was evident in the post-GFC 2007 period when several EMEs remained resilient to the onslaught of global instability. For EMEs, a regulatory framework must be an essential part of their general macroeconomic policy frameworks designed to achieve specific economic growth objectives. We have observed during the GFC 2007 that all those economies which had improved their regulatory institutions and put in place necessary frameworks and adopted the macroprudential approach/measures, absorbed the shocks with resilience as compared to their counterparts where such arrangements were non-existent. Although the empirical evidence on the effectiveness of macroprudential measures to manage capital flows and contain asset prices (booms and busts) is still preliminary, yet research has established that EMEs have used macroprudential instruments most frequently. Some macroprudential tools (e.g. countercyclical capital buffers) can reduce the potential systemic risks associated with capital inflows without targeting inflows *per se*. Similarly, caps on loan-to-value and debt-to-income ratios can be applied to discourage the erosion of lending standards in an economy. Further, discouraging short-term wholesale funding (which is more destabilizing in nature and usually termed as 'hot money' flows) by taxes or quantitative caps can lead to dampening the demand for such funding sources (Cerutti *et al.* 2015). In the same vein, Zhang and Zoli (2014), after analysing the 13 Asian and 33 other economies since 2000, posit that macroprudential measures like loan-to-value ratio caps, housing tax measures, and foreign currency-related measures have helped housing price growth, equity flows, credit growth, and bank leverages to subside. Similarly, Bruno *et al.* (2014) investigate the effectiveness of macroprudential policies and capital flow management policies for selected Asia Pacific economies and establish that bond market capital flow management policies are quite useful in dampening the unstable flows of bonds. They further posit that the effectiveness of macroprudential measures increases when they are complemented by proper monetary policy.

The EMEs of the Latin American region have taken a pioneering role among the EMEs and have upgraded their macroprudential policy frameworks over the years.

It is not surprising that the banking sector of these economies remained resilient to the global meltdown of 2007 and they even weathered the taper tantrum in a better way. Latin American EMEs have a long tradition of using macroprudential tools, and countries like Chile, Mexico and Uruguay have created dedicated institutional arrangements (e.g. financial stability councils) in the post-2007 GFC period to focus on the application of more macroprudential tools. These councils have an explicit mandate to monitor the systemic risks to the system and can make recommendations to use macroprudential policy tools to mitigate these risks.

Conclusion

Liberalized financial markets of EMEs were and will always be prone to the booms and busts of the global financial system. It is not possible for EMEs to reap the benefits of integration in a big way, but then protect themselves completely when there are bouts of instability. Advantages and disadvantages of interconnectedness are there, and advanced economies will consider their own economies first while taking any policy decisions, instead of taking care of the impact on EMEs. Therefore the best way for EMEs is to improve their own economies and put in place the requisite institutional arrangements that can minimize the impact of any spillovers. Emerging market economies are required to address the weaknesses in macroeconomic fundamentals through coherent and credible macro policy frameworks. A more sustainable way to improve the macro economy is by increasing the prospects of growth together with consolidation of the fiscal sector: if growth prospects are good, any bouts of volatility would be slowed because growth is the only variable that can help to reduce vulnerabilities in a more sustained manner by enhancing the policy space. Furthermore, EMEs need to address the inherent weakness of their domestic financial markets which are shallow and lack the proper legal infrastructures. Adopting the macroprudential policy tools/measures has improved the policy response of EMEs. In ever-evolving global financial conditions, EMEs need adequate policy buffers and requisite institutional safeguards to face the challenges in policy reversals.

Notes

1 Disclaimer: the views expressed in this chapter are those of the author and do not necessarily represent those of the Prime Minister's Performance Delivery Unit or the Prime Minister's Office of Pakistan.
2 The US Federal Reserve raised interest rates on 16 December 2015, a new target range for the federal funds rate at 0.25 per cent to 0.5 per cent, up from zero to 0.25 per cent.
3 Turkey, South Africa, India, Indonesia, Argentina, Russia and Chile were the most affected during the first period of taper talk after May 2013, and then again most of these were jolted in September 2015. Fitch, the credit rating agency, coined the term *'fragile five'* in 2013, consisting of Brazil, India, Indonesia, Turkey and South Africa.
4 From 2009 to the end of 2012, the gross capital flows to the EMEs reached almost 4.5 trillion US dollars.
5 This resulted in deregulation and liberalization in most EMEs in the follow up of *Washington Consensus* policies. Since then, EMEs have weathered various episodes of financial instability.

6 For a more recent discussion on capital flows and related regulatory policy challenges, see Reinhart and Reinhart (2009), Cardarelli *et al.* (2010), Ostry *et al.* (2010) and Forbes and Warnock (2012).
7 In May 2013, the Federal Reserve for the first time hinted about the possibility of the US central bank tapering its securities purchases from 85 billion US dollars a month to a lower amount. On 22 May 2013, Ben Bernanke, then Chairman of the Federal Reserve, talked about tapering (slowing of the Federal Reserve's QE) in his testimony to Congress which had a sharp negative impact on economic and financial conditions in emerging markets.
8 See also Demirgüç-Kunt and Huizinga (1998); Levine (1999); Morck *et al.* (1999); Herring and Chatusripitak (2000).

References

Aizenman, J., Mahir, B. and Hutchison, M. (2014). "The Transmission of Federal Reserve Tapering News to Emerging Financial Markets", NBER Working Paper No.19980.

Alfaro, L., Kalemli-Ozcan, S. and Volosovych, V. (2008). "Why Doesn't Capital Flow from Rich to Poor Countries? An Empirical Investigation", *Review of Economics and Statistics*, 90(2): 347–368.

Annunziata, M. (2013). "India and the Emerging Market Crisis", *Vox*, CEPR's policy portal, posted 1 September 2013. Available at: www.voxeu.org/article/india-and-emerging-market-crisis (accessed 12 December 2015).

Bagehot, W. (1873). *Lombard Street: A Description of the Money Market*. London: John Murray.

Basu, K., Eichengreen, B. and Gupta, P. (2014). "From Tapering to Tightening: The Impact of the Fed's Exit on India", World Bank Policy Research Working Paper WPS7071.

Beck, T. and Levine, R. (2003). "Legal Institutions and Financial Development", NBER Working Paper No. 10126.

Bruno, V. and Shin, H. S. (2013). "Capital Flows, Cross-Border Banking and Global Liquidity", NBER Working Paper 19038.

Bruno, V., Shim, I. and Shin, H. S. (2014). "Comparative Assessment of Macroprudential Policies", BIS Working Paper No. 502, October.

Caballero, J. (2011). "Do Surges in International Capital Inflows Influence the Likelihood of Banking Crises?", mimeo, University of California, Santa Cruz.

Calvo G., Leiderman, L. and Reinhart, C. (1993). "Capital Inflows and Real Exchange Rate Appreciation in Latin America: The Role of External Factors", *IMF Staff Papers*, 40(1): 108–151.

Cardarelli, R., Elekdag, S. and Kose, M. A. (2009)."Capital Inflows: Macroeconomic Implications and Policy Responses", IMF Working Paper WP/09/40, March.

Cerutti, E., Claessens, S. and Laeven, L. (2015). "The Use and Effectiveness of Macroprudential Policies: New Evidence", IMF Working Paper WP/15/61.

Chinn, M. and Ito, H. (2008). "A New Measure of Financial Openness", *Journal of Comparative Policy Analysis* 10(3): 309–322.

Choi, W. G. (2013). "Current Policy Challenges Faced by Emerging Market Economies and Korea", paper presented at the Federal Reserve Bank of San Francisco 2013 Asia Economic Policy Conference, San Francisco, CA, 3–5 November. In R. Glick and M. M. Spiegel (Eds), *Prospects for Asia and the Global Economy*. Available at: www.frbsf.org/economic-research/files/Prospects-for-Asia-and-the-Global-Economy-full-text.pdf (accessed 14 October 2015).

Demirgüç-Kunt and Huizinga. H. (1998). "Determinants of Commercial Bank Interest Margins and Profitability: Some International Evidence", World Bank Policy Research Working Paper No. 1171.

Diaz-Alejandro, C. (1985). "Good-bye Financial Repression, Hello Financial Crash", *Journal of Development Economics*, 19(1–2): 1–24.

Dorrucci, E., Meyer-Cirkel, A. and Santabárbara, D. (2009). "Domestic Financial Development in Emerging Economies: Evidence and Implications", European Central Bank Occasional Paper No. 102, April.

Eichengreen, B. and Mussa, M. (1999). "Capital Account Liberalization and IMF", *Finance and Development* 35(4). Available at: www.imf.org/external/pubs/ft/fandd/1998/12/index. htm.

Eichengreen, B. and Gupta, P. (2014). "Tapering Talk: The Impact of Expectations of Reduced Federal Reserve Security Purchases on Emerging Markets", World Bank Policy Research Working Paper No. WPS6754.

Fernandez-Arias, E. and Montiel, P. J. (1995). "The Surge in Capital Inflows to Developing Countries: Prospects and Policy Response," World Bank Policy Research Working Paper No. WPS1473.

Forbes, K. J. and Warnock, F. E. (2012). "Capital Flow Waves: Surges, Stops, Flight, and Retrenchment", *Journal of International Economics*, 88(2): 235–251.

Fratzscher, M., Duca, M. L. and Straub, R. (2012). "On the International Spillovers of US Quantitative Easing", European Central Bank Working Paper No. 1557, June.

Gelos, R. G., Sahay, R. and Sandleris, G. (2011). "Sovereign Borrowing by Developing Countries: What Determines Market Access?", *Journal of International Economics*, 83(2): 243–254.

Hallwood, C. P. and MacDonald, R. (eds) (2000). *International Money and Finance*. Cambridge, MA: Blackwell Publishers.

Herring, R. J. and Chatusripitak, N. (2000). "The Case of the Missing Market: The Bond Market and Why it Matters for Financial Development", Asian Development Bank Institute Working Paper No. 11.

International Monetary Fund (2014). "Emerging Market Volatility: Lessons from the Taper Tantrum", IMF Staff Discussion Note SDN/14/09.

Internationational Monetary Fund (2015). "Monetary Policy in the New Normal", remarks at 2015 China Development Forum Panel Discussion by Christine Lagarde, Managing Director, IMF, Beijing, 22 March 2015. Available at: www.imf.org/external/np/speeches/2015/032215a.htm (accessed on 15 December 2015).

Jeanne, O., Subramanian, A. and Williamson, J. (2012). *Who Needs to Open the Capital Account?* Washington, DC: Petersen Institute for International Economics.

Kalemli-Özcan, S. Papaioannou, E. and Perri, F. (2012). "Global Banks and Crisis Transmission," NBER Working Paper No. 18209.

Kawai, M. and Takagi, S. (2008). "A Survey of the Literature on Managing Capital Inflows". ADB Institute Discussion Paper No. 100, March. Tokyo: Asian Development Bank Institute.

Lane, T., Ghosh, A., Hamann, J., Phillips, S., Schulze-Ghattas, M. and Tsikata, T. (1999). "IMF Supported Programs in Indonesia, Korea and Thailand: A Preliminary Assessment", IMF Occasional Paper No. 178.

La Porta, R., Lopez-de-Silanes, F., Shleifer, A. and Vishny, R. (1997). "Legal Determinants of External Finance", *Journal of Finance*, 52(3): 1131–1150.

La Porta, R., Lopez-de-Silanes, F., Shleifer, A. and Vishny, R. (1998). "Law and Finance", *Journal of Political Economy*, 106(6): 1113–1155.

La Porta, R., Lopez-de-Silanes, F., Shleifer, A. and Vishny, R. (2000). "Investor Protection and Corporate Governance", *Journal of Financial Economics*, 58(1–2): 3–27.

Levine, R. (1999). "Law, Finance, and Economic Growth", *Journal of Financial Intermediation*, 8(1–2): 8–35.

Levine, R. (2005). "Finance and Growth: Theory and Evidence" in P. Aghion and S. N. Durlauf (Eds), *Handbook of Economic Growth*, Volume 1, Part A. Amsterdam: Elsevier, pp. 865–934.

Levine, R., Loayza, N. and Beck, T. (1999). "Financial Intermediation and Growth: Causality and Causes", World Bank Policy Research Working Paper 2059.

McKinnon, R. I. (1973). *Money and Capital in Economic Development*. Washington, DC: Brookings Institution.

McKinnon, R. I. (1993). *The Order of Economic Liberalisation: Financial Control in the Transition to a Market Economy*. 2nd edn. Baltimore, MD: The Johns Hopkins University Press.

Minsky, H. P. (1992). "The Capital Development of the Economy and the Structure of Financial Institutions", Working Paper No. 72, Levy Economics Institute of Bard College, Annandale-on-Hudson, New York.

Mishkin, F. S. (2008). *The Next Great Globalization: How Disadvantaged Nations Can Harness their Financial Systems to Get Rich*. Princeton, NJ: Princeton University Press.

Mishra, P., Moriyama, K., N'Diaye, P. and Nguyen, L. (2014). "Impact of Fed Tapering Announcements on Emerging Markets", IMF Working Paper WP/14/109.

Morck, R., Yeung, B., and Yu. W. (1999). "The Information Content of Stock Markets: Why Do Emerging Markets Have Synchronous Stock Price Movements?", Harvard Institute of Economics Research Paper No. 1879.

Murray, J. (2013). "Exits, Spillovers and Monetary Policy Independence", speech to the Canadian Association for Business Economics, Kingston, Ontario, 27 August. Available at: www.bis.org/review/r130828d.pdf (accessed 15 December 2015).

Obstfeld, M. (2009). "International Finance and Growth in Developing Countries: What Have we Learned?", *IMF Staff Papers*, 56(1): 63.

Orhangazi, Ö. and Gökçer, Ö. (2015). "Capital Flows, Finance-Led Growth and Fragility in the Age of Global Liquidity and Quantitative Easing: The Case of Turkey", PERI Working Paper No. 397, Political Economy Research Institute, University of Massachusetts Amherst.

Ostry, J. D., Ghosh, A.R., Habermeier, K., Laeven, L., Chamon, M., Qureshi, M. S. and Reinhardt, D. B. S. (2010). "Capital Inflows: The Role of Controls", IMF Staff Position Note SPN/10/04.

Portes, R. (2009). "Global Imbalances" in M. Dewatripont, X. Freixas and R. Portes (Eds), *Macroeconomic Stability and Financial Regulation: Key Issues for the G20*. London: Centre for Economic Policy Research, pp. 19–26.

Powell, J. (2013). "Advanced Economy Monetary Policy and Emerging Market Economies", speech given at the Federal Reserve Bank of San Francisco 2013 Asia Economic Policy Conference, San Francisco, CA, 4 November.

Prasad, E. S. and Rajan, R. (2008). "A Pragmatic Approach to Capital Account Liberalization", NBER Working Paper No. 14051, June.

Rajan, S. R. (2001). *Relevance of Currency Crisis Theory to the Devaluation and Collapse of the Thai Baht*, Princeton Studies in International Economics No. 88. Princeton, NJ: International Economics Section, Princeton University.

Reinhart, C. and Reinhart, V. (2009). "Capital Flow Bonanzas: An Encompassing View of the Past and Present", NBER Working Paper 14321.

Reinhart, C. and Rogoff, K. (2011). *This Time Is Different: Eight Centuries of Financial Folly*. Princeton, NJ: Princeton University Press.

Robinson, J. (1952). "The Generalization of General Theory," in *The Rate of Interest, and Other Essays*. London: Macmillan, pp. 67–142.

Rodrik, D. (1998). "Who Needs Capital-Account Convertibility?", in *Should the IMF Pursue Capital-Account Convertibility?*, Princeton Essays in International Finance No. 207. Princeton, NJ: International Finance Section, Princeton University, pp. 55–65.

Rodrik, D. (2000). "Institutions for High-Quality Growth: What they Are and How to Acquire them," NBER Working Paper No. 7540.

Rojas-Suarez, L. (2014). "Towards Strong and Stable Capital Markets in Emerging Market Economies", BIS Paper No. 75: 13–20.

Sachs, J. (1995). "Alternative Approaches to Financial Crisis in Emerging Markets", Background Paper for discussion during meetings in Basel, Switzerland, December 9–10.

Shaw, E. S. (1973). *Financial Deepening in Economic Development*. New York: Oxford University Press.

Uygur, E. (2010). *The Global Crisis and the Turkish Economy*. TWN (Third World Network) Global Economy Series No. 21. Available at: www.twn.my/title2/ge/ge21.pdf (accessed 14 October 2015).

Volz, U. (ed.) (2012). *Financial Stability in Emerging Markets. Dealing with Global Liquidity*. Bonn, Germany: German Development Institute, DIE. Available at: www.stephanygj.net/papers/AvoidingCapitalFlightToDevelopingCountriesACounterCyclicalApproach2012.pdf (accessed 12 December 2015).

World Bank (2015). *Global Economic Prospects: The Global Economy in Transition*. Washington, DC: World Bank.

World Economic Forum (2015). *Accelerating Emerging Capital Markets Development. Corporate Bond Markets*. Geneva, Switzerland: World Economic Forum.

Zhang, L. and Zoli, E. (2014). "Leaning Against the Wind: Macroprudential Policy in Asia", IMF Working Paper WP/14/22.

Annex A

Table 4.1.1 Phases of quantitative easing and tapering by the United States Federal Reserve

	First round (QE1) (Nov. 2008–Jun. 2010)	Second round (QE2) (Nov. 2010–Jun. 2011)	Third round (QE3) (Sep. 2012–Dec. 2013)	QE tapering (Jan. 2014)	QE tapering (Feb.–Mar. 2014)	QE tapering (Apr. 2014)
US Bonds	$300 billion	$600 billion	$540 billion ($45 billion/month*)	$40 billion/month	$35 billion/month	$30 billion/month
MBS**	$1.25 trillion	–	$640 billion ($40 billion/month)	$35 billion/month	$30 billion/month	$25 billion/month
Others	$175 billion	–	–	–	–	–
Total	$1.725 trillion	$600 billion	$1.18 trillion ($85 billion/month*)	$75 billion/month	$65 billion/month	$55 billion/month

Source: Document publicized by the Federal Reserve Board.

Notes

* During the QE3, the Federal Reserve Board started purchasing US bonds in January 2013.

** Mortgage-backed securities.

5   Towards de-financialization

Malcolm Sawyer[1]

Introduction

The financial sector has grown substantially over the past few decades, and done so in terms of its economic, political and social importance. Using the definition provided by Epstein (2005: 3), "financialization means the increasing role of financial motives, financial markets, financial actors and financial institutions in the operation of domestic and international economies", this can be viewed as a process of financialization. The term financialization is used in a range of social sciences (though not usually mainstream economics) and in a range of ways. Van der Zwan (2014: 101–102), for example, views financialization in three dimensions:

1   financialization as a regime of accumulation;
2   financialization of the modern corporation (emergence of shareholder value as the main guiding principle of corporate behavior); and
3   the financialization of the everyday (the diverse ways in which finance is grounded in practices of everyday life).

The second and third dimensions could be seen as elaborations of the ways in which financialization on the Epstein definition is revealed. The first indicates a more systemic approach and accords with those who view financialization in terms of a different era of capitalism. Our focus in using the term financialization here will be in the general sense of Epstein rather than as portraying a different era of capitalism.

Financialization (and variants) is a relatively new term (from the early 1990s[2]) and as Epstein (2005) notes, often relates to the period since the 1970s; others have focused on the period since 1980.[3] During the period since circa 1980, the financial sector has grown substantially and also it has been characterized by de-regulation and liberalization and by the development of a range of financial products, derivatives and securitization and of trading in those financial products. There has been a general growth of household debt. Financialization can be viewed in terms also of the dominance of finance over industry. It has been accompanied by rising inequality of income and wealth.

However, finance and the financial sector have generally experienced growth, and financialization is of long standing. Vercelli (2014) labels the period since circa 1980 as the second financialization, where the first was in the period of the last decades of the nineteenth century into the twentieth century until around 1930, brought to an end with the Wall Street crash and the banking collapses.

After a period in the industrialized capitalist economies of what may be termed de-financialization in the period from the early 1930s to the mid-1950s, the processes of financialization gathered pace from the mid-1950s. The pace quickened from circa 1980 onwards, and financialization spread to many other countries, notably the former Communist countries of Central and Eastern Europe (from 1990), Latin American and East Asian countries. These processes of financialization were much more than 'more of the same' coming from further expansion of the banking system. It has been the case that the banking sector has continued to grow, at least as judged by measures such as the ratio of bank deposits to Gross Domestic Product (GDP). Other features of this period of financialization have been the growth of the stock market relative to the banking system, and the development and growth of derivatives and securitization and the growth of 'fictitious' capital, with the much larger ratios of financial assets and liabilities to GDP and to productive assets (see Brown *et al.* 2015 for some details). There has been a general shift in the direction of de-regulation and liberalization. In terms of ownership there have been moves away from public ownership (though reversed temporarily by the bail-out and nationalization of banks in the aftermath of the financial crisis of 2007–2009), and from mutual forms of ownership, though countries started (and indeed finished) with rather different patterns of ownership.

In this chapter, the main focus is on the relationships between finance, financialization and economic growth and development. There is a long literature which has been concerned with what is often termed financial development or financial deepening and economic development and growth: "Financial development occurs when financial instruments, markets, and intermediaries ameliorate – though do not necessarily eliminate – the effects of information, enforcement, and transactions costs and therefore do a correspondingly better job at providing the five principal functions" (Levine 2005: 869–70).

A related literature has developed in which financial liberalization and the relaxation of so-called financial repression are examined. Financial development has often been viewed as held back by 'financial repression' – government regulations and restrictions on the banking system on, for example, interest rates which can be charged on loans, paid on deposits, the products which can be supplied by banks, and the volume and direction of loans. Financial liberalization and de-regulation are then viewed (as in the McKinnon [1973] and Shaw [1973] hypothesis) as releasing financial development, and thereby stimulating economic development. These can be seen as a feature of financialization involving de-regulation and the promotion of the efficiency of markets and of the unregulated financial system, and promoting the growth of the financial sector. As such, financial liberalization can be examined in terms of its effects on investment, growth and also on credit expansion and financial crisis.

Financialization and economic growth

Ross Levine (2005) remarks that:

> Economists disagree sharply about the role of the financial sector in economic growth. . . . Nobel Laureate Robert Lucas (1988, p.6) dismisses finance as an 'over-stressed determinant of economic growth'. Joan Robinson (1952, p.86) famously argued that 'where enterprise leads finance follows'. From this perspective, finance does not cause growth, but at the other extreme, Nobel Laureate Merton Miller (1998, p.14) argues that, '[the idea] that financial markets contribute to economic growth is a proposition too obvious for serious discussion'. Drawing a more restrained conclusion, Bagehot (1962 [1873]), Schumpeter (1926 [1912]), Gurley and Shaw (1955), Goldsmith (1969), and McKinnon (1973) reject the idea that the finance-growth nexus can be safely ignored without substantially limiting our understanding of economic growth.
>
> (Levine 2005: 867)

The growth of banks in the context of financial development can be interpreted in terms of banks providing the main vehicle for savings (in the form of bank deposits) which are then allocated for investment purposes. The perceived benefits of this arise from the pooling of savings, the monitoring functions of the banks, etc.

Schumpeter is an early author supporting the view that financial development leads to economic development. He developed a credit theory of money (as opposed to a money theory of credit) which placed the need for credit to enable production to come to fruition. In this process, the banker is the key agent: "The banker, therefore, is not so much primarily the middleman in the commodity 'purchasing power' as a producer of this commodity . . . He is the ephor of the exchange economy" (Schumpeter 1911: 74). This involves the credit creation process, and links with the endogenous view of money. It is the ability of banks to create spending power through loans which is a feature of growth and expansion.

The manner in which the financial sector (and its development) has been argued to facilitate economic growth can be seen in terms of the effects on savings behaviour, investment funding and the 'quality' of investment. Levine, for example, argues that the financial system provides the following functions: to "produce information ex ante about possible investments and allocate capital; monitor investments and exert corporate governance after providing finance; facilitate the trading, diversification and management of risk; mobilize and pool savings; ease the exchange of goods and services" (Levine 2005: 869). He has recently argued that "finance promotes economic growth primarily by improving the efficiency of capital allocation, not by increasing investment" (Levine 2011: 272). The financial sector is then seen in terms of being a facilitator in linking together savings and investment, and stimulating savings through the provision of financial assets in which the savings can be held, and in performing a range of monitoring roles.

The significant element here is, of course, that a well-functioning financial sector is postulated to raise the rate of growth (through more and higher-quality investment). The empirical difficulty is measuring the performance of those functions, whereas what is often measured is some dimension of the size of the financial sector (e.g. bank deposits relative to GDP). The question that may be also asked is whether the manner in which the financial sector has grown in the past three decades through securitization and in the ratio of assets and liabilities to GDP has improved those functions and aided economic growth.

Growth may be constrained by credit creation in less developed financial systems; in more sophisticated systems, finance is viewed as endogenous, responding to demand requirements. This line of argument suggests that the more developed a financial system is, the higher the likelihood of growth causing finance. The growth of the stock of money (and indeed the evolving forms of money) could be anticipated to be closely related with the monetization of the economy and the development of trade.

The development of the financial sector encourages saving through the provision of liquid financial assets as a vehicle for saving and raises the quality of investment through monitoring, etc. The combination of those would raise the rate of growth of the economy. These are predominantly theoretical arguments on the linkages from the financial sector to the real sector, and the question must be whether the financial sector works in the ways envisaged in the theoretical arguments. Further, financial development is often measured in terms of the scale of the financial sector such as bank deposits (relative to GDP), and stock market valuation. When bank deposits are the major vehicle for savings, then it could be expected that there will be some relationship between bank deposits (relative to GDP) and growth – the scale of the relationship depending on the degree to which bank deposits are the major form of savings and the degree to which savings and investment are related.

However, the major questions should be whether the financial system does operate in the ways envisaged, and whether the ways in which the financial systems have expanded and evolved in the past few decades are conducive for the encouragement of savings and investment, and the direction of finance and funds towards productive investment.

Financial repression and financial liberalization

Liberalization and de-regulation of the financial sector have featured strongly in the ways in which the financial sector has changed and grown in the last three to four decades. Ideas such as those expressed by McKinnon (1973) and Shaw (1973) have had a major influence and been drawn up to promote de-regulation. The ideas of McKinnon (1973) and of Shaw (1973) argued that government regulations on the banking system restrain the activities of the banks with regard to interest rates and the allocation of credit, which in turn limits the funds allocated to investors and lowers the quantity and quality of investment, and thereby growth. The recommendation of the financial liberalization proponents was the removal of ceilings on interest rates and scrapping of credit allocation policies. This would enable equilibrium between savings and investment to be established since "there is widespread agreement that flows of saving and investment should be voluntary and significantly decentralized in an open capital market at close to equilibrium interest rates" (McKinnon 1991: 12, quoted in Rousseau and Wachtel 2011: 276).

Financial liberalization and de-regulation have been viewed as important ingredients in the present financialization era, and hence the arguments of authors such as McKinnon and Shaw are highly relevant as setting out some general arguments for the favourable impacts on the real economy of financial liberalization. In turn, financial liberalization and de-regulation are viewed as important elements of financialization, particularly in the period since the mid-1970s.

The advocacy of financial liberalization is often based on a model of banking in which deposits make loans, and does not make any allowance for the credit creation processes which may be unleashed by financial liberalization and the relaxation of controls over the volume of credit. The processes of financial liberalization (and a general trend towards de-regulation, though there are also changes in the form of regulation involved) may well exacerbate the tendencies towards instability. This was expressed as:

> Financial liberalization produces an upward step-change in the intensity of the domestic drive towards financial innovation . . . It thereby speeds up the process by which debt ratios of commercial concerns and financial institutions rise, escalating financial fragility, and it hastens the day when banking and financial crises loom.
>
> (Arestis and Glickman 2002: 244–245)

Financial deepening and economic growth: the empirical results

Financial deepening has generally been measured in terms of the scale of the financial sector to GDP, such as the ratio of bank deposits to GDP, stock market valuation to GDP, and a combination of such ratios.

Levine (2005), in his extensive review of the empirical literature, concluded that:

> A growing body of empirical analyses, including firm-level studies, industry-level studies, individual country-studies, time-series studies, panel-investigations, and broad cross-country comparisons, demonstrate[s] a strong positive link between the functioning of the financial system and long-run economic growth. While subject to ample qualifications and countervailing views noted throughout this article, the preponderance of evidence suggests that both financial intermediaries and markets matter for growth even when controlling for potential simultaneity bias. Furthermore, microeconomic-based evidence is consistent with the view that better developed financial systems ease external financing constraints facing firms, which illuminates one mechanism through which financial development influences economic

growth. Theory and empirical evidence make it difficult to conclude that the financial system merely – and automatically – responds to economic activity, or that financial development is an inconsequential addendum to the process of economic growth.

(Levine 2005: 921)

Ang (2008) surveys the main findings of cross-country analyses and maintains that even though these studies provide significant contributions to the literature for understanding the finance–growth nexus and suggest that financial development exerts a positive impact on economic growth, their results are subject to several criticisms; for example, lack of attention to causality issues and difficulties of reflecting institutional differences between countries.

The relationship between financial development and economic growth in the past three decades or so in the industrialized world is of particular interest. Casual observation may suggest that the general growth of the financial sector and the enhanced size of that sector have not obviously been associated with any faster growth. Indeed it is often argued that growth in the Western industrialized economies has been somewhat slower over the past three decades of financialization. Further, the literature on financialization has indeed suggested a variety of ways in which the processes of financialization may have diminished investment. For example, Hein (2012) argues that:

> Regarding investment in capital stock, financialisation has been associated with increasing shareholder power *vis-à-vis* management and labourers, an increasing rate of return on equity and bonds held by rentiers, and decreasing managements' animal spirits with respect to real investment, which each have partially negative effects on real investment of firms.

(Hein 2012: 180)

Authors working within the mainstream traditions have reported a mixture of weakening of the links between financial development and economic growth, and reversal of the signs of the relationship, from positive to negative, at high levels of financial deepening summarized in a quadratic relationship. This is often based on econometric evidence and regressions which are estimated to span many years.

Rousseau and Wachtel (2011) argue that

> although the finance-growth relationship is now firmly entrenched in the empirical literature, we show that it is not as strong in more recent data as it was in the original studies with data for the period from 1960 to 1989.

(Rousseau and Wachtel 2011: 276)

They consider a range of explanations. There is the increased incidence of financial crises which are often followed by recession and lost output which is never recovered. They then state that rapid growth of credit may have led to both inflation and weakened banking systems which in turn gave rise to growth-inhibiting financial crises.

Another study documents

> that the size of the financial sector has increased dramatically in both the developed and developing world in combination with a high volatility of the financial sector relative to the economy as a whole. In line with previous research we find that in the long run financial intermediation increases growth and reduces growth volatility. Both effects have, however, become weaker over time. The size of the financial sector while controlling for the level of intermediation in an economy does not seem to affect long-run growth or volatility. Our analysis also shows that neither the size of the financial sector nor intermediation is associated with higher growth in the medium run. This result obtains despite a positive growth effect of the size of the financial sector and the non-intermediation component in the subsample of high-income countries. Critically, financial system size, especially non-intermediation services, has a positive relationship with volatility in high-income countries over the medium-term.
>
> (Beck *et al.* 2014: 62)

A study from the Bank for International Settlements (BIS) came to two conclusions:

> First, financial sector size has an inverted U-shaped effect on productivity growth. That is, there comes a point where further enlargement of the financial system can reduce real growth. Second, financial sector growth is found to be a drag on productivity growth. Our interpretation is that because the financial sector competes with the rest of the economy for scarce resources, financial booms are not, in general, growth enhancing. This evidence, together with recent experience during the financial crisis, leads us to conclude that there is a pressing need to reassess the relationship of finance and real growth in modern economic systems. More finance is definitely not always better.
>
> (Cecchetti and Kharroubi 2012: 14)

Sahay *et al.* (2015: 5) state that using "a new, broad, measure of financial development . . . [underscores] that many benefits in terms of stability can still be reaped from further financial development in most [emerging markets]". But they document that

> the effect of financial development on growth is bell-shaped; it weakens at higher levels of financial development. This weakening effect stems from financial deepening, rather than from greater access or higher efficiency. The empirical evidence also suggests that this weakening effect reflects primarily the impact of financial deepening on total factor productivity growth, rather than on capital accumulation.
>
> (Sahay *et al.* 2015: 5)

Further, it appears that the pace of financial development matters: "When it proceeds too fast, deepening financial institutions can lead to economic and financial instability" (Sahay *et al.* 2015: 5).

Cournède *et al.* (2015: 6), in an OECD study, note that, "over the past fifty years, credit by banks and other intermediaries to households and businesses has grown three times as fast as economic activity". Based on 50 years of data for OECD countries, they conclude that, "in most OECD countries, further expansion [of the financial sector] is likely to slow rather than boost growth".

Financial liberalization and de-regulation: some empirics

Bumann *et al.* (2012: 43) summarize the position with regard to the "hotly debated" relationship between financial liberalization and economic growth in the following terms:

> [W]hereas some have claimed that liberalisation of financial markets contributes to the efficiency with which these markets can transform saving into investment, which ultimately fosters economic growth, others have pointed out that these liberalisations have contributed to various financial and economic crises in the past. . . . The evidence that emerges from these studies [of the relationship] remains inconclusive.
>
> (Bumann *et al.* 2012: 43)

These authors undertake a meta-analysis based on 60 empirical studies. Their

> meta-regression analysis provided the following main results: First, the unconditional mean of the t-statistic of the financial liberalisation variable equals 1.42, which is highly significant. Using a chi-squared test we also have to reject the null hypothesis that the average t-statistic equals 1.96. . . . Hence, we conclude that although our results indicate that, on average, there is a positive effect of financial liberalisation on growth, the significance of this effect is only weak. Second, for most of the variables that may help [in] explaining the heterogeneity of results about the relationship between financial liberalisation and economic growth we do not find any significant results. There are two exceptions. Our analysis suggests that data from the 1970s generate more negative financial liberalisation coefficients which suggests that financial liberalisation policies carried out during the 1970s seem to have a stronger negative relationship with growth. Moreover, our results show that studies that take into account a measure of the level of development of the financial system report lower t-statistics for the relationship between liberalisation and growth.
>
> (Bumann *et al.* 2012: 43–45)

Arestis and Stein (2005) draw attention to the linkages between financial liberalization and subsequent financial crisis, fuelled by rapid credit expansion following de-regulation and often asset price bubbles. They report on the work of Demirgüç-Kunt and Detragiache (1998) who surveyed a total of 53 countries, covering the period between 1980 and 1995, whose experiences resulted in financial and banking crises.

> In fact, Demirguc-Kunt & Detragiache (1998) find that 78% of all banking crises were linked to periods of financial liberalisation. The results of those crises were catastrophic. Interest rates exceeded 20%, a number of 'bad' debts and waves of bank failures and other bankruptcies ensued, associated with extreme asset volatility, and with all the financial systems involved reaching a near collapse stage. As a consequence the real sectors of the affected economies entered severe and prolonged recessions. On the whole, financial liberalisation in those and other countries had a destabilising effect on the economy and [was] abandoned. Since the mid-1990s there have been major crises in Argentina, Ecuador, Thailand, Russia, Turkey, Uruguay, Col[o]mbia, Indonesia, Kenya and South Korea. Much of this instability has been associated with rapid financial liberalisation, without exception. Interestingly enough, and in contrast to the earlier period referred to above in the case of South Korea, the crisis of November, 1997 in this country, followed the deregulation of interest rates, the opening of the capital market, foreign exchange liberalisation, the granting of new banking licenses and the dismantling of government monitoring mechanisms that were part of the policy loan system.
>
> (Arestis and Stein 2005: 384)

A more general conclusion on financial liberalization and its effects is drawn by Ghosh, who argues that

> [I]t is evident from this discussion that complete financial liberalization – in the sense of implementing all of the various internal and external measures described here, is neither necessary nor desirable. In fact, such extreme measures have not been implemented by the more successful developing country industrializers. In fact, the examples of those countries that have successfully industrialized – from the nineteenth century onwards, and continuing to date – is instructive, because there are two features which are common to all of them: some degree (usually substantial) of directed credit; and some controls on cross-border capital flows.
>
> (Ghosh 2005: 15)

He then concludes:

> So, there is a strong case for developing countries to ensure that their own financial systems are adequately regulated with respect to their own specific requirements, which may vary substantially, depending upon the size and nature of their economies, the extent of external integration, the relative importance of the banking system vis-à-vis the capital market, and so on.
>
> (Ghosh 2005: 16–17)

The size of financial sector: now too large?

The financial sector is not, as illustrated in Brown *et al*. (2015), a great generator of jobs and employment. Some of the expansion of employment in the financial sector has been in jobs such as call centres, but there are also highly trained mathematicians and physicists employed on Wall Street and elsewhere who could have been more socially useful employed as scientists and engineers. Tobin (1987) has written that:

> I confess to an uneasy Physiocratic suspicion, perhaps unbecoming in an academic, that we are throwing more and more of our resources, including the cream of our youth, into financial activities remote from the production of goods and services, into activities that generate high private rewards disproportionate to their social productivity.
>
> (Tobin 1987: 294)

Epstein and Crotty (2013: 5) extend that suggestion of Tobin by arguing that "a broader perspective, based in different ways on the works of Karl Marx and Hyman Minsky, would suggest that the financial sector can have more sinister impacts: that it can engage in exploitation and also destroy value." They continue by producing a

> very preliminary range of estimates [which] suggests that the financial sector in the United States is extracting 2–4 times as much income relative to the services it provides to the real sector in the decade of the 2000's as it did during the high growth period of the 1960's. This suggests that the financial sector may need to be only one-half to one-quarter as large as it is currently to serve the existing needs of the real sector.
>
> (Epstein and Crotty 2013: 13)

The financial sector, then, can be seen to absorb resources which are then not available for deployment in the real sector, and this raises the question of whether a larger financial sector detracts from the growth of the real sector. The empirical evidence cited above would be supportive of the view that there comes a point when the financial sector is in a sense too large, and that further expansion of the financial sector becomes detrimental to growth. This line of argument would suggest that further expansion of the financial system beyond a certain point would not be related with the savings–investment relationship. Since the link between financial development and economic development comes essentially from the savings–investment links, then the relationship is called into doubt. This can be conveniently summarized by the following quote:

> Finance is a powerful tool for economic development but with important non-linear effects. Critically, [a] poorly designed regulatory framework can reinforce the fragility inherent in financial systems, and cause economic

damage. This also implies that the financial sector can grow too large for society's benefits. Even twenty to thirty years after financial liberalisation, high-income countries still have to learn how to live with the genies they let out of the bottle and harness it to the benefit of their societies.

(Beck 2013: Conclusions)

In general, in industrialized countries, the ratios of savings and of investment to GDP have not risen over the past three decades, and growth has tended to be somewhat lower than previously. A key function for the financial sector is generally said to be the provision of financial assets as a vehicle for savings, the funding and monitoring of investment, and the linking together of savings and investment, enabling the stimulation of savings, and more effective and greater investment. As indicated above, the larger scale of the financial sector has not been matched by higher savings, investment or growth. The growth of the financial sector has come from the development of a wide range of financial assets and liabilities which have the effect of placing more steps in the passage of funds from savers to investors, and the growth of trading in existing financial assets. For example, in many countries, there has been not only a growth of the stock market in terms of the ratio of stock market valuation to GDP, and much of that may reflect the retention of profits by corporations rather than the issue of new equity and the raising of funds through the stock market. But this has also often been accompanied by a rise in the volume of transactions on the stock market and the rate of turnover of stocks. Thus resources are used in the trading of existing financial assets, but without additional funds being generated and allocated to investment.

Proposals for de-financialization

The general approach taken here is that the financial sector has become 'too large', and has moved away from its key function of linking savers and investors. Although this has not been discussed above, it is not just a matter of the quantity of funds but the allocation of such funds. Indeed, it could be argued that growth will be need to be much slower in the future as ecological and climate change concerns are addressed. A set of tax policy proposals are first considered which could be used with the aim of reducing the size of the financial sector. This is followed by alternative structures for financial institutions.

Taxes

A financial transactions tax is a means of reducing the financial sector's trading activities in existing financial assets, which can be argued to be unrelated to what should be the key functions of the financial sector – the financing and funding of investment.[4] The trading of existing financial assets, the growth of 'fictitious capital', and the rise of assets and liabilities (relative to GDP) contribute little to that key role. The resources which are engaged in such trading would be released for more productive activities, and there can be beneficial effects on the volatility and fragility of such markets. The essential rationale for a financial transactions tax remains and is indeed reinforced by financialization and the specific direction which financialization has taken in the past three decades with the growth of securitization and derivatives.

The financial sector can be said to be undertaxed relative to the non-financial sector in that, as a general rule (at least within the European Union), while value added tax (VAT) is levied on much of the non-financial sector, it is not levied on the financial sector. A financial activities tax[5] would address that difference, and the associated distortion where one sector is more taxed than another, leaving the former smaller and the latter larger than would otherwise be the case. There is a distortionary taxation which promotes the size of the financial sector at the expense of the non-financial sector. A financial activities tax is a substitute for a value added tax. It would be possible to adjust the financial activities tax to address some other issues such as the rent gained by the financial sector. For example, the European Commission (2011) considered three variants of a financial activities tax – (i) profits of financial institutions in cash-flow terms plus remuneration paid by the sector; (ii) as (i) with remuneration replaced by the notion of 'excessive remuneration'; (iii) sum of cash-flow profits above a specified return on capital and 'excessive' remuneration.

Alternative financial institutions

The financial sector, perhaps more than any other sector, has had a mix of different forms of ownership – public, private, and mutual and co-operative. Different types of financial institutions can have different functions and different sets of customers;,for example, savings banks versus investment banks, firms as customers versus households as customers. Thus, complementarities between financial institutions arise with each type having their own functions and specialisms.

Financial institutions determine the terms on which loans, credit, etc. are provided to the non-financial sector, whether to corporations, small and medium-size enterprises (SMEs) or households. This is not only a matter of what are the costs of finance, including the rates of interest to be charged, but also how credit rationing operates. It is an inevitable feature of the provision of credit, loans and funds that the lender has to be concerned over the risks of default, late payment and non-performing loans. It is then an inevitable feature that (formal or informal) credit ratings are made by lenders, with consequent effects on the cost and availability of funds.

There is an array of alternative financial institutions, alternative that is, to the profit-oriented private banks. Mutual organization and state-owned ones may be considered to have objectives other than the maximization of profits, but do have to at least break even (what exactly that would mean depends on how costs are evaluated) and in that sense, pay regard to the 'bottom line'. Further, such organizations have a range of other objectives – serving particular income groups, providing funds to specified groups, etc. Notable examples here would be institutions such as credit unions, micro-finance institutions, etc. These alternative forms of financial institution are often, but not always, organized on a more localized level than profit-seeking institutions.

The local aspect of this is stressed by Sikka (2014) when he writes that

> banks should be part of local communities. They should not be permitted to up sticks and leave local communities in the lurch. Maintaining a socially desirable network of branches should be a necessary quid pro quo for a deposit-taking licence and the state's deposit protection guarantee. Each branch closure must be sanctioned by the regulator, and banks must be required to demonstrate that after closure, the local community's access to banking services will not suffer.
>
> (Sikka 2014: 24)

One of the relevant features of these alternative financial institutions is that they are banks with relatively close contact with their customers rather than operating through financial markets. They are focused on the role of linking together savers and investors which has been argued above should be the key role of the financial sector.

Guided lending

The ways in which funds are allocated and how well those allocations serve broader social and economic objectives are important considerations. This can involve some degree of guided lending for banks – that is, requirements that a specified proportion of their lending is for investments which may be deemed 'green' and address environmental concerns. This could draw on the US experience of the Community Reinvestment Act (CRA), introduced in 1977 and revised in 1995, whereby banks and other financial institutions are legally required to direct a portion of funds to lending to the local community:

> The Community Reinvestment Act is intended to encourage depository institutions to help meet the credit needs of the communities in which they operate, including low- and moderate-income neighborhoods, consistent with safe and sound operations. The CRA requires that each depository institution's record in helping meet the credit needs of its entire community be evaluated by the appropriate Federal financial supervisory agency periodically. Members of the public may submit comments on a bank's performance. Comments will be taken into consideration during the next CRA examination. A bank's CRA performance record is taken into account in considering an institution's application for deposit facilities.
>
> (Federal Reserve 2014)

Such policies can go alongside the view that

> government has an active role to play in allocating credit to finance productive economic activity, and it should use a full range of policy tools including

interest rate subsidies, loan guarantee programs, and tax incentives to assure that capital flows in the most productive directions.

(Block 2014: 13)

Development banks

The advantages of a development bank model include the clear setting of objectives for the way in which funds are to be allocated, and which sectors and activities are to be favoured. It can enable funds to be provided on more favourable terms than would be forthcoming from private financial institutions through implicit government subsidy of its operations (e.g. the mark-up of the interest rate charged over the costs of funds in the capital market is kept low). The range of investments funded by a development bank could also focus on the type of investments which are shunned by the financial markets. These would include investments which have a long-term rather than short-term pay-off, and those subject to high degrees of uncertainty: a notable example here would be research and development activities. There are, of course, examples of banks operating along such lines, including the German KfW Development Bank, the UK's Green Investment Bank and the European Investment Bank.

A State development bank has the potential for the prioritizing of funds for socially desirable investments. This is not to underestimate the obstacles of assessing the social desirability of investment projects, nor the threat of 'mission creep' whereby those financial institutions which initially have wider objectives than profit maximization become focused on profits.

Concluding remarks

Financialization involves the increasing political power as well as economic scope of the financial sector. In this chapter it has been argued that in a number of dimensions the financial sector has become too large. Some proposals have been made for diminishing its size through the use of taxes specific to the financial sector. The arguments for a more diverse banking system and financial institutions were made, in which financial institutions are more focused on the key role of intermediating between savings and investment. This could involve the encouragement and development of alternative financial institutions including credit unions, and micro-finance, mutual organization, local and regional financial institutions as well as State development banks. These are general ideas and any specific proposals would need to be mindful of the specific characteristics of the country concerned. It has to be recognized that the major barriers to any serious reforms of the financial sector come from the political power and influence which that sector can yield.

Notes

1 Acknowledgments: this chapter draws on the results of research undertaken within the project Financialisation, Economy, Society and Sustainable Development (FESSUD), which received funding from the European Union Seventh Framework Programme (FP7/2007–2013) under grant agreement No. 266800. The views expressed in this chapter are mine, and do not reflect the views of the partners within the FESSUD project nor those of the European Commission.
2 See Sawyer (2014) amongst others for discussion of the origin and usage of the term.
3 This has been the case with the studies within the project Financialisation, Economy, Society and Sustainable Development (details at www.fessud.eu).
4 For an overall assessment of financial transactions taxes see, for example, Arestis and Sawyer (2013).
5 See Sawyer (2015) for some discussion.

References

Ang, J. B. (2008). "A survey of recent developments in the literature of finance and growth", *Journal of Economic Surveys* 22(3): 536–576.

Arestis, P. and Glickman, M. (2002). "Financial crisis in South East Asia: Dispelling illusion the Minskyan way", *Cambridge Journal of Economics*, 26(2): 237–260.

Arestis, P. and Stein, H. (2005). "An institutional perspective to finance and development as an alternative to financial liberalisation", *International Review of Applied Economics*, 19(4): 381–398.

Arestis, P. and Sawyer, M. (2013). "The potential of financial transactions taxes", in P. Arestis and M. Sawyer (Eds), *Economic Policies, Governance and the New Economics.* Basingstoke, UK: Palgrave Macmillan.

Bagehot, W. (1962 [1873]). *Lombard Street.* Homewood, IL: Richard D. Irwin.

Beck, T. (2013). "Finance and growth: too much of a good thing?", *Vox*, CEPR's policy portal, posted 27 October. Available at: www.voxeu.org/article/finance-and-growth (accessed August 2014).

Beck, T., Degryse, H. and Kneer, C. (2014). "Is more finance better? Disentangling intermediation and size effects of financial systems", *Journal of Financial Stability*, 10: 50–64.

Block, F. (2014). "Democratizing finance", *Politics & Society*, 42(1): 3–28.

Brown, A., Passarella, M. and Spencer, D. (2015). "The nature and variegation of financialisation: A cross-country comparison", FESSUD Working Paper No. 127.

Bumann, S., Hermes, N. and Lensink, R. (2012). *Financial Liberalisation and Economic Growth: A Meta-analysis. Technical Report.* London: EPPI-Centre, Social Science Research Unit, Institute of Education, University of London.

Cecchetti, S. G. and Kharroubi, E. (2012). "Reassessing the impact of finance on growth", BIS Working Paper No. 381.

Cournède, B., Denk, O. and Hoeller, P. (2015). "Finance and Inclusive Growth", *OECD Economic Policy Papers*, No. 14. Paris: OECD Publishing.

Demirgüç-Kunt, A. and Detragiache, E. (1998). "Financial liberalization and financial fragility", IMF Working Paper WP/98/83.

Epstein, G. (2005). "Introduction: Financialization and the World Economy", in G. A. Epstein (Ed.), *Financialization and the World Economy.* Cheltenham, UK: Edward Elgar Publishing, pp. 3–16.

Epstein, G. and Crotty, J. (2013). "How big is too big? On the social efficiency of the financial sector in the United States", PERI Working Paper No. 313, Political Economy Research Institute, University of Massachusetts Amherst.

European Commission (2011). *Impact Assessment Accompanying the Document Proposal for a Council Directive on a Common System of Financial Transaction Tax and Amending Directive* 2008/7/EC. SEC(2011)1102. Brussels: European Commission.

Federal Reserve (2014). Community Reinvestment Act (CRA). Available at www.federalreserve.gov/communitydev/cra_about.htm (accessed March 2014).

Ghosh, J. (2005). "The economic and social effects of financial liberalization: a primer for developing countries", UN DESA Working Paper No. 4, ST/ESA/2005/DWP/4, October.

Goldsmith, R. (1969). *Financial Structure and Development.* New Haven, CT: Yale University Press.

Gurley, J. G. and Shaw, E. S. (1955). "Financial aspects of economic development", *American Economic Review*, 45(4): 515–538.

Hein, E. (2012). *The Macroeconomics of Finance-dominated Capitalism – and its Crisis.* Aldershot, UK: Edward Elgar Publishing.

Levine, R. (2005). "Finance and Growth: Theory and Evidence", in P. Aghion and S. N. Durlauf (Eds), *Handbook of Economic Growth.* Amsterdam: Elsevier, pp. 866–934.

Levine, R. (2011). "Regulating Finance and Regulators to Promote Growth", paper presented at Federal Reserve Bank of Kansas City Annual Economic Symposium, 25–27 August, Jackson Hole, Wyoming, USA. Available at: www.kansascityfed.org/publicat/sympos/2011/Levine_final.pdf (accessed August 2014).

Lucas, R. (1988). "On the mechanics of economic development", *Journal of Monetary Economics*, 22(1): 3–42.

McKinnon, R. I. (1973). *Money and Capital in Economic Development.* Washington, DC: Brookings Institution.

McKinnon, R. I. (1991). *The Order of Economic Liberalization.* Baltimore, MD: The Johns Hopkins University Press.

Miller, M. H. (1998). "Financial markets and economic growth", *Journal of Applied Corporate Finance*, 11(3): 8–14.

Robinson, J. (1952). "The generalization of the *General Theory*", in J. Robinson, *The Rate of Interest and Other Essays*, London: Macmillan, pp. 67–142.

Rousseau, P. L. and Wachtel, P. (2011). "What is happening to the impact of financial deepening on economic growth?", *Economic Inquiry*, 49(1): 276–288.

Sahay, R. Čihák, M., N'Diaye, P., Barajas, A., Bi, R., Ayala, D., Gao, Y., Kyobe, A., Nguyen, L., Saborowski, C., Svirydzenka, K., and Yousefi, S. R. (2015). "Rethinking financial deepening: Stability and growth in emerging markets", IMF Staff Discussion Note SDN15/08.

Sawyer, M. (2014). "What Is Financialization?", *International Journal of Political Economy*, 42(4): 5–18.

Sawyer, M. (2015). "Taxation of financial activities", FESSUD Deliverable D4.13 (available from www.fessud.eu).

Schumpeter, J. (1911). *The Theory of Economic Development: An Inquiry into Profits, Capital, Credit, Interest and the Business Cycle* (1934 translation). Cambridge, MA: Harvard University Press.

Schumpeter, J. A. (1926 [1912]). *Theorie der wirtschaftlichen Entwicklung*, 2nd edn. München und Leipzig: Duncker & Humblot. [English edn (1934). *The Theory of Economic Development.* New York: Oxford University Press.]

Shaw, E. S. (1973) *Financial Deepening in Economic Development*. New York: Oxford University Press.

Sikka, P. (2014). "Banking in the public interest: Progressive reform of the financial sector", CLASS Policy Paper No. 24, February.

Tobin, J. (1987). "On the efficiency of the financial system", in P. M. Jackson (Ed.) *Policies for Prosperity; Essays in a Keynesian Mode*. Cambridge, MA: The MIT Press, pp. 282–295.

Van der Zwan, N. (2014). "State of the Art: Making Sense of Financialisation", *Socio-Economic Review*, 12(1): 99–129.

Vercelli, A. (2014). "Financialisation in a Long-Run Perspective: An Evolutionary Approach", *International Journal of Political Economy*, 42(4): 19–46.

6 A common currency for the common good

Sergio Rossi

Introduction

The global financial crisis that erupted in 2008, after the demise of Lehman Brothers, is not simply the result of a lack of appropriate regulation of bankers' forms of behaviour, as generally claimed. To be sure, misbehaviour can give rise to a variety of financial or economic crises, but cannot originate a systemic crisis, which is a crisis that affects the economic system as a whole. For such a crisis to occur, there must be a structural flaw, to wit, a system-wide disorder. Indeed, this is what a truly macroeconomic analysis can reveal, if we consider the monetary architecture that exists to date to carry out payment orders at the national or international level (Cencini and Rossi 2015).

This chapter explains, notably, that the global financial crisis originated in the structure of domestic payment systems, which are also used for international settlements despite the purely accounting nature of bank money. In the next section we will argue that the nature of bank money is purely scriptural, so that a monetary system is a closed system essentially: a flight of bank deposits cannot occur in this framework; only their holders may be located outside the relevant banking system. However, as the third section will show, payments that concern residents in two distinct monetary systems affect both of them negatively, contributing to financial instability within as well as between them. As a matter of fact, to date, emerging market economies have been suffering from the lack of payment finality at international level, both when they are net exporters (because they are not paid finally for their net exports) and when they are net importers (owing to the credit bubble that this inflates domestically). In the fourth section, we will elaborate on this analysis to show how the architecture of the payments system should be structurally reformed at the international level, to avoid both problems that have been the origin of a systemic financial crisis across the global economy in 2008. The key to this structural reform lies in making sure that all transactions on foreign-exchange markets respect the nature of money as a purely numerical means of payment, instead of denaturing it into an object of trade and speculation. In this regard, emerging market economies can decide, individually, bilaterally or as a group, to shield themselves from the present non-system for international payments, setting up an international settlement institution in charge of issuing a supranational means of payment finality for their foreign trade. Such a system will contribute to financial stability domestically and internationally, thereby supporting economic development in a sustainable way, and the benefits of this will increase employment levels around the world.

The nature of money

There is no doubt, today, that money is issued by the banking system (see McLeay *et al.* 2014). Also, there should be no problem in understanding that money is issued through a credit operation, which results from banks' double-entry system of accounts. Indeed, a payment needs money to be finalized, so that "a seller of a good, or service, or another asset, receives something of equal value from the purchaser, which leaves the seller with no further claim on the buyer" (Goodhart 1989: 26). In this perspective, as already noted by Hicks (1967: 11), "[e]very transaction involves three parties, buyer, seller, and banker". This clearly explains that the banking system neither buys nor sells anything when it intervenes in order for a payment to occur finally. The number of money units issued by banks to carry out payments does not add to the income or wealth available in an economic system. Money is purely a numerical counter, debited and credited to those agents that are involved in the relevant payment. Hence,

> [m]oney therefore *only comes into existence the moment a payment is made.* At that moment, in one and the same act, money is created, the borrower becomes a debtor to the bank and the agent receiving a payment becomes the creditor of the same bank.
>
> (Graziani 1990: 11, emphasis in original)

Let us illustrate it through the relevant bank ledgers (Table 6.1).

As a result of the payment, the payer is indebted to the domestic banking system, which has a debt against the payee for the same amount, in the form of the corresponding bank deposit (say, £x). This shows that loans create deposits, as Schumpeter (1970) famously explained. In fact, bank deposits cannot move outside the banking system that generates them, because each payment implies a double entry in the banks' books: when a deposit is debited to the relevant payer (say, a wage-earner), an identically equivalent amount is credited, simultaneously, to the bank account of the payee (say, a company). As Table 6.2 shows, there can be no "leakages" (or "deposit flight") from the banking system, which, as a matter of fact, is a closed system "always and everywhere".

Table 6.1 The result of a payment carried out by the domestic banking system

Domestic banking system	
Assets	*Liabilities*
Loan to payer £x	Deposit of payee £x

Table 6.2 The domestic banking system is a closed system

Domestic banking system	
Assets	*Liabilities*
	Deposit of payer −£x
	Deposit of payee +£x

The fact that the banking system is a closed system does not exclude the possibility that the owner of a bank deposit resides elsewhere; that is, in a different monetary space. As a matter of fact, a number of bank deposits in a country like Switzerland are owned by a variety of non-residents (both European and non-European citizens), who have decided, notably for banking secrecy reasons, to move (part of) their financial wealth into a "safe place" like Switzerland (Table 6.3). This off-shore relationship might also exist as a result of a cross-border payment between any two agents, as Table 6.4 illustrates.

There can be no doubt that the entries in Table 6.4 epitomize a final payment as regards the two agents involved, which can be an importer in country A and the corresponding exporter in country R. Recalling the Goodhart (1989: 26) definition of payment finality quoted above, we see that the payee (resident in country R) has no further claim on the payer (resident in country A): the latter has indeed transferred to the former a claim on the amount of the transaction between them, this amount being recorded in the form of equivalent bank deposits (let us assume that x MA = y MR).

To sum up, money is a purely numerical counter, issued by banks any time a payment needs to be carried out between any two agents (the payer and the payee). Bank loans give rise to bank deposits, whose ownership may then be transferred from an agent to another as a result of the relevant payment order. No bank deposit can therefore leave the banking system that originates it, although the ownership of this deposit might be transferred from a resident to a non-resident in the same

Table 6.3 The result of a wealth transfer between two different monetary spaces

Bank A (banking system of country A)	
Assets	*Liabilities*
	Deposit of client I −x MA
	Deposit of bank R +x MA

Bank R (banking system of country R)	
Assets	*Liabilities*
Deposit with bank A +x MA	Deposit of client I +y MR

Note: MA = money of country A; MR = money of country R.

Table 6.4 The result of a payment across two different monetary spaces

Bank A (banking system of country A)

Assets	Liabilities	
	Deposit of payer	−x MA
	Deposit of bank R	+x MA

Bank R (banking system of country R)

Assets		Liabilities	
Deposit with bank A	+x MA	Deposit of payee	+y MR

Note: MA = money of country A; MR = money of country R.

monetary space that generates this deposit. Cross-border payments are in any case final for the agents involved, since the payee has no further claims on the payer once the payment has been carried out by the relevant payment and settlement systems. Let us turn now to the pathological issues raised by cross-border payments for the countries involved thereby.

The structural origin of the current international monetary disorder

The purely numerical nature of money makes it plain that money cannot be considered as an object exchanged against some other (non-monetary) items. As Schumpeter used to say, nobody would agree to supply an umbrella in exchange for a number (especially when it rains). In this regard, it is worth considering the essential distinction between the means of payment (money) and the record of its purchasing power (bank deposits). The former is issued by banks within payments – which are instantaneous events, because it takes just an instant of time to record the result of the relevant payment in the assets and liabilities of the bank(s) carrying out the payment order – while the latter actually exists between any two payments within the banking system of the relevant monetary space as a memory item: the owner of a bank deposit knows that she can dispose of a purchasing power when the latter is needed to finance a payment. In other words, money carries out payments, while the stock of bank deposits finances them (see Rossi 2007a: Chapter 2).

Against its own nature, money is considered as if it were a good (or an asset) whenever it intervenes in an international (commercial or financial) transaction. Let us consider in this respect once again the entries in Table 6.4. Suppose that country A represents the US economy, and country R is an emerging market economy such as China. In this stylized case, country A imports from R commercial goods that it does not pay for finally, since the banking system of country R merely records the "image" of the bank deposit (worth x MA) that, in fact, remains within the banking system of the importing country (A). As already noted by Rueff

(1963: 323–324), there is thus a "duplication" of the bank deposit resulting from the payment by agent I (importer in country A) for those items sold by agent II (exporter in country R): "Entering the credit system of the creditor country, but remaining in the debtor country, the claims representing the deficit are thus doubled" (Rueff 1963: 324). This is why the US economy may record deficits "without tears" (Rueff 1963: 323) in its balance of payments. In fact, these trade deficits elicit equivalent "payment deficits" for the net importing country (Machlup 1963: 256). As a result, then, the net exporting country only receives a promise of payment (an "IOU"), rather than being paid finally for the efforts its residents made in producing those commercial items that were exported eventually (see Rossi [2009] and Piffaretti and Rossi [2012] for analytical elaboration as regards the United States–China case).

This duplication of the bank deposits involved in the cross-border payment between the importer in country A and the exporter in country R induces an inflationary increase in the financial capital recorded in the banking system of the exporting country:

> Financial capital increases *twice* in the net exporting country; in national money and in foreign exchange. One of the two increases can only be *fictitious* since the national economy's gain *vis-à-vis* the rest of the world equals the amount of net commercial exports – not *twice* this amount.
>
> (Schmitt 1984: 43, my translation)

The entries in Table 6.4 illustrate this problem with respect to country R: as a result of the amount of money A entered as an asset (official reserves) in its ledger, R's banking system issues an equivalent amount of money R. This amount is just the numerical equivalent of the official reserves earned by country R as a whole owing to its commercial exports. "Deprived of any real content, it pathologically increases the financial capital of country B [country R in our stylized case] and is thereby the cause of an inflationary gap of international origin" (Cencini and Rossi 2015: 208).

To be sure, this inflationary gap does not materialize through an increase in the goods' market prices necessarily. As a matter of fact, the stock of bank deposits generated by the monetization of the country R's external gain (as a result of its net exports) is as a general rule remunerated by banks, which have therefore an incentive in expanding as much as possible the volume of their lending to any kind of agents. This expansion of bank loans can thus generate a credit bubble, notably when – as in the United States in the decade preceding the bursting of the "subprime" crisis in August 2007 – a number of borrowers are not really creditworthy (witness the Chinese bubble that burst in the summer of 2015). This is particularly the case when, owing to financialization and a series of financial innovations, a large number of banks abandon their original business model ("originate and hold") to adopt a predatory approach through which they "originate and distribute" (across the global financial market) an excessive volume of loans (Rossi 2011, 2015). This lending strategy does not only affect the country whose banks adopt it: it originates a variety of international externalities, particularly when it affects those emerging market economies that suffer therefore from extreme exchange-rate volatility or "sudden stops" and "flight to quality" effects (see, for instance, Calvo 1998; Tavasci and Ventimiglia 2015).

Further, the lack of payment finality between any two different monetary spaces (say, A and R) affects also the net importing country negatively. Suppose, again, that country A – for instance, an emerging market economy like Turkey – records a trade deficit. If a local importer pays this deficit with an amount of so-called "key currencies" (such as the US dollar), this is not going to be a final payment, but represents only a promise of payment for the countries concerned, as explained above: the circulation of an IOU does not (and cannot) transform a promise of payment into a final payment, unless the issuer (the US economy, in our case) accepts its own IOUs in exchange for commercial or financial items. In this case, there would be a barter trade once the IOUs have come full circle (that is, once the net importing country issuing the IOUs has become a net exporting country, to absorb and destroy these IOUs). If, by contrast, the local importer disposes of a number of domestic money units (to wit, Turkish lira), the situation is analogous to that in Table 6.4: there is a transfer of ownership for the relevant amount deposited within the domestic banking system, which provides for payment finality at the agents' level, but does not do so for the countries involved thereby. The net importing country, in this case, is affected by an inflationary gap insofar as the payer obtains a credit line that increases the available stock of bank deposits without increasing simultaneously produced output on sale. As a matter of fact, the goods imported from country R do not pertain to country A's output. Hence, they cannot be considered in the money-to-output relationship existing in the net importing country, whose amount of bank deposits is therefore excessive with respect to its output – epitomizing thereby an inflationary gap (Rossi 2001). Once again, however, this discrepancy in the money-to-output relation might not be revealed by the evolution of consumer prices (and their indices), because the excessive bank deposits can be spent on (real and financial) asset markets, thereby inflating "asset bubbles" that increase the financial fragility of the domestic economy as time goes by (see Rossi 2010 and 2013).

A structural reform to re-establish international monetary order

As pointed out by Keynes (1980: 18), "[every] trading transaction must necessarily find its counterpart in another trading transaction sooner or later". Keynes's own idea was to revert to the structure of the international gold standard system, which was "a means for trading goods against goods" (1980: 12). This led Keynes to draft his famous plan for an international clearing union, which he presented (unsuccessfully) at the Bretton Woods conference in July 1944. More than 70 years later, the spirit of this plan can inspire the urgently needed international monetary reform, to provide payment finality between monetary systems that issue different (hence heterogeneous) means of payment (see, for instance, Rossi 2007b).

Waiting for a new "Bretton Woods conference" to be gathered at a global level (an event that will not happen before too long), emerging market economies may decide to shield themselves, individually, bilaterally or as a group, from the non-system for international payments that exists today. Their source of inspiration can be the Keynes plan presented at Bretton Woods in 1944, which should be elaborated upon considering the advances in monetary macroeconomics, particularly regarding endogenous money and the workings of payment and settlement systems (see Rossi 2007a, for a comprehensive overview and analytical elaboration of these research fields).

Let us explore in this section the individual and bilateral solutions, before arguing that a regional solution for emerging market economies can provide a welcome mimetic effect as regards international payment finality and, therefore, financial stability at the domestic as well as global level.

A single country, say Brazil, can indeed autonomously decide to set up an international department in the book-keeping of its central bank, in charge of recording, in a separate international currency, the result of its residents' payment orders regarding their imports from all over the world (or from a part of it only). Table 6.5 illustrates the working of this payment system's reform.

Let us assume that a Brazilian importer disposes of an amount of x reals (the Brazilian currency) to pay the seller of the relevant items finally. As this occurs through a bank in Brazil, the latter bank sends a payment order to the national central bank (instead of sending it to the corresponding bank in the country where the exporter resides, as this occurs to date). Hence, the Domestic department (DD) – to be created with the proposed reform – of the central bank of Brazil debits the payer's bank for the amount of the transaction ($-x$ reals), which it simultaneously credits to the Foreign department (FD) of the same central bank. This is so because, according to our reform proposal, the FD will be in charge of carrying out the international segment of any cross-border transaction, issuing the number of international money units (IMU) that corresponds to the amount of local currency involved thereby. As the nature of bank money is purely numerical, there

Table 6.5 The result of an international payment for a country's imports

Central bank of Brazil Domestic department (DD)

Assets	Liabilities	
	Deposit of payer's bank	$-x$ reals
	Deposit of FD	$+x$ reals

Central bank of Brazil Foreign department (FD)

Assets		Liabilities	
Deposit with DD	$+z$ IMU	Deposit of country R	$+z$ IMU

Note: IMU = international money units.

Table 6.6 The result of an international payment for a country's exports

Central bank of Brazil Domestic department (DD)

Assets	Liabilities	
	Deposit of FD	−x reals
	Deposit of payee's bank	+x reals

Central bank of Brazil Foreign department (FD)

Assets		Liabilities	
Deposit with DD	−z IMU	Deposit of country R	−z IMU

Note: IMU = international money units.

is no particular problem in allowing the FD of the Brazilian central bank to issue a number of international money units for the final payment of its foreign peer (the central bank of country R, which is the exporting country in this stylized case). The relevant entry in the FD shown in Table 6.5 is merely a memory item, recalling that country R has a claim on Brazil, which will be replaced by some Brazilian output when the latter country exports to R part of its own production or, alternatively, some financial assets that R's residents are willing to purchase. As Table 6.6 shows, indeed, the balances in the FD are cleared if and when country R imports from Brazil commercial or financial items, for an amount equivalent to the positive balances previously recorded in the same FD.

This (single country) solution has the merit to avert considering the real as an object of trade, since it is – as is any national currency – a means of payment only. It also avoids speculation on the volatility of the real, as its exchange rate (against the IMU as well as in regard to other national currencies) will be decided and announced by the central bank – so that it will be stable without being definitively fixed over a relevant period of time. It goes without saying, however, that the decision to set the exchange rate at a given level, which does not need to induce balanced trade necessarily, will not be an easy task. It has to involve all stakeholders democratically, considering also the likely effects beyond the country's borders. This is the main reason in favour of a bilateral, if not group, solution.

There might be an initial agreement between, say, China and Brazil, to set up a bilateral settlement facility whereby their trade relations are going to be paid finally owing to the issuance of the relevant number of international money units (IMUs), issued either by the FD of their national central banks or by a dedicated joint institution. If so, then all imports and exports concerning these two countries will be paid finally, in local currency as regards their residents and in international money units between the two national central banks. Let us imagine the creation of a Sino–Brazilian settlement institution in that regard, and consider its workings for the final payment of Brazilian imports from China (Table 6.7).

Table 6.7 The working of a bilateral settlement institution for emerging countries

Central bank of Brazil Domestic department (DD_B)

Assets	Liabilities	
	Deposit of payer's bank	$-x$ reals
	Deposit of FD_B	$+x$ reals

Central bank of Brazil Foreign department (FD_B)

Assets		Liabilities
Deposit with DD_B	$+z$ IMU	
Deposit with BSI	$-z$ IMU	

Bilateral settlement institution (BSI)

Assets	Liabilities	
	Deposit of FD_B	$-z$ IMU
	Deposit of FD_C	$+z$ IMU

Central bank of China Foreign department (FD_C)

Assets		Liabilities	
Deposit with BSI	$+z$ IMU	Deposit of DD_C	$+z$ IMU

Central bank of China Domestic department (DD_C)

Assets		Liabilities	
Deposit with FD_C	$+y$ yuans	Deposit of payee's bank	$+y$ yuans

Note: IMU = international money units; we suppose that x reals = z IMU = y yuans.

As regards those payments that concern importers (in Brazil) and exporters (in China), it does not really matter whether they are carried out between commercial banks (as is the case today) or involving also their national central banks (as we propose in this section). Any cross-border payment concerning Brazil and China, however, will also induce an international payment that will be finalized by the Sino–Brazilian settlement institution, which will issue the number of (z) international money units necessary to carry out the payment between the two central banks involved.

In the importing country (Brazil), the DD of the national central bank debits the account of the payer's bank with the relevant amount of domestic currency (x reals), and credits, not the account of the exporter's bank or banking system, but the account of its own FD. The latter, indeed, is in charge of carrying out the international segment of this payment, as already noted above. Contrary to the single-country solution, however, in the bilateral solution investigated at this stage, the FD of the Brazilian central bank gets in touch with the Sino–Brazilian settlement institution, asking it to carry out the international payment, through which the FD of the Brazilian central bank is debited by the relevant amount of international currency (hence the negative deposit in the ledger of the settlement facility shown in Table 6.7), while the FD of the central bank of China is credited with the same amount (recorded as a positive deposit in the same ledger). Clearly, starting from a *tabula rasa* means that Brazil obtains a credit from the Sino–Brazilian settlement institution, up to some bilateral limit that has to be agreed initially, and that can be amended over time depending on a number of contingencies also to be defined *ex-ante*.

Contrary to today's non-system for international payments (in which no such limits are defined legally, but, in fact, exist as regards a country's risks and the credibility of its commitments to repay its debt), the framework established by the bilateral settlement facility proposed here is able to provide for international payment finality, and thereby reduces financial fragility and financial instability both within and between the countries concerned. It can also be a factor increasing bilateral trade, particularly when (as in the Keynes plan) the bilateral settlement institution charges a fee to those balances (either positive or negative) that in its accounts lie above a pre-determined threshold over a given period (see Rossi 2007b).

This trade-inducing effect, and the ensuing benefits as regards both economic growth and employment levels – with their positive impact on the general government sector through higher tax receipts and lower public expenditure for the welfare state – could convince an increasing number of other (emerging market) economies to join in with such an international settlement facility, particularly those countries that aim at severing their current links with the US-centred monetary regime. Indeed, if the number of countries entering into such a (regional) payment system increases as time goes by, the benefits that each of them may obtain from its daily working will also increase, because of its multilateral character that makes it easier to "recycle" any positive balance with the international settlement institution through the purchase of either real goods or financial assets from any other participating countries. Hence, contrary to the euro-area "top-down" approach imposing monetary unification a-democratically (indeed, there has been no democratic vote to adopt the euro as a single European currency in its many countries), the international monetary reform that we propose in this chapter follows a "bottom-up" approach that, moreover, leaves national currencies in their place, simply introducing a common currency for the common good. The differences between these two approaches cannot be more striking, particularly considering the deep, severe and dramatic euro-area crisis (see Mastromatteo and Rossi [2015] for analytical elaboration on that).

Conclusion

This chapter has explained that money and payments are crucial for the working of any economic system, both when they are instrumental for "systemic" order and when they originate monetary–structural disorders – as in the current non-system for international payments. This is why any attempt at eradicating the flaws of this state of affairs has to begin with a sound understanding of money and banking. The first section has therefore pointed out the accounting nature of money, its essential link with bank credit, and their being instrumental to carry out any payment orders within an economic system. In light of this, we have been in a position to address the monetary–structural shortcomings of today's international monetary regime, which originate a pathological financial capital as a result of the payments elicited by foreign trade. Referring to the case of emerging market economies, we showed that the latter suffer from these shortcomings both when they are net exporters and when their trade balance records a deficit. In both cases, their banking systems record an excessive amount of deposits with respect to saleable output in these countries. A structural–monetary reform is thus mandatory, in order to establish monetary order within and between them, thereby avoiding financial instability and thus reducing the risk of economic and financial crises. The last section presented the basics of this reform, which has been illustrated with stylized cases considering net importing as well as net exporting countries pertaining to the category of emerging economies. It notably showed that a country may decide to shield its own economy from the negative consequences of the current non-system for international payments, setting up a kind of monetary "filter" between its domestic and foreign payments traffic. In doing so, it can avert both the "duplication" of foreign-exchange reserves when it is a net exporter, and the inflation of a credit bubble when its trade balance is negative.

Owing to a variety of externalities, however, this single-country solution is a second best with regard to those advantages that can result from a bilateral, if not multilateral, settlement facility among those (emerging market) economies that suffer most from the present non-system at the international level. This is why, at the end of the last section, we argued in favour of a multilateral settlement institution in which a rapidly growing number of countries will participate, in order to maximize the benefits resulting from a common currency to be used by their national central banks only. This would also do justice, more than 70 years later, to the spirit of Keynes's 1944 plan – which intended to give rise to "the least possible interference with internal national policies, and . . . should not wander from the international terrain" (Keynes 1980: 234). These objectives would also be fully in line with Keynes's *General Theory*, where he pointed out that:

> It is the policy of an autonomous rate of interest, unimpeded by international preoccupations . . . which is twice blessed in the sense that it helps ourselves and our neighbours at the same time. And it is the simultaneous pursuit of these policies by all countries together which is capable of restoring economic health and strength internationally, whether we measure it by the level of domestic employment or by the volume of international trade.
>
> (Keynes 1936: 349)

While a single currency for a variety of countries deprives all of them of their much-needed monetary sovereignty, a common currency can help each of them to achieve its own economic policy goals and improve thereby its economic performance in the interest of all stakeholders. The conceptual difference between a single currency and a common currency is subtle, although rather easy to understand, but its practical outcomes cannot be underestimated by all those who strive to make the world a better place to live in for its whole population. Let us hope that this chapter will contribute to the common good, delivering some inputs to induce a critical mass of emerging market economies to establish a multilateral settlement institution issuing a truly international means of final payment among them. If it works, the rest of the world will follow suit before too long, thereby averting the next systemic financial crisis – an occurrence, in the contrary case, which could be observed quite shortly, in light of the persistent financial turmoil at the time of writing.

References

Calvo, G. A. (1998). "Capital flows and capital-market crises: The simple economics of sudden stops", *Journal of Applied Economics*, 1(1): 35–54.

Cencini, A. and Rossi, S. (2015). *Economic and Financial Crises: A New Macroeconomic Analysis*. Basingstoke, UK and New York: Palgrave Macmillan.

Goodhart, C. A. E. (1989). *Money, Information and Uncertainty*, 2nd edn. London and Basingstoke, UK: Macmillan.

Graziani, A. (1990). "The theory of the monetary circuit", *Économies et Sociétés*, 24(6): 7–36.

Hicks, J. R. (1967). *Critical Essays in Monetary Theory*. Oxford: Clarendon Press.

Keynes, J. M. (1936). *The General Theory of Employment, Interest, and Money*. London: Macmillan.

Keynes, J. M. (1980). *The Collected Writings of John Maynard Keynes XXV, Activities 1940–1944. Shaping the Post-War World: The Clearing Union* (edited by D. E. Moggridge). London and New York: Macmillan and Cambridge University Press.

Machlup, F. (1963). "Reform of the international monetary system", in H. G. Grubel (Ed.), *World Monetary Reform: Plans and Issues*. Stanford, CA and London: Stanford University Press and Oxford University Press, pp. 253–260.

McLeay, M., Radia, A. and Thomas, R. (2014). "Money creation in the modern economy", *Bank of England Quarterly Bulletin*, 54(1): 14–27.

Mastromatteo, G. and Rossi, S. (2015). "The economics of deflation in the euro area: A critique of fiscal austerity", *Review of Keynesian Economics*, 3(3): 336–350.

Piffaretti, N. F. and Rossi, S. (2012). "An institutional approach to balancing international monetary relations: The case for a US–China settlement facility", *International Journal of Humanities and Social Science*, 2(17): 1–11.

Rossi, S. (2001). *Money and Inflation: A New Macroeconomic Analysis*. Cheltenham, UK and Northampton, MA: Edward Elgar Publishing.

Rossi, S. (2007a). *Money and Payments in Theory and Practice*. London and New York: Routledge.

Rossi, S. (2007b). "The monetary-policy relevance of an international settlement institution: The Keynes plan 60 years later", in A. Giacomin and M. C. Marcuzzo (Eds), *Money and Markets: A Doctrinal Approach*. London and New York: Routledge, pp. 96–114.

Rossi, S. (2009). "International payment finality requires a supranational central-bank money: Reforming the international monetary architecture in the spirit of Keynes", *China–USA Business Review*, 8(11): 1–20.

Rossi, S. (2010). "The 2007–9 financial crisis: An endogenous-money view", *Studi e Note di Economia*, 15(3): 413–430.

Rossi, S. (2011). "Can it happen again? Structural policies to avert further systemic crises", *International Journal of Political Economy*, 40(2): 61–78.

Rossi, S. (2013). "Structural reforms to reduce systemic financial fragility", in N. Karagiannis, Z. Madjd-Sadjadi and S. Sen (Eds), *The US Economy and Neoliberalism: Alternative Strategies and Policies*. London and New York: Routledge, pp. 153–163.

Rossi, S. (2015). "Structural reforms in payment systems to avoid another systemic crisis", *Review of Keynesian Economics*, 3(2): 213–225.

Rueff, J. (1963). "Gold exchange standard a danger to the West", in H. G. Grubel (Ed.), *World Monetary Reform: Plans and Issues*. Stanford, CA and London: Stanford University Press and Oxford University Press, pp. 320–328.

Schmitt, B. (1984). *La France souveraine de sa monnaie*. Paris, France and Albeuve, Switzerland: Economica and Castella.

Schumpeter, J. A. (1970). *Das Wesen des Geldes*. Göttingen, Germany: Vandenhoeck and Ruprecht.

Tavasci, D. and Ventimiglia, L. (2015). "Sudden stops", in L.-P. Rochon and S. Rossi (Eds), *The Encyclopedia of Central Banking*. Cheltenham, UK and Northampton, MA: Edward Elgar Publishing, pp. 468–470.

7 A capital market without banks

Lending and borrowing in Hennaarderadeel, Friesland, 1537–1555

Merijn Knibbe and Paul Borghaerts

Introduction

Around 1540, the economy of the coastal zone of Friesland (a province in the northern part of the Netherlands), of which Hennaarderadeel is a part, was thoroughly monetized, specialized and quite market-orientated. A few arable farmers produced and sold wheat, but purchased rye for their own consumption, while a much greater number of livestock farmers purchased horses in the spring, but sold them again in the autumn to save on precious hay – which was used to feed milk cows (Knibbe 2006: 194–202). In villages and towns, quite a number of cobblers, wagon makers, blacksmiths and the like made a living, and in 1505, commercial project developers from Holland diked and drained the large Bildt area, a 5,000 hectare mudflat outside the dikes. At a price. This area would soon be characterized by (for the time) large arable farms which exported their barley and wheat not just to nearby cities like Franeker and Leeuwarden, but also to the rapidly growing cities in Holland and notably to the booming centre of the grain trade, Amsterdam (Kuiken 2013). Comparable statements can be made about the thriving land market: people had clear legal title to the land and land was often sold and purchased, though there were strict 'family first, neighbours second' rules about who had the first right to buy. Such rules, of course, influenced the allocation of land and the number and kind of transactions, but this did not make the land market less of a market – every market is guided by ever-changing rules and habits which influence what happens. The point about a market is not that such – arbitrary – rules exist. The point is that, contrary to other human exchange systems, like gift exchange or gender-based systems of division of labour, prices are set *before* transactions are finalized and these rules clearly enabled this. An exceptionally large part of the available land was rented. Clearly, land was not just bought to use for farming, but also for patrimonial reasons and to use it as an economic 'asset'. This resembled the situation in the clay soil area of coastal Flanders (Soens and Thoens 2009), but differed from the situation in many other parts of Europe, where households bought and sold land to adapt available 'capital' to the number of family members of working age (to name only a few studies, see Pfister 2007; Fertig 2009; Vermoesen 2010; Ogilvie *et al.* 2012).

There was, however, a limitation to the extent of the market. As far as we know – information is scarce – the labour market was somewhat limited at the beginning of the sixteenth century (Postma and Spahr van der Hoek 1956). Living-in servants were common, but as far as we can say, day labourers working on the hay or grain harvest or in construction were, around 1540, a pretty novel sight (see also wage data in Nijboer 2007: 131–134). And at least in 1505, the project developers mentioned above had to bring in labourers from Holland . . . But even living-in servants were in no way indentured and often switched from employer to employer (mainly larger farmers) while, though the larger part of their income consisted of board and lodging, they also did receive a money wage. The main thing which strikes the present-day historian, especially when he or she compares this area with other European areas of the time, is the absence of all kinds of feudal ties on land and labour.

As in all market-orientated, monetary societies, a capital market existed, too. Even a quick glance in the sources shows that lending and borrowing were common. Remarkably, even though sources on the capital market are relatively abundant – for instance, when compared with the labour market – little is known about this capital market. Lending and borrowing were common, but how common? Who were the lenders? Who were the borrowers? Why did people lend and borrow? How much did people lend and borrow? What was the interest rate? How did 'matching' take place; i.e. how did supply and demand for funds meet? Were interest rates comparable with those in other places and other times? Did women take part in the capital market? We do not know and this chapter sets out to shed some light on these questions. We do know, however, one important thing. There were no banks. It would take another 300 years before the first serious banks would be established in Friesland, though seventeenth-century Leeuwarden knew a pawn shop (exploited by the Leeuwarden orphanage) and the extensive and dependable tax investigation of 1749 does show that in Leeuwarden – the capital of Friesland which had about 14,000 inhabitants – two people called themselves 'bankers'. In the sixteenth century, banks were of course not unheard of – the names of sixteenth-century banking dynasties like de Medici and Fugger still resound – but there were no banks in Friesland. Matching between lenders and borrowers took place – but banks did not play any role. 'Textbook' economics states that the unique mission of banks is to match the supply of funds with the demand for funds – but it seems that sixteenth- to eighteenth-century Frisians did not need this service, and the question arises: why not? Are there situations when people do just not need banks and is this 'unique mission' possibly less general than is sometimes supposed? In the discussion, this problem will be tackled. First, however, we will try to give at least part of an answer to the other questions posed above.

Other regions

Before answering the questions, it is good to investigate the available literature. The history of the pre-1700 capital market in particular is still somewhat under-researched, but recently an interesting crop of new studies has become available. The common thread of these studies is a focus on the household and on an active, long-term participation of these households in the capital market. Households did not just borrow (and lend!) out of desperation – for instance, because a cattle plague had wiped away their stock of cows – but used lending and borrowing as strategies to 'make ends meet in the long term'. In fact, when it comes to normal, day-to-day village trade, the economy was even almost entirely credit-based, which is shown for Friesland by the large amount of financial 'note books' which kept track of all kinds of petty debts mentioned in probate inventories (Knibbe 2007); and which for Flanders is shown by, for instance, Ronsijn (2014: 103–109). Vermoesen (2010: 21) even shows a picture of a 'clearing book' which was used to enable mutual cancellation of such debts in Flanders – in this case, no money at all was involved in these transactions! Aside from these 'trade' debts for groceries, shoes, the blacksmith and wages, there was, however, also a 'loanable funds' market where people borrowed and lent larger amounts of money, which is what this chapter is about. Compared with most of those studies (on which more below), the Frisian data are early, as most of them consider seventeenth- and eighteenth-century societies, while our data are for the second quarter of the sixteenth century, but a comparison with other studies is enlightening nevertheless – we can at least say something about the question as to whether Friesland was special or part of a larger pattern. One remark has, however, to be made: many of these studies use the 'permanent income' approach to lending and borrowing – borrowing now and paying back later, when your income is higher. One drawback of this vision of lending and borrowing is that it looks at the total debts of the household while, in reality, lending and borrowing took place in different spheres. One of these was the sphere of day-to-day trade mentioned above. In this sphere (the bakery, the blacksmith, local labour), credit was not just common – it was the norm (and still is; even in the Netherlands, there is living memory that small local grocers provided this kind of credit to their customers . . .). But aside from this day-to-day sphere, there was a lending and borrowing sphere for larger purchases. Crucially, the first sphere (nowadays this might be called the credit card sphere) relied on your 'reputation' (see Nijboer 2007, for more information about this); while in the second sphere, official collateral was required. This collateral consisted mainly of land and real estate (the mixture depending on the area, as we will see below), but also all kinds of household durables – especially those of pewter, copper, silver and gold and the (expensive!) beds – were required, while also (and contrary to the first sphere) interest was charged. This chapter is, as stated, about the second sphere, which, however, does *not* imply that in Friesland, the day-to-day trade sphere was not important (see Postma [1962] who, however, mentions that very large credits were sometimes turned into interest-bearing obligations).

With this in mind, we can mention the study of a remote seventeenth-century 'small' farmers' village in the Black Forest by Ogilvie *et al.* (2012) which shows that most borrowing took place for investments, especially to purchase houses (including some land and a '*Gemüsegarten*' or vegetable garden), but also land and raw materials (there was quite a production of textiles). Also, the richer (or less poor) households were the ones which were borrowing and lending; borrowing clearly was not just a 'last resort' strategy for poor households. And it turns out that total debts were higher at the time of dying than when people established a household, with most borrowing going on between the ages of 40 and 50. The amount of debt was positively correlated with wealth, except for cash (obviously . . .) and, interestingly, cattle. Did cattle function as a kind of money? *As for all other studies below, it is also important what we do not see: usury. There were, no doubt, 'non-performing loans' and the like, and people surely could lose their collateral, but lending was not at all the prerogative of a village usurer.*[1]

Another study (Vermoesen 2011) focuses on the County of Aalst in Flanders, Belgium in the period between 1650 and 1794. Vermoesen shows that lending and borrowing were very much located in and around the village: most lending and borrowing took place within 10 kilometres of the village (2011: 60) and 50–60 per cent of obligations were due to fellow villagers (2011: 128). He also shows that the trade debts mentioned above (including wages due) were inter-twined with a dense network of economic and social relations. The data, however, also show that quite a bit of lending was going on with parties outside the village – it was not only a local affair. He points out the importance of literate local elders, men with an official position and superior knowledge about the financial affairs of people, who often served as a kind of matchmaker – a profitable function.

Pfister (2007) investigates an area near Zürich, Switzerland and investigates whether small farming/cottage industry households there tried to optimize 'income', but, departing from the strictly economic definition of income, on the understanding that households also produce a lot of goods and services for them-selves, while producing market income was often also located within the house-hold, which means that there was a trade-off between investing in land and the household and income. This trade-off was decisively influenced by the life cycle of the household, which as it grew larger and children became somewhat older, tried to secure more land and other assets.

Zuijderduijn *et al.* (2011) and De Moor and Zuijderduijn (2013) investigate the (at that time small) town of Edam between circa 1480 and 1564 and find a lively credit market which, as in the Zürich case, comprised a system of credit tied to the life cycle of households, though specific circumstances (more wage labour, for instance, in the ship-building sector) cause a somewhat different pattern: poor, small, young households – instead of somewhat older households as around Zürich and in the Black Forest – were active borrowers too, while old households at the end of the life cycle seem to have sold assets and lent money to obtain a kind of pension. The money raised by these young, poor households was, among other things, often used to buy a house, but also to buy a boat, a prime means of produc-tion in this coastal town. The timing of borrowing differed from that of the other areas, but the purpose was the same: establishing a viable living. A clear legal title to land and relatively low transaction costs (everybody knew everybody, while sanctions for free riding and criminal behaviour existed) enable efficient lending and borrowing.

Nijboer (2007) investigates a wholly different social-economic group, but during a period and in a place close to our time and place: the Leeuwarden 'burghers' between 1590 and 1720. Remarkably, he finds that for the rich members of this group, collateral was less important (at least, as long as you were a member of the 'in crowd') and reputation was everything; for less wealthy people (or at least people who were assumed to be less wealthy), the possession of collateral was important. Postma (1962) gives information on the taste in clothes for the richer members of this group, which was expensive. Consumption-orientated lending among this group seems to have been important. For poorer inhabitants, owning collateral like gold, silver or pewter was, however, crucial to be able to borrow. In the course of time, a process started in which the weight of, for instance, jewellery became less important, and the way it was 'fashioned' came to the fore. Still later, debt contracts became more 'paper'-orientated in the sense that debt contracts themselves became more important as collateral.

Paping (1995) investigates for a comparable region in nearby Groningen, but at a much later period (1770–1860), the nature of lenders, and states that quite a few older farmers sold their farms and used the money as a kind of pension, investing it in loans.

Summarizing, we see lively capital markets which in the countryside were mainly directed at investments in, especially, land and buildings, but in Edam also in shipping. This lending and borrowing was clearly tied to the life cycle of the household, though there were large differences in the shape of 'life cycle lending and borrowing'. Much lending and borrowing, but surely not all of it, had a local nature and it seems that literate local administrators often had a crucial (and, may we say, profitable) function when it came to matching at least part of the demand and supply. Taking into account the special nature of our area – which unlike the other areas was dominated by a relatively egalitarian structure of (for the time) large and specialized farms – we have to take the points above into account when looking at and understanding the data.

Sources

Hennaarderadeel was a county of Friesland, a province which is part of the present- day Netherlands, but was at that time a semi-independent state owned by the Habsburgs. In the counties, the '*Grietman*', a kind of shire reeve and head of the local lower court, was responsible for writing deeds, like inscribing debt contracts into a kind of register.[2] Ideally, in the case of debt contracts, these deeds (which are not the contracts!) contain the names of the lender(s) and borrower(s), the place where they live, the amount, the maturity, the interest rate and the collateral (mostly land, but in some cases, also houses or personal belongings). Often, one or more of these variables is missing. There is, however, no reason to doubt the reliability of the data though they may not be entirely representative, as there are clear signs that contracts were disproportionately inscribed in the ledger whenever a debtor had died or was seriously ill. The actual contracts were generally written down by a trusted and literate 'neighbour', often '*soenluiden*' (who had the honorary, but real function to arbitrate whenever conflicts arose) or '*baarsluiden*' (who were a kind of lower judge who could not only arbitrate, but who could also decide in minor legal issues).[3] In the period and region covered here, about 1,400 such contracts might have been made, of which about 300 are inscribed in the ledger. This suggests that the ledger was a kind of additional 'certainty' to establish the rights of the creditor. The series starts in 1537 and runs well into the seventeenth century: in the first years, a limited number of deeds is available (three in 1537 and only one in 1539) which is no doubt due to the (at that time) new character of this system, but the number rapidly increases to about 30 to 60 per year in the 1540s and 1550s. A database of the deeds has been made which does not contain the names, but which does contain all other data (as far as these are available): the information below is, unless stated otherwise, based upon this set of data. The sources are transcribed as part of Paul Borghaerts' project which is discussed on his website (see the References list); part of the sources are also published on this website. The interested reader can consult it to investigate technical details. For this study, only the '*proclamatieboeken*' were used, especially the '*proclamatie en recesboek*' 36, 37 and 38 as available in the Tresoar archive, Leeuwarden. The *proclamatieboeken* contain deeds which were orally proclaimed three times in the church or in the local county house, to enable everybody in this – still to a large extent – illiterate society to be present at sales and auctions or to establish rights connected to goods and lands which were sold or auctioned.

A genuine capital market?

First, we have to investigate the kind of transactions which were financed by lending and borrowing in more detail. On 27 May 1555 (Julian calendar), Doecke Tijesse from Wirdum, Douue Sercx from Wommels and Tijaerdt Poppe (son) from Menaldum became custodians of the youngest children (orphans) of Jelte Menne and Ebel Poppe (daughter) (Ebel was in all probability the sister of Tijaerdt).[4] Their farm building, including the right to rent certain parcels of land, as well as all the animals and the appurtenances were sold during a '*boelgoed*' (a kind of yard sale); the farm (as well as the compost heap and available manure in the shape of manure as well as '*dompen*', brick-shaped manure-based fuel) was sold during an auction in an inn (which we know as the buyer did not only have to pay for the house, but also for the drinks during the auction) on 15 June, probably 'by the burning candle'. The inventory is not explicit about this last custom, but some of the other deeds are. It was, after some bidding, sold for 390 guilders of 28 stuivers, of which 100 were paid the next day. This indicates that it might well have been the case (and, considering the sources, was the case) that in such instances, which occurred on a regular basis, people had to be able to raise quite a bit of money at short notice. And the bidding at this and other auctions shows that quite a few people could raise the money. There were good reasons to borrow and people did do so.[5] But can we call this lending and borrowing a capital *market*? The example suggests it is, but we need more thorough information to confirm this.

A market can be described by looking at its participants and the social and economic structure of society; at the institutions governing a market, like the nature of money (fiat or not) and property and contract rights; and at the matching mechanism which itself is of course also guided by all kind of institutions. A genuine capital market should also show transactions and prices; in this case, loans and interest rates. Below, we will investigate the capital market in Hennaarderadeel. We will start with transactions and prices and continue with analysing the participants in this market: was this indeed a market in the sense that economists use the term, in which one transaction influences all others as it, even if only slightly, influences supply, demand and the information people have about the market? Or one where these transactions are just haphazard and basically random events or a kind of forced loan ordained by a local chieftain or the government? After the transactions, we will investigate the participants and the matching mechanism.

The interest rates

Figure 7.1 shows the unweighted average interest rate (weighting with the amounts of the loans did not yield any meaningful differences which, on the Ockham's razor principle, made us choose the simplest average). The series is compared to four other series:

1   one for Amsterdam (medium-run loans; see Dehing 2012);
2   one for the city of Leeuwarden, which was quite close to Hennaarderaadeel, but which does not consist of rural loans backed by (mainly) land as collateral, but comprises 'urban' loans, often backed by 'reputation' (Nijstad 2007);
3   one for the coastal zone of Groningen which, of all other regions of the Netherlands, is the region most comparable to the Frisian coastal zone, and which also consists of 'rural' loans, but is for a much later period (but also before the advent of banks in this area); and
4   one for Dutch government bonds.

Unlike the situation in the Black Forest as described by Ogilvie *et al.* (2012), there was no maximum interest and no government interference with the right to borrow; the prices should be understood as the consequence of private actions, though the government was an active borrower itself (at a higher interest rate, for instance, in the case of the nearby city of Franeker in 1538). As can be seen, the series do match, while the increase of the Hennaarderadeel series and the decrease of the Leeuwarden series might indicate the consequences of the 'sixteenth-century price revolution' (which, in Friesland, only genuinely started after 1543; see Knibbe 2014). The tentative conclusion must be that the series itself, as well as a comparison with the other series, indicate that there was a genuine capital market in Hennaarderadeel in the first half of the sixteenth century.

Figure 7.2 shows the individual interest rates of the contracts. A remarkable aspect of the graph is its 'decimal' nature. We see a cluster at 5 per cent as well as at 6 per cent, and for the latter period a decreasing number of contracts with rates

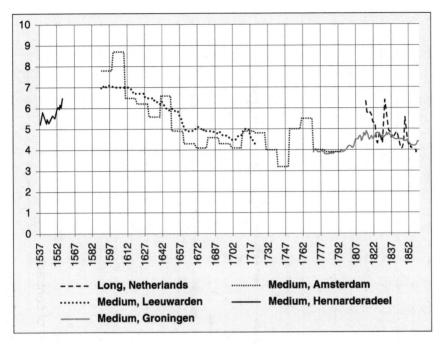

Figure 7.1 Rural interest rates (%) in the Netherlands, 1537–1860.

below 6 per cent and an increasing number with rates above 6 per cent. The deeds almost invariably state the interest rate as 6 gold guilders per 100 gold guilders or 3 per 50 guilders – many contracts, indeed, use 'neat' sums like 50, 100 or 200 guilders for the loan. In a society with limited numeracy and still using roman numbers this might have been a strategy to make contracts more transparent.[6] Considering the interest rate as a 'market price', this suggests that there were going rates (5 per cent and 6 per cent) which were well known, and deviations for special circumstances (one of these being the situation when there was no land, but a house [without underlying land, see below] as collateral). There is a tendency especially for the 6.7 per cent, the 7.5 per cent and the 8 per cent rates to be connected to small loans, but there were also quite a number of small loans with 'normal' rates, while very low rates often also were for small loans.

Looking at averages, the standard loans of *exactly* 50 guilders and *exactly* 100 guilders were actually slightly more expensive than loans between 50 guilders and 100 guilders (Table 7.1) – also recall that the up-front payment for the auctioned farm was 100 guilders while the price was 390 guilders, which goes some way to explain the large number of 50 guilder and 100 guilder debts. Even when purchase prices differed, instalments could be nice round sums. We could not discover any meaningful connection between the kind of collateral or the gender of the borrower with the interest rate.[7] Using past prices as input as a main source of information for present prices is of course characteristic for asset prices.

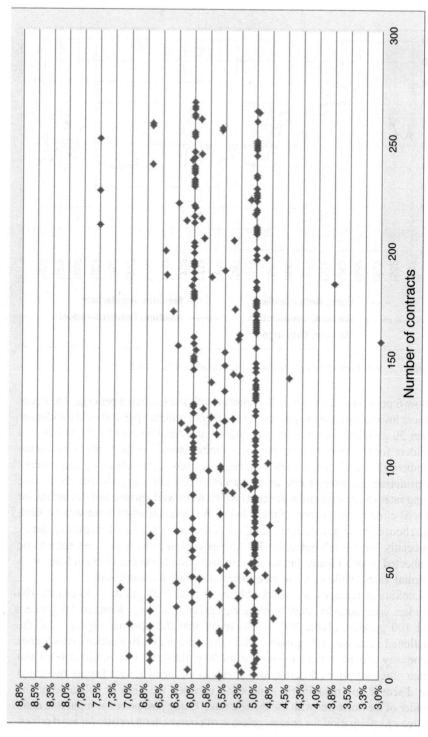

Figure 7.2 Interest rates of individual loan contracts, chronologically ordered, 1537–1556.

Table 7.1 Amounts borrowed and average interest rate

Amount (gold guilder of 28 stuivers)	Contracts	Interest rate
≤ 10	8	5.68%
10 < 50	131	5.69%
50	95	5.93%
50 < 100	102	5.58%
100	156	5.84%
100 < 400	87	5.91%

All this information seems to underscore that there was a transparent market, with clear, well-known market-wide 'standard' prices like 5 per cent and 6 per cent.

Who borrowed, why and how much?

Households were often acting as lender as well as borrower. An example: on 27 March 1556, a probate inventory was made of the belongings of the deceased farmer Wopke Gerbens, living in Wommels. The inventory of course listed cows, a horse, pigs, ducks, geese, bees and chickens, but it also listed 'in-debts' (receivables) as well as 'out-debts' (payables). Aside from out-debts of 10 guilders to Sybe Anne because of wages and some smaller debts, there were genuine interest-bearing loans, one of 120 guilders owed to Andle Abbes and one of 126 gold guilders owed to Wijbe Doeckes. But Wopke and his wife had been lending, too, and the inventory also lists in-debts of 80 guilders at 6.25 per cent from Laes te Remswert; 100 guilders at 5 per cent from Wisse Epes te Arum; 50 guilders at 6 per cent from Douwe Pijbes te Hennaard; 120 guilders at 6 per cent as well as 63 guilders without specified interest but called 'a bond' from Trijn (a woman) te Braard, as well as 100 guilders at 6 per cent and 33 guilders from Trijn Broers. Aside from this, there were three more loans without specified interest of 50 guilders, 30 guilders and 33 guilders, the last one being a bond. The total number of people involved in lending and borrowing, including the deceased man, was 18, but, as lending and borrowing were collateralized by the belongings of a couple and not just those of the lender or borrower, this number might approximately have to be doubled. And this household was not an exception.[8] This is shown by Table 7.1. By far the largest number of loans were between 50 guilders and 250 guilders (all in gold guilders of 28 stuivers), which (as well as the interest rates) fits nicely with the data of the probate inventory. And when we look at the names of the lenders and borrowers, it shows that the same people often borrowed or lent such sums more than once. An important question is: how much money was this? There is not too much information available about prices in Friesland around this time, but probate inventories and sales of cows, horses, land and houses do, however, give some idea about the purchasing power of such sums.

In probate inventories (for information about these, see Knibbe 2006) and records of 'yard sales' (Dutch: *boelgoed*, sale of the inventory of a farm), which often took place when custodians of orphans decided that orphans were too young

Table 7.2 House prices (gold guilders)

Price	Number of houses
10 < 20	7
20 < 25	8
25 < 30	8
30 < 40	5
40 < 50	3
50 < 100	5
100–195	6
210	1

to handle a farm, cows (not heifers or calves) were valued and sold for about 8–18.5 gold guilders (of 28 stuivers, end of our period).[9] These cows were probably about the size of present-day Scottish highland cattle, but had even at that date probably a somewhat higher milk yield. Horses were valued at around 20–25 gold guilders (though for some reason or other, their price was always quoted in Philippus guilders of 25 stuivers); and one '*pondemaat*' of land (about 0.35/0.4 hectares) was sold at between 50 and 80 gold guilders. Prices of houses were more variable; differences were no doubt partly caused by the building materials (loam and manure for traditional houses, bricks for modern houses). Even then, the low value of houses (not the land underlying it, villages somewhat resembled a modern-day trailer park with much of the land often owned by the church) is remarkable (Table 7.2).

These indirect data suggest that most of the loans were not used to buy houses or livestock or something of the kind, but land, which is corroborated by more direct data. The way the land market was regulated probably enabled 'informal' matching of lenders and borrowers. Land was freely tradeable, but as in all markets, exchange was guided by rules and customs. The right of '*Niaar*' (etymologically related to the English 'near') stipulated that family had the first right to buy, neighbours had the second right; only after these parties, were other people allowed to buy. Whenever land came up for sale, a sale had to be proclaimed three times in church as well as in the lower court to enable people with a right of *Niaar* or any other right to stake their claim, which of course added to transparency.[10] Since, in a rural society like Hennaarderadeel, everybody knew everybody else, it was well known who were willing and able to buy, while some people might have had an information advantage, as shown by the probate inventory of Hugo Upckes, a pastor, which lists dozens upon dozens of loan contracts and who himself clearly was an active lender, too.[11] For one thing, he must have known when payments were due which gave him an information advantage about who was possibly willing to (re)lend this money. One identifiable group which very often lent money was '*mombers*', or the financial custodians of orphans, who had to manage the estate of these orphans until they came of age and who often lent the money after a *boelgoed* – something which people no doubt were aware of.[12]

As inheritances were equally divided among children (including females), ownership of land had the tendency to fragment. Economies of scale in the hay harvest as well as cheese making, however, discouraged small farms and farm sizes were pretty stable, which was enabled by a system where most lands used for farming were rented. At the same time, a system of ownership where people, for instance, owned one third of one seventh of an undivided parcel led to high transaction costs and a lively trade in such ownership rights existed, which, partly due to *Niaar'*, led to a more consolidated system of ownership than one would have expected based upon inheritance rights alone. The amounts of land sold were often between 1 and 6 *pondematen*, which had values of between 50 and 500 gold guilders, which coincides reasonably well with the data on loans.[13]

Geographical information can add a little more clarity to this. Figure 7.3 shows for three villages (Lutkewierum, Wommels and Kubaard) for which a reasonable number of deeds are available, the places where borrowers living in or close to such a village borrowed. The map shows Friesland around 1830; between 1530 and 1830, the population of Hennaarderadeel increased only by about 30–40 per cent; every dot on the map is a house or a cluster of houses (Figure 7.3).

Four things can be noted. First, lending and borrowing was rural business. Some lenders did live in small cities like Bolsward, Harlingen or Franeker and the slightly larger capital of Friesland, Leeuwarden. But most of them were, like the borrowers, village dwellers. Second, close inspection of the map (the networks of lines linking borrowers and lenders) reveals that there were in fact two circles of lenders. One was a somewhat smaller circle with lenders which could be visited in one day (say about twenty kilometres back and forth) and then there was a larger one, which could extend thirty kilometres or even more. Interestingly, it can be shown that this second circle of lenders consisted almost solely of family members. Third, lending was common. The deeds written down by the *Grietman* only cover part of the loans, but even then it is clear that lending and borrowing were not exceptional in these villages. Fourth, these circles overlap and as a circle can be drawn for every village on this map (not just the three examples illustrated), it is clear that there must have been an integrated market for this entire area, a market which probably extended along the coast of the North Sea up to Denmark.

Conclusion and discussion

As far as we are concerned, the capital market in Hennaarderadeel, and in a large area around this rural backwater, was genuine. And it was important. People with access to this market – a precise estimate is not possible at this moment, but this must have been a large part of the population – could use this capital market to further their aims, like buying a farm or establishing a trade. All kinds of rules and habits to facilitate matching and to guarantee ownership rights were in place. This also indicates that the background of lending and borrowing was, in most cases, an economic one. People did not borrow for military reasons or (as far as these data go) to finance conspicuous consumption. We should not extend this some-what rosy picture to later periods. As far as we know, 'conspicuous consumption'

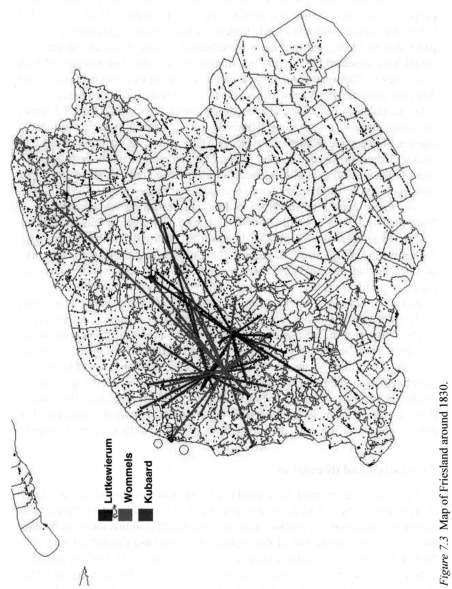

Figure 7.3 Map of Friesland around 1830.

Lutkewierum

Wommels

Kubaard

became more important over time (Nijboer 2007), while the number of people with access to the credit market might have decreased over time, especially in the growing cities of Friesland where (at least in 1749) a disproportionately large number of the poor (often single women) lived. And in the same period, the Habsburg government did borrow (at a higher interest rate than the average farmer) to finance its wars and tried to extract tribute from the area. Rural borrowing, however, clearly had an economic nature. Borrowing might also have funded farm improvements and especially the change from farm buildings made of loam and wood to brick buildings (which, beneath their brick hull, however, still sometimes hide ancient wood structures), an expenditure which was part consumption and part investment. But whatever the reason for borrowing and lending – there is no doubt that this can be called a genuine capital market.

Above all, however, the consistently positive link between the value of assets and the value of debts hammers home the fact that borrowing in this early modern economy was not associated with poverty or distress. Rather, it was linked to ownership of the single largest and most important piece of real property (a house and its appurtenances), to precious metals, to financial assets, and to large amounts of valuable furniture (the most durable of household moveables). It seems likely that these very pronounced and consistent links arose from the fact that these asset categories provided collateral to support higher borrowing.

Remarkably, 'matching', or the way market institutions enabled lenders and borrowers to meet and to make a transaction, did not require banks. To an extent, literate people like Hugo Upckes, mentioned above, may have served as a kind of proto-banker. Local knowledge and family ties seem to have been enough to enable matching of supply and demand for funds and a kind of peer-to-peer lending and borrowing system existed in Hennaarderadeel, just like in the other regions mentioned in the text. Extensive capital markets could clearly exist without banks. Which raises the question: why do banks exist? Answering this question is not the purpose of this chapter. But based upon the information above, it can be stated that 'matching supply and demand of funds' is not the answer, not even in the 'loanable funds market' of sixteenth- to eighteenth-century Europe.

Notes

1 Without elaborating this: the land market was sometimes characterized by extreme increases in prices or, especially after the introduction of French laws in the Netherlands around 1800, 'rent sharking'.
2 This official was officially elected, each 'old' farm having one vote. In reality, the people who were elected came from a limited number of families. Even then, it was not officially hereditary.
3 This was part of the common law system, as opposed to the conflict-orientated Roman law system which increasingly came to dominate written law in Friesland.
4 Transcription Borghaerts, Tresoar, weesboeken Hennaarderadeel Swijns 1555, Hen-20-109.
5 Bear in mind that the farm was for the larger part bought 'on credit'!
6 Five per cent is the 20th stuiver, 6.7 per cent is the 15th stuiver. This is consistent with 'age heaping' in marriage contracts of the time. People tended to round their age to the nearest five or zero (De Moor and van Zanden 2008).

7 De Moor *et al.* (2011) split the interest rate into a risk part, a transactions cost part and a 'pure' time preference part. If this is meaningful, it seems that small loans were, on average (!), not riskier than large loans, though the few high-priced ones may have been riskier.

8 Unpublished transcription of probate inventories from Hennaarderadeel by Jan Post, available from Merijn Knibbe.

9 A history of prices for Friesland at this time is not in its infancy, but still in the womb (but see Post 2002). A quick glance in the probate inventories mentioned above, however, yielded 62 prices of cows with an average of 12.01 guilders, a modus of 11 guilders, and a lowest and highest price of 8 and 18.5 gold guilders for inventories from 1553 and 1554.

10 Like Hoite Hoits, an innkeeper in whose inn an auction was held 'by the burning candle', who in 1542 asserted his right to be paid by the buyer for the wine (not a local product!) used during the auction.

11 Transcription by Jan Post.

12 It is outside the scope of this chapter, but it does seem to have been the case that some of these custodians ended up with quite a bit of the land of the orphans, bought at a relatively low price.

13 As quite a few parcels of land were burdened with all kinds of taxes in money or in kind, often to maintain roads and bridges and dikes, as well as other taxes or religious dues, the purchase value of land was not always a precise estimate of its economic value.

References

(Sources: transcriptions as described and partly available on the website www. hennaerderadeel.nl/home/.)

Dehing, P. (2012). *Geld in Amsterdam. Wisselbank en wisselkoersen, 1650–1725* [*Money in Amsterdam. The Bank of Exchange and Exchange Rates, 1650–1723*]. Hilversum, the Netherlands: Verloren.

De Moor, T. and van Zanden, J. L. (2008). "Van fouten kan je leren. Een kritische benadering van de mogelijkheden van 'leeftijd-stapelen' voor sociaal-economisch onderzoek naar gecijferd-heid in het pre-industriële Vlaanderen en Nederland" ["Learning from mistakes. About the possibilities of 'age heaping' as a guide to the study of numeracy in pre industrial Flanders and Holland"], *Tijdschrift voor Sociale en Economische Geschiedenis*, 5(4): 55–86.

De Moor, T. and Zuijderduijn, J. (2013). "Preferences of the poor: Market participation and asset management of poor households in sixteenth-century Holland", *European Review of Economic History*, 17(2): 239–255.

Fertig, C. (2009). "Urban capital and agrarian reforms: Rural credit markets in nineteenth-century Westphalia", in P. R. Schofield and T. Lambrecht (Eds), *Credit and the Rural Economy in North-western Europe c. 1200–1850*. Turnhout, Belgium: Brepols Publishers, pp. 169–196.

Knibbe, M. (2006). *Lokkich Fryslan. Landpacht, arbeidsloon en landbouwproductiviteit in het Friese kleigebied, 1505–1830* [*Agricultural Rents, Agricultural Wages and Agricultural Productivity in Friesland, 1505–1830*]. Groningen: NAHI.

Knibbe, M. (2007). "Geen lezers maar Schrijvers. Uitingen van verschriftelijking van de cultuur in Hennaarderadeel rond 1560" ["Writers, not readers. Signs of increasing literacy in Hennaarderadeel around 1560"], *Fryslan*, 13(4): 10–13.

Knibbe, M. (2014). "De kerk, de staat en het vredesdividend. Pachtopbrengsten van kerkelijke goederen in Friesland" ["The church, the state and the peace dividend. Rents of ecclesiastical land in Friesland"], *De Vrije Fries*, 94: 251–278.

Kuiken, K. (2013). *Het Bildt is geen eiland. Capita cultuurgeschiedenis van een vroegmoderne polder* [*Het Bildt Is No Island. Capita Cultural History of an Early Modern Polder*]. Groningen: self-published.

Nijboer, H. (2007). *De fatsoenering van het bestaan. Consumptie in Leeuwarden tijdens de Gouden Eeuw* [*An Increasingly Fashionable Existence. Consumption in Leeuwarden during the Golden Century*]. Groningen: Rijksuniversiteit Groningen.

Ogilvie, S., Küpker, M. and Maegraith, J. (2012). "Household debt in early modern Germany: Evidence from personal inventories", *The Journal of Economic History*, 72(1): 134–152.

Paping, R. (1995). *Voor een handvol stuivers. Werken, verdienen en besteden: De levensstandaard van boeren, arbeiders en middenstanders op de Groninger klei, 1770–1860* [*For a Fistful of Stuivers. Labouring, Earning and Spending: The Standard of Living of Farmers, Labourers and the Self-employed on the Groningen Clay 1770–1860*]. Groningen: NAHI.

Pfister, U. (2007). "Rural land and credit markets. The permanent income hypothesis and proto-industry: Evidence from early modern Zurich", *Continuity and Change*, 22(3): 489–518.

Post, J. (2002). "De waarde van een koe. Prijsreeksen voor koeien in Friesland" ["The value of a cow. Price series for cows in Friesland"], unpublished mimeo, Leeuwarden, the Netherlands.

Postma, O. (1962). "Slechte betalers in de gouden eeuw" ["Bad debtors in the golden age"], *De Vrije Fries*, 45: 155–160.

Postma, O. and Spahr van der Hoek, J. J. (1952). *Geschiedenis van de Friese landbouw* [*History of Agriculture in Friesland*]. Drachten, the Netherlands: Laverman.

Ronsijn, W. (2014). *Commerce and the Countryside. The Rural Population's Involvement in the Commodity Market in Flanders, 1750–1910*. Ghent: Academia Press.

Thoen, E. and Soens, T. (2009). "Credit in rural Flanders c. 1250–c.1600: Its variety and significance", in: P. R. Schofield and T. Lambrecht (Eds), *Credit and the Rural Economy in North-western Europe c.1200–1850*. Turnhout, Belgium: Brepols Publishers, pp. 19–38.

Vermoesen, R. (2010). "Paardenboeren in Vlaanderen" ["Farmers owning a horse in Flanders"], *Tijdschrift voor Sociale en Economische Geschiedenis*, 7(1): 3–37.

Vermoesen, R. (2011). *Markttoegang en commerciële netwerken van rurale huishoudens. De regio Aalst 1650–1800* [*Access to the Market and Commercial Networks of Rural Households in the Aalst Area 1650–1800*]. Ghent: Academia Press.

Zuijderduijn, J., De Moor, T. and van Zanden, J. L. (2011). "Small is beautiful. On the efficiency of capital markets in late medieval Holland", CGEH Working Paper No. 11. Utrecht, the Netherlands: University of Utrecht.

8 Financial liberalization, financial development and instability in emerging economies

What lessons for the franc zone?

Aboubakar Sidiki Cisse

Introduction

Financial development is defined "as the accumulation of financial assets, diversification of financial assets and financial institutions, improving efficiency and competition in the financial sector, access of the population to financial services" (Department for International Development 2004).

Financial development thus implies that the financial system is large (the accumulation of financial assets), deep and liquid (diversification of financial assets and financial institutions and enhancing competition in the financial sector). In the standard theory, financial development is conceivable in a liberalized financial environment. Hence, financial liberalization and financial development are two inseparable notions (standard theory). Such a development would allow the freeing up of more flexible financing, more adaptable to the diverse needs of the economy and especially to diversify funding sources, while providing a bulwark against various risks. It is in this mindset that since the 1970s, financial liberalization – as a means to achieve financial development – is advocated by international financial institutions (the International Monetary Fund [IMF], the World Bank, etc.) and backed by the dominant theory. However, with the recurrence of financial instabilities in emerging economies, the position of the consensual dominant theory on the relationship between financial liberalization, financial development and economic growth is called into question (Ülgen 2014). Furthermore, economic theory seems to minimize the idea that there may be links between the volatility of macroeconomic variables and financial instability. Indeed, in developing countries in general, and in those of the franc zone – West African Economic and Monetary Union (WAEMU); Central Africa Economic and Monetary Union (CAEMU) – in particular, it seems that financial instability is the result of a dysfunctioning of the real economy.

This chapter aims to show that if financial development has a positive impact on economic growth, the instability that may result lessens its effect on the real economy. Macroeconomic stability and the sustainability of the development process in developing countries are major concerns in this respect. The chapter then especially insists on the relevance of a gradual and controlled financial liberalization in the countries of the franc zone.

Financial development and economic growth: a literature review

Although the purpose of this chapter is not only to discuss the direction of causality between the financial sphere and the real economy, a review of the literature on this point is necessary to address the issue in more general terms. In this section, we show that the essential issue is not the direction of causality, but the structural interdependence between financial variables and real variables.

Joan Robinson's approach: economic growth as a financial development factor

Unlike many authors, Joan Robinson supports the idea that it is the real variables that cause the development of the financial sector, with statements such as: "where enterprise leads, finance follows" (Robinson 1952: 86). Growth is essential for the initiation of development. This is accompanied by the emergence of new needs in the economy (increased investment, increased credit, diversification of financial portfolios, banking in the economy, the emergence of financial markets, future financialization of the economy) facing the financial system as they develop. Therefore, it is economic development that brings about financial development, and the financial system appears as an endogenous response to the request made by economic agents. A healthy economy means healthy companies that sell their products more easily. New jobs can be created. The consequences of this mechanism are those of Keynes's (1936) effective demand – namely, an increase of consumption due to the increase in household purchasing power, economic growth, lower unemployment, etc. This stimulates the financial system since the increase in consumption is accompanied by a marked increase in the demand for money or loanable funds.

Schumpeter's approach: the financial system leads to economic growth

Schumpeter, in his various works, makes no reference to the financial efficiency of the financial system and the latter is reduced mainly to banks. However, the definition of the entrepreneur and resulting assumptions refer to certain criteria which are at the roots of economic development. The entrepreneur is defined as the economic agent whose function is to execute new combinations (innovations); which means that any individual who does not realize new combinations is not an entrepreneur.

The Schumpeterian entrepreneur is also a capitalist since she takes risks by running new combinations. The Schumpeterian entrepreneur plays a central role in the evolution of the capitalist system. Indeed, it is he who by his strategies helps to cope with competition between firms and generates industrial evolution. Indeed, if the entrepreneur cannot finance herself, she must find external funding. This must be provided by the banking system and the form of credit to allow the entrepreneur to acquire the means of production necessary for the implementation of its new combination. Credit must therefore be central to the economic system as its main function is to allow the economy to enter new channels: to bring innovations and/or improvements in the means of production.

Schumpeter (1961 [1934]: 103) states that "no one else is a debtor by the nature of his economic function" and one "can only become an entrepreneur by previously becoming a debtor" (1961 [1934]: 102). The granting of credit should not be based on past performance of the company, and the repayment guarantee must neither be based on the expected currency nor on present products or on goods, but on the balance sheet of the company. The availability of the financial system to finance companies is an essential condition for economic growth.

Unlike Robinson, for Schumpeter, causality runs from financial variables to real variables. In this causality, the two main players are entrepreneurs and bankers, the first through their financing needs and the latter through their ability to satisfy those needs. The banker should not be considered as an intermediary, but as the producer of what Schumpeter calls "purchasing power or command authority". It makes possible the implementation of new combinations with the decision whether or not to grant credit to the entrepreneur. The banker's refusal to give credit to the entrepreneur can be a brake on economic development. Economic and industrial development rests on the credit supply. The financial system leads to economic growth through the financing of innovation which is the key driver of growth in Schumpeter's model. In development policies, emphasis should be placed on the development of the banking system; that is to say, a system able and always willing to finance the economy.

The impact of financial development on the trade balance and productivity of factors of production

Financial development is accompanied by financial liberalization and the opening up of the economy to the rest of the world. Financial liberalization primarily consists of free interest and exchange rates as well as free capital movements. This would result in a greater monetization of the economy with new tools of payment, reducing delays and transaction costs. Exchange hedging mechanisms can be strengthened. The banking system must play its full role there. It can do this by facilitating credit conditions not only to export companies, but also to individuals involved in import and export; and thus enable the country to strengthen its international specialization and increase its trade volumes.

Studies on the role of the financial system on the productivity of factors of production also focus on the links between technology and productivity (Alfaro *et al.* 2009). Bank financing allows companies to invest in technological progress, which may lead to further innovation and increase productivity. For example, new information technologies facilitated in the last decades significant increases in productivity in a number of countries like the United States and other countries that are members of the Organisation for Economic Co-operation and Development (OECD) (Colecchia and Schreyer 2001).

Financial development can also improve the factors of production. Labour (L) can be improved when financial development allows a rich economic growth in terms of the number of jobs and their quality. Capital movements can generate an increase of productivity by increasing the volume of investments arising from financial development. The latter, indeed, emphasizes the country's attractiveness in terms of capital and investment including risk management through the reduction of transaction costs (Levine 1997).

Positive relationship between financial development and economic growth

The contribution of Gurley and Shaw has been theorized in *Money in a Theory of Finance* (1974). This can be considered as one of the pioneers in the study of the contribution of financial development to economic growth: "A financial system which is not mature is a problem for economic progress" (Gurley and Shaw 1974: 46, my translation from the French edition). Immaturity means restrictions on loans and borrowing. This approach is part of a liberal framework in which there is no place for financial repression. The considered economy is a basic economy with three agents – consumers, enterprises and the government; and three markets – the labour market, the market of goods and services and that of the currency. In this basic economy, the financial system is inefficient; that is to say, there are no financial assets to encourage savings, no financial market to allocate savings to investment, the currency is the only financial asset. The purpose of the model is to show that financial innovations contribute to economic progress. The development of financial intermediaries contributes to economic growth through two channels: the first is the transfer of savings of households (surplus agents) to enterprises (deficit agents); and the second is monetary policy. Through savings transfer, financial intermediaries contribute to raising the level of savings and investment. The collected savings will be used so as to cope with investment opportunities. This transfer is facilitated by financial innovations that accompany financial development. The monetary policy channel is about stabilization of prices and interest rates. Indeed, after financial liberalization, monetary policy will no longer be conducted in order to meet the needs of public authorities, but it is to act directly on money in circulation through the control of inflation and adequate administration of interest rates. The agents' revenues increase, savings and credit supply also increase. According to Gurley and Shaw (1974), monetary policy must be implemented in order to facilitate the funding of the real economy.

In a similar way, the analysis of King and Levine (1993a, 1993b) is based on a liberal model of perfect competition where the financial structure is not very important. What is important is the combination of different financial structures. Noting the lack of valid measurements of global financial development, the authors consider several other possibilities. They use two indicators to calculate the magnitude of the financial sector (current liabilities of the financial system as a percentage of Gross Domestic Product [GDP] and the amount of credit extended to private enterprises – both by the private sector banks and the central bank – as a percentage of GDP); and two indicators to assess the financial system's efficiency (proportion of total credit actually provided by private sector banks without the central bank; and the share of total credit granted to non-financial companies). This corresponds to the situation of an open and competitive market economy. In such an economy, the banking system is essentially private as it is assumed that private economic units would be more efficient than public lenders.

Indeed, financial liberalization, following the seminal works of McKinnon (1973) and Shaw (1973), is central to the work of King and Levine. This is to ensure that the financial system is free of any financial repression, which – according to the authors – hinders financial development. The aim of this liberalization is not the exclusive achievement of higher interest rates, but to open the economy to foreign capital, liberalize interest rates and attract more bank deposits. King and Levine present a model which assumes that deposits (savings of agents) do determine the investment. In this context, the liberalization is a prerequisite for financial development, which in turn, does enhance economic growth.

King and Levine (1993b) define the functions of a good financial system through five key concepts:

1   facilitation of coverage and risk diversification;
2   better allocation of resources;
3   monitoring of managers and businesses;
4   mobilizing savings;
5   the facilitation of trade of goods and services.

The authors find a positive and statistically significant correlation between financial development variables and economic growth. The originality of King and Levine's work is that they have been able to show econometrically that financial development predicts future economic growth; that is, the level of financial development of a country in the period T predicts future growth in the period T + n.

The importance of the financial structure for per capita income

According, for instance, to Luintel *et al.* (2008), financial structure has a positive impact on per capita income. This work shows, from a Post-Keynesian perspective, that beyond the financial development, the financial structure is the best explanation of the role of finance in economic growth. The authors take into account three financial systems:

1   bank-based (emphasis on the crucial role of banks in development financing);
2   market-based (liberalized financial operations and institutions efficiently reducing the bank's power in the financing process); and

3   financial-services-based (emphasis on the efficiency of the way that financial services are provided, and not on the source of finance).

The study focuses on six developing or newly developed countries[1] and is conducted over a period of 30 years for all the countries except Greece (39 years). The variables considered in the study are: level of production, labour, capital, financial structure, the gross fixed capital formation, the size of population. The aggregate measure of financial structure suggested in this work is the weighted sum of two ratios: the ratio of Stock Market Total Value Traded to Private Credit; and the ratio of Stock Market Capitalization to Private Credit. If the ratio is greater than 1, the financing of the economy is supposed to be mainly provided by financial markets. Otherwise, it is the banking system which is the main financing source of the economy. Gross fixed capital formation in turn gives the level of investment and largely depends on bank intermediation (bank-based system) or financial markets (market-based system).

Many examples of studies are then conducted on Germany (bank-based financial system), the United Kingdom and the United States (market-based financial systems) (Luintel *et al*. 2008). These studies seek to explain the effectiveness of a financial system through economic growth. Finally, results are mixed because the growth rates in the three countries are roughly close to each other. Beck and Levine (2002), among other authors, maintain that the comparison between different financial structures is not relevant since the significant effect on economic growth is exerted by the overall financial development. For this kind of approach, mainly resting on market efficiency, financial systems must be liberalized since it is assumed that large, liquid and unconstrained markets are prone to innovations and then facilitate risk management. In fact, we notice that most developing countries have financial systems dominated by bank intermediation. The efficiency of this intermediation may be questioned, but it has to be recognized that banks play an important role in those countries. Gerschenkron (1962) in his study of the history of industrialization, points to the importance of the banking system, more than markets, in the early stages of economic development. The role of the government is particularly important since it should help the financial system to finance projects, to create a climate of trust in business, essential to the granting of loans which are based on the expectations about the evolution of the economy. Financial markets are even more important as countries develop (Boyd and Smith 1998). From this perspective, the issue is whether developing countries should basically focus their development policies on the expansion of their financial markets. The countries that have the most developed financial markets also have the strongest banking institutions. One could say that countries with developed financial markets are also those which are financially and economically developed. The direction of the causality between finance and growth then seems to be a very confused matter.

Luintel *et al*. (2008) put more emphasis on the complementarity between the two financial systems. Their work highlights the importance of the financial structure for per capita income. Indeed, their study shows that the financial structure had a positive effect on income over the period for all the countries studied except the Philippines. The authors explain this by the level of development of this country. They also show differences within the countries included in the study. For example, in countries like Greece, India, South Korea and Taiwan, the development of financial markets has been accompanied by a significant increase in per capita income; while in South Africa, per capita income increased with the banking development. The financial system improves the per capita income by allowing and facilitating the financing of investments and private initiatives.

This review of the literature shows that the financial system plays a positive role in economic growth through improvement of the trade balance, the attractiveness of the economy, increased productivity and competitiveness and finally the increase in per capita income. This rosy picture should not, however, hide another reality: financial instability greatly reduces the possible positive impact of finance on the real economy.

Financial development versus financial instability

Are there obvious and linear links between financial development and financial stability? In a prudent fashion, conventional models (for instance, Levine 1997; Khan and Senhadji 2000) argue that financial instabilities in developing and emerging financial systems (during the 1980s and 1990s) can largely be explained by their weak financial development. However, Kpodar and Guillaumont Jeanneney (2006) maintain that financial development is often accompanied by financial instability. Indeed, the development of financial systems relies on financial liberalization and is accompanied by financial innovations which encourage large risk taking that generates financial instabilities both in emerging and developed economies. The increase of bank credit is used as an indicator to predict financial crises (Kaminsky and Reinhart 1999). Financial liberalization and the opening up of bank and financial markets result in an increase in the number of financial institutions and this strengthens competition between the different groups. This often puts banks up to engage in a battle for market shares at the expense of stable long-term financing relations with their customers. Increased competition then pushes banks to take several diverse risks; banks develop products and processes to attract potential customers, while the quality of information deteriorates since banks in their role of financial engineers no longer give correct information to their customers and enter into various manoeuvres to attract capital and customers. Speculative activities gain strength with the development of markets for securities and interest rates can reach new heights to attract investors. Furthermore, when the legal environment is weak and bank supervision is defective, as is the case in developing economies such as the franc zone countries, markets plunge in unstable phases and *"banks develop an incentive to moral hazard behavior, generator of financial crises"* (Kpodar and Guillaumont Jeanneney 2006; emphasis added). This analysis is in accordance with Stiglitz and Weiss (1981). According to these authors, the normal behaviour of a bank dealing with uncertainty is to voluntarily limit its rate, ration credit in a context of asymmetric information and reduce monitoring costs. It is on this basis that McKinnon (1988) shows that in countries where the legal environment and banking supervision are lacking in a context of macroeconomic instability, banks adopt a moral hazard behaviour that causes them to make very risky loans at exorbitant rates and to take currency and maturity risks beyond their capacity to manage them. This constitutes the main channels of transmission of financial instability. The common point between the crisis of the 1990s in Europe and Japan, the Asian crisis of 1997, the Russian crisis of 1998, the Turkish crisis of 2001, the Argentinian crisis of 2001–2002 and the subprime crisis of 2007–2008 is the financial liberalization and markets' openness which first preceded financial development and financial crisis as well.

Reinhart and Rogoff (2008) analyse the financial crises that occurred in 120 countries between the nineteenth century and 2008. The main common explanation (for all crises), they suggest, is the degree of liberalization which usually coincides with a period of high international capital mobility. Thus, they find strong correlation between the circulation of capital movements, credit and asset prices (real estate prices and stock prices). In 18 of the 26 banking crises identified and analysed, the financial sector had been liberalized in the five years preceding the beginning of the crisis. In the less advanced economies, a financial crisis, as we usually know it, is rare. These countries may be affected by the negative externalities coming from their northern partners as was the case from 2009 with lower global growth.

Economic development versus financial stability

There is a reciprocal relation between economic development and financial development, but also between economic development and financial stability. Economic development is a bulwark against financial instability. But without financial stability, no sustained growth and economic development are possible. Financial instability does not only affect developing economies, its impacts on economic growth also reduce the expected effects of financial liberalization and financial development.

If the relationship between financial development and economic development is widely studied and debated, the question of financial instability is usually set aside. However, it appears that financial stability is the link between these two concepts. Without it, we do not see how financial development could positively affect economic development. Unfortunately, financial instability is usually neglected in the literature on financial development and economic development. In most analyses, this issue is related to financial underdevelopment in developing economies with weak and primitive financial mechanisms. Therefore, it is difficult to understand financial instabilities in developed countries since one assumes that financial system development would lead to financial stability and economic development. This contradiction comes from the fact that financial instability is treated separately from the subject of financial development. There is a virtuous circle of finance when everything works normally (financial stability accompanying financial development) and a vicious circle of financial development when it is obstructed by financial instability.

Financial crises do not strike all economies in the same way. Indeed, according to whether a country is rich or poor, the economy is affected differently because the instability manifests itself differently. This represents a break with the usual interpretation that the economies most vulnerable to crises are those that are less advanced in terms of financial development. This break rests on the fact that it is not because the financial system is liberalized, deep and liquid that it is stable and efficient with regard to the aim of sustainable/durable economic growth and development.

If all economies may be subject to financial instabilities either directly or indirectly, the most interventionist states are the least affected by financial instability. The recurrence of the crisis is stronger in countries that have gone a long way in terms of financial openness and liberalization. This is not an apology for interventionism, but only a sufficiently broad observation that calls into question the relevance of financial liberalism in the process of economic development. Numerous works – Berthélemy and Varoudakis (1996), Deidda and Fattouh (2002), Rioja and Valev (2004a, 2004b), Samargandi *et al.* (2013) – put forward the idea that the impact of financial development on economic growth depends on the level of economic development, such that the impact of financial development is greater in emerging economies than in developed and developing countries.

Parallel to this, the recurrence of financial crises is greater in developing and emerging economies than in developed economies. The fundamental difference between those economies in the face of financial instabilities lies in the irreversibility of economic development at short-run. Whatever the scale of a financial crisis, an economy that is already developed will remain so. In emerging and developing countries, efforts made and progress provided for years may collapse within months of financial crisis. This happened in several countries in Asia and Latin America. While in developed countries, instabilities lead to recession and increasing unemployment, in developing countries, this is a real step backwards, increasing poverty, dislocating the development process and narrowing the expected effects of financial development. From this perspective, numerous works (for example, Klein and Shabbir 2006; Das 2009, to quote but a few) point to the causes and costly consequences of financial crises in emerging market economies.

Some lessons for the franc zone

Financial development and financial instability affect the economy in several ways. First, financial development is a long-lasting process that depends on initial structural conditions and does not obviously generate growth and development, especially in less developed regions like sub-Saharan Africa (Kpodar 2005, 2008). Second, financial instability usually results in the disruption of the economic system, more or less deeply according to the extent of the crisis. The system of payments deteriorates (currency depreciates, increasing the burden of debt and

Table 8.1 Cost of banking crises in the public sector (% of GDP)

Countries	Period	Initial cost	Net cost
Emerging and developing countries			
Indonesia	1997–2003	56.8	52.3
Thailand	1997–2000	43.8	34.8
Chile	1981–1983	52.7	33.5
South Korea	1997–2000	31.2	23.1
Ecuador	1998–2001	21.7	21.7
Mexico	1994–1995	n.a.	19.3
Developed countries			
USA	Savings and Loans 1984–1991	3.7	2.1
France	Crédit Lyonnais 1993–1995	1.2	1
Japan	1990–2005	20	15–20
Norway	1987–1989	2.5	0
Sweden	1991–1993	4.4	0

Source: Icard (2007).

causing deteriorating terms of trade), transaction costs increase and the confidence of agents in financial and banking institutions is affected, especially when the crisis is reflected in a lack of liquidity in the economy and when financial and banking institutions are no longer able to meet their commitments. This results in a panic in the money market and puts the economy in a deep need for funding. This is what we call a "monetary crisis of confidence" (Cisse 2012: 196). Another consequence is disintermediation or marketization that could draw attention to the fact that banks' intermediation remains a major source of funding, both in developed economies and in developing economies. In developing countries like those in the franc zone, intermediation is the main source of funding to the extent that other means of financing are in an embryonic state. When intermediation is affected, it is the entire system of financing of the economy which is severely weakened. As a consequence, enterprises cannot have access to domestic bank-financing and must self-finance their activities (without sufficient resources to meet their needs) or borrow from abroad at high rates, which further increases the dependence of the financial system *vis-à-vis* foreign capital. Self-financing and borrowing abroad may be further complicated with instability as foreign lenders lose confidence in a shaky economy. When instability hits the banking system, the consequence is immediately transmitted to credit allocation mechanisms through more rationing as banks' lending capacity and willingness substantially reduce or because some banks disappear. On the foreign exchange market, instability will result in lasting asset price volatility with rising real interest rates which reduce the volume of investments. As for companies involved in international trade, financial instability is also felt as the costs for hedging foreign exchange risks increase, and financial and commercial contracts with companies abroad are revised. Icard (2007: 75) sums up the impact of financial instability on the real economy in the following terms: "in total, instability of institutions hinders the development of the financial system, increases the cost of funding, reduces lending capacity, hampers the efficient allocation of resources and ultimately slows down growth". Basically, financial instability destroys everything that financial development was previously expected to bring to the real economy.

What lessons can we draw from this for the franc zone? Financial liberalization and financial development could lead to economic development in a context of financial stability. Recent experience, however, shows that financial liberalization and deregulation provoke financial instability. The banking crisis of 1985 was the result of a multidimensional crisis that has shaken the economies, public finances and the payments system of all countries in the franc zone. The causes of this multi-dimensional crisis were also multiple. Anchoring the CFA franc into the French franc caused it to suffer from the instability of the latter *vis-à-vis* major currencies. The instability of the French franc resulted in a deterioration of the region's terms of trade and a heavier debt burden. Furthermore, as the franc zone mainly exports primary products (cotton, gold, coffee, cocoa and oil, for instance), the drop in prices for these commodities in the1980s degraded public finances (exporting companies were public), increased unemployment, and thus increased poverty, especially in the Sahelian zone countries. The banking sector, which was largely public, was challenged by the lack of economic activity on the one hand and by exacerbated government interventionism on the other hand. It was the beginning of the great banking crisis of the franc zone and of a new financial repression.

In 1986, at least 25 banks and financial institutions (mainly development banks) were in default. The first solutions were proposed through structural adjustment policies (SAPs). Regarding the financial sector, the remedy provided by SAPs was liberalization and financial openness. This resulted in a strong bank restructuring in the 1990s. Countries in the region sought to strength their regulatory systems. The Banking Commission (the world's first experiment in banking regulation) was created in 1990 and placed under the control of the central bank in the western part of the franc zone (WAEMU). The creation of this Commission facilitated the strengthening of micro-prudential and macro-prudential tools. Commissions to harmonize national economic policies and to strengthen regional integration were created (WAEMU and CAEMU). Today, financial development continues and the number of banks and financial institutions included within the zone is increasing (a 6 per cent increase in 2013; total bank loans to the real economy increased by 18 per cent in 2013). The bond market also continues to develop. The volume of bonds issued increased by 24.9 per cent between 2012 and 2013 (Banque Centrale des États de l'Afrique de l'Ouest 2014). Bonds are about to become the primary source of internal funding for the states of the franc zone. The financial market, still in development, is now unified within the WAEMU.

The franc zone authorities' concern is financial stability through increased financial regulations. But more broadly, financial stability is also related to eco-nomic stability. Indeed, financial stability reflects the normal functioning of the financial system without major disruption of the capital market which would lead to rising risks and an inefficient allocation of resources. In the franc zone, a particular emphasis must be placed on banking stability which is the main component of the financial system. In addition, the unification of the financial market in the area increases the risk of contagion. The anchoring of the currency on the euro today and its unlimited guarantee provided by the French Treasury give it some stability. However, the risk of financial instability could come from economic variables as in 1985. The WAEMU economies now depend on three variables that go beyond the strictly financial framework: rainfall, world prices of primary products and official development assistance (ODA). Good rainfall – a natural resource for agriculture – is the guarantee of good economic growth. What symmetrically this means is that poor rainfall can destabilize the economies of the zone via a decline in agricultural production which simply results in a decline in economic activity (fewer cotton exports, for example; fewer currency entries; fewer activities for banks, etc.). Falling commodity prices simply reduce states' revenues (export earnings), but also consumption and savings. The ODA addiction is still strong and can contribute to the deterioration of public finances.

These three factors are destabilizing for both the real and the financial sector. Therefore, the search for financial stability should be strengthened by the stability of these three real variables since there is a very close interdependence between the sustainability of the real economy and the durability of financial tools that must sustain economic growth and development financing.

Note

1 Greece, India, South Korea, the Philippines, South Africa and Taiwan.

References

Alfaro, L., Kalemli-Ozcan, S. and Sayek, S. (2009). "FDI, productivity and financial development", *The World Economy*, 32(1): 111–135.

Banque Centrale des États de l'Afrique de l'Ouest (2014). *Rapport annuel*. Dakar, Senegal: BCEAO.

Beck, T. and Levine, R. (2002). "Industry growth and capital accumulation: Does having a market- or bank-based system matter?", *Journal of Financial Economics*, 6: 147–180.

Berthélemy, J.-C. and Varoudakis, A. (1996). *Politiques de développement financier et croissance*, Série "Croissance à long terme". Paris: Centre de développement de l'OCDE.

Boyd, J. H. and Smith, B. D. (1998). "The evolution of debt and equity markets in economic development", *Economic Theory*, 12(3): 519–560.

Cisse, A. (2012). "Faible financement bancaire dans la zone UEMOA: Une analyse des causes de ce mal récurrent", MPRA Paper No. 40821. Available at: http://ideas.repec.org/p/pra/mprapa/40821.html

Colecchia, A. and Schreyer, P. (2001). "ICT investment and economic growth in the 1990s: Is the United States a unique case? A comparative study of nine OECD countries", *Science, Technology and Industry Working Papers*, No. 7. Paris: OECD Publishing.

Das, D. K. (2009). *Two Faces of Globalization: Munificent and Malevolent*. Cheltenham, UK: Eward Elgar Publishing.

Deidda, L. and Fattouh, B. (2002). "Non-linearity between finance and growth", *Economics Letters*, 74(3): 339–345.

Department for International Development (2004). "The importance of financial sector development for growth and poverty reduction", Policy Division Working Paper. Available at: www.ncrc.org/global/europe/UK/UKArticle7.pdf.

Gerschenkron, R. W. (1962). *Economic Backwardness in Historical Perspective: A Book of Essays*. Cambridge, MA: The Belknap Press of Harvard University Press.

Gurley, J. G. and Shaw, E. S. (1974). *La monnaie dans une théorie des actifs financiers*. Paris: Editions Cujas.

Icard, A. (2007). *Stabilité financière et banques centrales*. Paris: Economica.

Kaminsky, G. L. and Reinhart, C. M. (1999). "The twin crises: The causes of banking and balance-of-payments problems", *American Economic Review*, 89(3): 473–500.

Keynes, J. M. (1936). *The General Theory of Employment, Interest and Money*. London: Macmillan.

Khan, M. S. and Senhadji, S. A. (2000). "Financial development and economic growth: An overview", IMF Working Paper No. WP/00/209, December.

King, R. and Levine, R. (1993a). "Finance and growth: Schumpeter might be right", *The Quarterly Journal of Economics*, 108(3): 717–737.

King, R. and Levine, R. (1993b). "Finance, entrepreneurship and growth: Theory and evidence", *Journal of Monetary Economics*, 32(3): 513–542.

Klein, L. R. and Shabbir, T. (Eds) (2006). *Recent Financial Crises. Analyses, Challenges and Implications*. Cheltenham, UK: Edward Elgar Publishing.

Kpodar, K. (2005). "Le développement financier et la croissance: L'Afrique Subsaharienne est-elle marginalisée?", *African Development Review*, 17(1): 106–137.

Kpodar, K. (2008). *Développement financier, instabilité financière et croissance économique: Implications pour la réduction de la pauvreté*. Paris: Edilivre.

Kpodar, K. and Guillaumont Jeanneney, S. (2006). "Développement financier, instabilité financière et croissance économique", *Économie et Prévision*, 174(3): 87–111.

Levine, R. (1997). "Financial development and economic growth: Views and agenda", *Journal of Economic Literature*, 35(2): 688–726.

Luintel, K. B., Khan, M., Arestis, P. and Theodoridis, K. (2008). "Financial structure and economic growth," *Journal of Development Economics*, 86(1): 181–200.

McKinnon, R. I. (1973). *Money and Capital in Economic Development*. Washington, DC: Brookings Institution.

McKinnon, R. I. (1988). "Financial liberalization in retrospect: Interest rate policies in LDC's", in G. Ranis and T. P. Schultz (Eds), *The State of Development Economics: Progress and Prospectives*. New York: Basil Blackwell, pp. 386–415.

Reinhart, C. M. and Rogoff, K. S. (2008). "Is the 2007 US sub-prime financial crisis so different? An international historical comparison", *American Economic Review*, 98(2): 339–344.

Rioja, F. and Valev, N. (2004a). "Finance and the sources of growth at various stages of economic development", *Economic Inquiry*, 42(1): 127–140.

Rioja, F. and Valev, N. (2004b). "Does one size fit all? A reexamination of the finance and growth relationship", *Journal of Development Economics*, 74(2): 429–447.

Robinson, J. (1952). *The Rate of Interest and Other Essays*. London: Macmillan.

Samargandi, N., Fidrmuc, J. and Ghosh, S. (2013). "Is the relationship between financial development and economic growth monotonic for middle income countries?", *Brunel University Economics and Finance Working Papers Series*, Working Paper No. 13-2. London: Department of Economics and Finance, Brunel University.

Schumpeter, J. (1961 [1934]). *The Theory of Economic Development*. Cambridge, MA: Harvard University Press.

Shaw, E. S. (1973). *Financial Deepening in Economic Development*. New York: Oxford University Press.

Stiglitz, J. E. and Weiss, A. (1981). "Credit rationing in markets with imperfect information", *The American Economic Review*, 71(3): 393–410.

Ülgen, F. (2014). "Liberalised finance and instability: 'Does it drop out as a matter of logic?' LIMES plus", *Journal of Social Sciences and Humanities*, 11(3): 11–28.

9 Depositor myopia and banking sector behaviour

*Ozan Bakis, Fatih Karanfil
and Sezgin Polat*

Introduction[1]

Typically, banks provide liquidity insurance by pooling funds in exchange for demandable deposit contracts, and diversify away idiosyncratic credit risk by financing different investment projects (Diamond and Dybvig 1983; Diamond 1984; Kashyap *et al.* 2002, to quote but a few). Demand deposit contracts, which offer liquidity insurance, make banks prone to runs, leading to insolvency, due to early liquidation of long-term debt contracts. In this study, our main intention is to understand how the bank behaviour interacts with the depositor behaviour, given the conditions of financial constraint on both the demand and cost sides of bank credit. Although bank runs are more likely to be an issue for the banking sector, especially in a developing country like Turkey, where several exchange rate crises were associated with recurrent banking crises,[2] our focus will not be on the deposit drain, which is the case in the classical bank-run framework. We rather draw attention to the possible shortening of deposit maturity by risk-averse depositors due to increased uncertainty over real asset returns. Both theoretical and empirical studies consider the likeliness of bank runs in the absence of (full-coverage) deposits insurance. However, few studies deal with the deposit composition of banks varying from longer-termed time deposits to immediately demandable deposits. Kashyap *et al.* (2002) and Gatev and Strahan (2006) argue that synergies between credit lines and deposit taking enable banks to keep safe from the likelihood of runs and thus reduce their liquid asset holdings. However, in the case of full insurance, the deposit holders might give priority neither to the solvency nor to the liquidity risk of the individual bank, but to the price stability in the financial system. For a small open economy, the depositors' concern for price stability can arise from exchange shocks or high public debt driven by default risk, which might worsen the expectations that either inflation would accelerate and/or nominal interest rates would increase. Having to face that nominal shock is likely; the depositors might switch to time deposits with shorter maturity, denominated either in dollars or in the national currency to avoid any loss in real terms. The motivation of the risk aversion might be either to minimize loss incurring from the perceived risk associated with the uncertainty arising from a default on the public debt; or to avoid any depreciation resulting from the high pass-through effect of exchange rates, which is very common among emerging countries which have suffered from high inflation in the past.[3] This framework is a close fit for many Latin American countries and Turkey. The inconsistent exchange rate regime and fiscal policy in these emerging countries give incentives to myopic behaviour (or short-termism) as the only financing pattern for the debt contracts.[4] Figure 9.1 shows how some major Latin American counties and Turkey suffer from private credit contraction under fiscal dominance. Note that in the 1990s, these countries several times attempted stabilization policies by adopting hard pegs in order to tame high inflation and sustain growth. Reversal movements of private and public debt can be attributed to the fiscal imbalances resulting from default risk and uncertainty. In the past two decades, an improvement in budgetary position has contributed to credit expansion in terms of Gross Domestic Product (GDP).

In the literature, maturity of private debt contracts has a greater significance than term structure of deposits due to the link between firms' problems and investment financing. There are two opposing claims regarding the consequences of short-term debt on economic performance. First, Calomiris and Kahn (1991) and Flannery (1994) assert that shortening of debt maturity is an effective way of disciplining bankers and mitigating agency problems inherent in banking: the threat of withdrawal of funds increases the likelihood of profitable investment opportunities. Second, Diamond and He (2014) and Diamond and Rajan (2012) claim that short-term debt harms the real economy by decreasing real investment levels. Diamond and He (2014) show that short-term debt can hinder current investment:

1   when the volatility of firm value is higher in bad times than in good times;
2   in a dynamic setting with future investment opportunities, when the reduction in equity value is very large as a result of a combination of bad times and shorter-term debt;
3   when investment benefits are inter-temporally linked, short-term debt may reduce future growth as a result of earlier future default.

In Diamond and Rajan (2012), uncertainty about households' income is the source of liquidity problems in the economy. This uncertainty increases households' withdrawals which cause an increase in the real interest rate, which in turn decreases bank net worth. If this loss is sufficiently high, this may terminate some otherwise profitable project financed by bank loans.

The consequences of myopic debt financing can be found in models based on a bank-run setting. Chang and Velasco (2000) discuss how short-term debt can be a source of fragility leading to a balance of payments crisis. Bussière *et al.* (2006) argue that higher economic or political uncertainty tightens solvency constraints and favours the short-term debt since debt maturity decreases with the uncertainty on investment returns. Furthermore, using a longitudinal data set, Jeanne and Guscina (2006) find that Latin American countries have very low shares of long-term domestic-currency debt, and argue that the reason for the high ratio of short-term domestic debt can be found in the history of monetary instability in these countries.

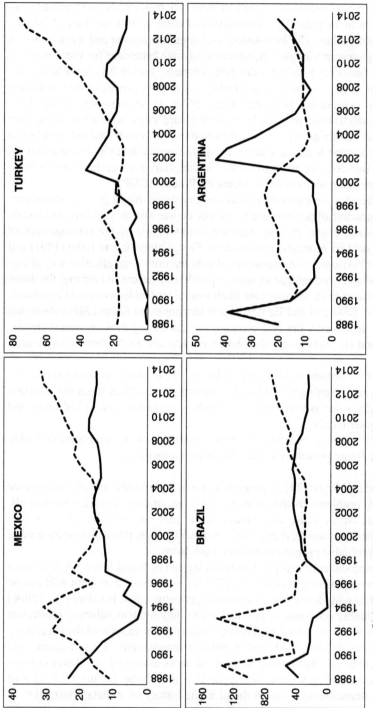

Figure 9.1 Public debt and credit expansion.

Source: Authors' creation, based on World Bank (2015).

—— Claims on central government, etc. (% of GDP)

--- Domestic credit to private sector (% of GDP)

We can clarify the possible interactions between the depositor and the banking sector in the following way. Banks will alter their asset composition unless the depositors' concerns are instantaneous or temporary. The compositional change in bank assets will probably be in favour of holding more assets like government bonds or treasury bills rather than debt contracts, which are less solvent and more risky in the short run. Thus, expectations about price stability in the financial system, whether derived from the depositors or the banking sector, will affect the credit market through the maturity channel. It is possible to make an analogy with the bank-run case: the maturity channel might not forcefully lead to a contraction in the funds (deposits) available to the banking sector, but it might lead to a contraction in the credit volume given the expectations of depositors and the reluctance of the banking sector to expand credits, which in turn can impede economic growth. In a similar fashion, in this study, our main hypothesis is that the systemic costs (which would appear in bank-run cases) are likely to emerge if the financial system runs into an unstable period due to increased uncertainty and risk perceptions over the asset-price stability.

Depositor behaviour can be a reflection of expectations in the financial markets, which in turn, contribute more to the short-term use of bank resources by creating a considerable cost effect for the banking sector. However, the degree of depositor myopia may change depending on expectations about the macroeconomic stability. It needs more inquiry at the individual bank level on how much banks decide to reduce the maturity gap[5] *vis-à-vis* the shortening of the deposit maturity. Nevertheless, it is reasonable to assume that banks will become more unwilling to finance investment projects. The contribution of this chapter is to assess the role of the price and maturity effects resulting from depositor myopia on the entire banking credit expansion. We try to show that macroeconomic imbalances like fiscal distress might undermine financial stability through shortening of the term structure of deposit maturity, and increasing the cost of funds with higher interest rates. We argue that bank behaviour does reflect and transmit the short-termism that governs the financial structure. The results that emerge from the Turkish case indicate that underdeveloped financial markets (with a heavy dependence on public debt) and recurrent banking crises, coupled with macroeconomic mismanagement, might lead to lower growth and shorter growth periods as well.

The remainder of this chapter is organized as follows. The second section discusses briefly the stability issue and the Turkish banking sector. The third section describes the data and the methodology used for testing the econometric model. The fourth section presents the results, and the fifth section concludes.

The banking sector and stability in Turkey

The banking sector in Turkey has a low capacity for credit creation. Indicators such as the ratio of commercial bank loans to GDP and the ratio of commercial bank loans to deposits are very low in comparison with Organisation for Economic Co-operation and Development (OECD) countries. As an example, the credit-to-GDP ratio was 35 per cent for Turkey, while it was 157 per cent for the EU-27 countries on average.

Table 9.1 Economic and financial indicators

	DIR	BIR	CR/GDP	DEP/GDP	CR/DEP	Growth	I/GDP	Inflation
Turkey	21	18.4	35	42	83	4.7	25.2	8.4
EU-27	4.3	4.5	157	136	116	4.6	25.2	3.6

Source: Turkish Statistical Institute (TURKSTAT).

Similarly, the deposit-to-GDP ratio was respectively 42 per cent and 136 per cent in 2007.[6] Combining both of these indicators, we see that the credit-to-deposit ratio was 83 per cent for Turkey, which is significantly lower than the EU-27 average of 116 per cent.

Table 9.1 provides a comparison of different economic and financial variables between the EU-27 countries and Turkey for 2007. European countries including Turkey are examples of bank-based economies where the main financial system works through credit institutions. Comparing Turkey with other European countries, we notice that the share of investment to GDP (I/GDP) – a proxy of finance demand – in Turkey is equal to the average value of European countries. However, there is a considerable difference in terms of financial variables – deposit interest rates (DIR), bond interest rates (BIR), ratios of credit to GDP (CR/GDP), deposit to GDP (DEP/GDP) and credit to deposit (CR/DEP) – which are more closely related to the credit availability of the banking sector.

According to Table 9.1, the ratios of deposit-to-GDP and credit-to-GDP are very high for the EU-27 countries. Compared with the case of Turkey, it is about 3.2 times higher for the first, and 4.5 times higher for the second ratio. The financial deepening indicators show evidence of the lower size of credit supply in Turkey. The same relatively low banking performance of Turkey can be traced when it comes to the low transformation rate of deposits to credit: the credit-to-deposit ratio is 1.4 times higher for the EU-27 countries.

From the development perspective, the financial liberalization that took place in the mid-1980s has not produced enough financial deepening in Turkey. The incapacity of the financial system to expand credits impeded economic development all through the 1990s. Although recent stable economic conditions facilitated a stronger banking sector (though there was a slight recession due to global recession in 2008), it is nevertheless evident that if the Turkish banking system were to catch up with the EU averages, all other things being equal, one would expect more investment and economic growth. Several studies in the literature support this view: Bencivenga and Smith (1991) develop a theoretical model where financial intermediation raises the economic growth rate. The basic idea in their paper is that without financial intermediaries, there will be an excessive holding of unproductive liquid assets that cannot be transformed into productive investment. As a result, financial intermediaries, by changing the composition of savings, produce higher investment and growth rates even without an increase in savings rates.[7] Levine *et al.* (2000) provide strong empirical evidence that a more efficient financial system which ameliorates information asymmetries and facilitates transactions promotes economic growth.

One of the main factors that may explain the underdevelopment of the Turkish banking system is the high uncertainty and volatility of the economy. Between 1994 and 2001, the Turkish economy underwent three serious subsequent economic crises; namely, in 1994, 1999 and 2001 (the severest one). These crises produced sharp downturns in economic activity and raised the question of public debt sustainability in the face of volatile interest rates and inflation. To give some figures by way of example, during the period between 1980 and 2007, the average inflation rate was 53 per cent and the debt requirement to GDP ratio was 5 per cent. Although GDP grew at a rate of 4 per cent on average, it followed a very unstable path: in 1994 and 1999, Turkey hit a growth rate of –4.7 per cent, while in 2001, it was even lower at –7.5 per cent.

A second factor might be the political instability. Between 1980 and 2008, 17 governments had been in power, and the average tenure is just about two years, since elections are held every five years, but an election can be called before that time. According to Kaufmann *et al.* (2009), Turkey has a score of –0.73 on the political instability index (which ranges from –2.5 to 2.5) while the EU-27 has 0.78 on average. This picture was even worse for Turkey in 1996, with a score of –1.49 compared to 0.81 for the EU-27 average. For the second index, showing whether governments design and implement policies and regulations that permit and promote private sector development, Turkey scores lower than the average for the EU-27 countries: in 2008, Turkey has an index number of 0.22 while the EU-27 average is 1.29. Interestingly, the Turkish government's regulatory quality is found to be higher in earlier years (e.g. 0.54 in 1996), meaning that the situation is worsening.

These economic and political uncertainties may strongly modify the composition and maturity of financial contracts, and thus generate a contraction in the volume of bank loans. From a small open economy perspective, higher interest rates – due to higher uncertainty – will not only reduce new investment, but also change the risk composition of new projects via credit rationing. Typically, when interest rates are higher, banks will be faced with the demand for loans for more risky projects. However, this is not the only effect of uncertainty on investment projects; it may also affect the maturity composition of deposits, which in turn shrinks the volume of credits. With rising uncertainty, depositors may be more averse to risk, and some of them may switch to shorter-term deposit contracts than they would choose in a more stable period. This curtailment in deposit maturity may also reallocate the funds available away from investment projects if banks' risk perception/aversion is affected by the maturity of deposits.

Data and methodology

Data description

We used monthly data covering a period of almost 20 years, starting from January 1990 up to October 2009, including the entire financially liberalized phase of the Turkish economy. Holding that data frequency is crucial in order to understand whether the compositional change on the asset side is affected by various financial variables, and especially from the liability side of the balance sheet in the short run, we limit the model to the data available on a monthly basis. Our main estimation strategy will be to test whether there is causality, in the sense of Granger, between short-term liabilities and long-term commitments as debt contract inside the banking sector. In order to eliminate the level effect of possible deposit drain, we chose to use the credit/deposit ratio as a proxy of bank behaviour. We excluded consumer credit, and kept the bank credit to the private sector (CRDP), which is supposed to be a longer-term commitment as debt contract. The deposit variable in the denominator consists only of deposits both in foreign and national currencies, with a maturity of one month and over. The maturity of deposit (MTDP) is the weighted average in days, and again it consists only of deposits with a maturity of one month and longer. In order to include the cost of funds in the model, we took the interest rate spread (IRSP) between one-month time deposits and the average monthly rate for short-term treasury bills. In order to include the credit demand, we used the monthly production index of the manufacturing sector (PROD) as a proxy. Along with the myopic (short-termism) hypothesis, we also consider the maturity of government bonds (TRES) that might serve as a major asset for the banking sector in the absence of more developed financial debt contracts. The exchange rate variable (EXCH) is also added to the model to reflect the probable nominal shocks in a small open economy. The next subsection discusses the methods to be used in establishing the causal relationships between the variables mentioned above.

Empirical methods

Our empirical strategy has two main objectives. The first one is to explain how the variables are related one to another over time. The second one is to provide an understanding of the causal relationships involved in different models. The pioneering study by Granger (1969) was the first to test for the direction of causality between two variables. The test, in its primitive form, is quite simple. Granger (1988: 200) gives the definition of causality in terms of predictability: considering two time-series, x and y, it is argued that "if y_t causes x_t, then x_{t+1} is better forecast if the information in y_{t-j} is used than if it is not used". Hence the standard causality test runs ordinary least squares (OLS) regression of a variable x in level form on the lagged levels of both x and y. Then a Fisher test is sufficient to check for Granger causality from y to x (*vice versa* for the inverse direction of causality). However, with non-stationary series it has been shown that the standard causality test can yield spurious causality results (see, among others, Granger and Newbold 1974).

Thus, each time-series analysis should begin by testing for the stationarity of the variables.[8] In the case of non-stationarity of the variables (with the proviso that they are integrated of the same order), Engle and Granger (1987) showed that any combination of these variables may be stationary, which means that there exists a cointegrating vector such that the linear combination of the variables formed using this vector is integrated of order zero. Thus, following the unit root tests, the second step of the analysis should consist of exploring the cointegration properties of the series, and the Johansen cointegration test procedure (Johansen and Juselius 1990) is widely used for this purpose. If a cointegrating relationship exists – that is, if we have a long-run equilibrium relationship between the variables involved in the analysis – then the dynamic Granger causality can be captured from a vector error correction model (VECM) derived from this cointegrating equilibrium relationship.[9]

Using the variables discussed above, the VECM can be expressed as follows:

$$\Delta CRDP_t = \psi_1 + \sum_{i=1}^{m} \beta_{11i} \Delta CRDP_{t-i} + \sum_{i=1}^{n} \beta_{12i} \Delta MTDP_{t-i} + \sum_{i=1}^{s} \beta_{13i} \Delta IRSP_{t-i}$$

$$+ \sum_{i=1}^{p} \beta_{14i} \Delta EXCH_{t-i} + \sum_{i=1}^{r} \beta_{15i} \Delta PROD_{t-i} + \sum_{i=1}^{s} \beta_{16i} \Delta TRES_{t-i}$$

$$+ \alpha_1 \varepsilon_{t-1} + u_{1t} \tag{9.1.1}$$

$$\Delta MTDP_t = \psi_2 + \sum_{i=1}^{m} \beta_{21i} \Delta CRDP_{t-i} + \sum_{i=1}^{n} \beta_{22i} \Delta MTDP_{t-i} + \sum_{i=1}^{o} \beta_{23i} \Delta IRSP_{t-i}$$

$$+ \sum_{i=1}^{p} \beta_{24i} \Delta EXCH_{t-i} + \sum_{i=1}^{r} \beta_{25i} \Delta PROD_{t-i} + \sum_{i=1}^{s} \beta_{26i} \Delta TRES_{t-i}$$

$$+ \alpha_2 \varepsilon_{t-1} + u_{2t} \tag{9.1.2}$$

$$\Delta IRSP_t = \psi_3 + \sum_{i=1}^{m} \beta_{31i} \Delta CRDP_{t-i} + \sum_{i=1}^{n} \beta_{32i} \Delta MTDP_{t-i} + \sum_{i=1}^{s} \beta_{33i} \Delta IRSP_{t-i}$$

$$+ \sum_{i=1}^{p} \beta_{34i} \Delta EXCH_{t-i} + \sum_{i=1}^{r} \beta_{35i} \Delta PROD_{t-i} + \sum_{i=1}^{s} \beta_{36i} \Delta TRES_{t-i}$$

$$+ \alpha_3 \varepsilon_{t-1} + u_{3t} \tag{9.1.3}$$

$$\Delta EXCH_t = \psi_4 + \sum_{i=1}^{m} \beta_{41i} \Delta CRDP_{t-i} + \sum_{i=1}^{n} \beta_{42i} \Delta MTDP_{t-i} + \sum_{i=1}^{o} \beta_{43i} \Delta IRSP_{t-i}$$

$$+ \sum_{i=1}^{p} \beta_{44i} \Delta EXCH_{t-i} + \sum_{i=1}^{r} \beta_{45i} \Delta PROD_{t-i} + \sum_{i=1}^{s} \beta_{46i} \Delta TRES_{t-i}$$

$$+ \alpha_4 \varepsilon_{t-1} + u_{4t} \tag{9.1.4}$$

$$\Delta PROD_t = \psi_5 + \sum_{i=1}^{m} \beta_{51i} \Delta CRDP_{t-i} + \sum_{i=1}^{n} \beta_{52i} \Delta MTDP_{t-i} + \sum_{i=1}^{o} \beta_{53i} \Delta IRSP_{t-i}$$

$$+ \sum_{i=1}^{p} \beta_{54i} \Delta EXCH_{t-i} + \sum_{i=1}^{r} \beta_{55i} \Delta PROD_{t-i} + \sum_{i=1}^{s} \beta_{56i} \Delta TRES_{t-i}$$

$$+ \alpha_5 \varepsilon_{t-1} + u_{5t} \tag{9.1.5}$$

$$\Delta TRES_t = \psi_6 + \sum_{i=1}^{m} \beta_{61i} \Delta CRDP_{t-i} + \sum_{i=1}^{n} \beta_{62i} \Delta MTDP_{t-i} + \sum_{i=1}^{o} \beta_{63i} \Delta IRSP_{t-i}$$

$$+ \sum_{i=1}^{p} \beta_{64i} \Delta EXCH_{t-i} + \sum_{i=1}^{r} \beta_{65i} \Delta PROD_{t-i} + \sum_{i=1}^{s} \beta_{66i} \Delta TRES_{t-i}$$

$$+ \alpha_6 \varepsilon_{t-1} + u_{6t} \tag{9.1.6}$$

where Δ is the difference operator, m, n, o, p, r and s are the number of lags determined by the Hannan–Quinn information criterion, ε_{t-1} is the lagged error correction term derived from the cointegration equation and u_{it} is a white noise.

This system of equation enables us to investigate multivariate Granger causality. As argued by Lutkepohl (1982), Granger non-causality tests in a bivariate system may be subject to the omitted-variable bias. In addition to this technical aspect, our model does not consider only credit-to-deposit ratio and maturity of deposits, but it takes into account interest rate spread, exchange rates, and the maturity structure of government bonds in order to capture the possible interactions inside the financial system.

Results and discussion

As described above, as a preliminary step, we test for unit root by means of the augmented Dickey–Fuller test (ADF; Dickey and Fuller 1981). Furthermore, we employ the Kwiatkowski *et al.* (1992) test, known as the KPSS test, for the null hypothesis of stationarity of a univariate time series. The results indicate that all variables involved are non-stationary in level, but stationary in first difference; that is, they are all I(1).[10]

Since the non-stationary variables are integrated of the same order, their linear combination may be stationary, indicating that the variables are cointegrated. We test for cointegration or long-run relationship between these variables employing the Johansen–Juselius test (Johansen and Juselius 1990; Johansen 1991). The results are given in Table 9.2. To check the robustness of the results, the Engle–Granger two-step procedure (Engle and Granger 1987) is also performed (not reported here in view of the similar findings).

As shown in Table 9.2, both trace and maximum eigenvalue statistics indicate the presence of two cointegrating equations at the 5 per cent level.

From Table 9.3, it follows that the error correction term is significant only for the CRDP equation. This means that if there is a deviation from the cointegrating relationship, this variable has the tendency to restore the long-run equilibrium,

Table 9.2 Johansen Test for the number of cointegrating relationships

Eigenvalue	$H_0 : r =$	Trace	L Max	Critical values at 95%	
				Trace	L Max
0.23288	0	127.32	62.83	82.49	36.36
0.13025	1	64.49	33.07	59.46	30.04
0.06218	2	31.41	15.21	39.89	23.80
0.0431	3	16.20	10.44	24.31	17.89
0.02365	4	5.76	5.67	12.53	11.44
0.00038	5	0.09	0.09	3.84	3.84

Note: r indicates the number of cointegrating relationships. The critical values for maximum eigenvalue and trace test statistics are given by Johansen and Juselius (1990). The model specification includes an intercept and no trend in the cointegrating equations.

Table 9.3 Temporal Granger causality test results

Sources of causation													
Short-run (F-statistics)						Long-run (LR-statistics)	Joint (short-run/long-run) (F-statistics)						
	CRDP	MTDP	IRSP	EXCH	PROD	TRES	ε_{t-1}	CRDP, ε_{t-1}	MTDP, ε_{t-1}	IRSP, ε_{t-1}	EXCH, ε_{t-1}	PROD, ε_{t-1}	TRES, ε_{t-1}
CRDP	–	0.10	2.54	0.33	0.6	0.73	7.66**	–	3.63*	4.33**	2.59	1.59	1.51
MTDP	0.09	–	1.90	0.07	0.35	0.56	0.18	0.11	–	1.31	0.10	0.32	0.46
IRSP	2.25	24.09**	–	1.33	0.10	0.42	3.47	2.39*	14.03**	–	1.87	0.72	1.11
EXCH	0.08	0.11	0.37	–	0.89	2.14	1.26	0.33	0.64	0.65	–	0.78	1.84
PROD	3.57**	0.12	0.11	0.82	–	0.82	0.48	2.88**	0.27	0.21	0.73	–	0.81
TRES	1.26	1.80	0.24	2.85	2.56*	–	1.82	1.72	1.66	0.70	2.34	3.19**	–

Note: * and ** denote significance at the 5 and 1 per cent level, respectively.

absorbing the effect of the shock to the system. Considering only Equation (9.1.1), we see that both in short and long runs (joint causality), Granger causality runs from MTDP and IRSP to CRDP. This finding implies that in the long run, credit supply in Turkey is affected by changes in the interest rate spread, but it is not preceded by the demand side, which is proxied by production index (PROD). Thus, it can be said that the credit market is greatly affected by cost-driven factors, given the considerable price of uncertainty.

Another important finding is that MTDP is found to be an exogenous variable, which means that none of the other variables involved in the analysis Granger-causes MTDP. This finding is crucial for the focus of our theoretical discussion. The expectations of depositors emerge as an exogenous factor affecting the bank behaviour in terms of credit creation. Considering the high volatility in the Turkish financial market, it is not surprising that expectations change quite frequently under a high inflation and rapid exchange rate adjustments. We argue that expectations of depositors contribute to the shift in the allocation of funds in terms of maturity. On the other hand, in the short- and long-run dynamics, our results indicate that interest rate spread changes should be considered as endogenous variables to both credit supply and deposit maturity. Furthermore, taking into account the results from Equation (9.1.1), we see that bi-directional causality exists between IRSP and CRDP, implying that the price effect and rationing of credits are mutually reinforcing, and give rise to circularity in terms of Granger causality.

Considering both Equations (9.1.5) and (9.1.1), we conclude that a uni-directional causal relationship exists between CRDP and PROD, and that the direction of causality is from the former to the latter. This finding provides enough evidence that the credit market is driven by the supply side rather than the demand side: throughout two decades of open economy experience, the economic cycle is constrained by credit market conditions.

Finally, from Equations (9.1.4), (9.1.5) and (9.1.6), it follows that a uni-directional causality runs from PROD to TRES, indicating that the government budget constraints weigh on the maturity of public financing. We can conclude that there is a connection between tax revenues and the default risk on public debt. As the growth of the economy accelerates and tax revenues increase, the default risk on public debt decreases, leading to a greater facility in terms of maturity for public finance.

Conclusion

In this chapter, we focused on the relationship between the banking sector credit expansion and myopic depositor behaviour in Turkey during the period from 1990 to 2009. Considering the high macroeconomic instability resulting from the two major imbalances (budget deficit and inflation), the past two decades under financial liberalization have not contributed enough to deepen the credit market compared to other countries' experiences.

The multivariate causality analysis provides evidence of a circular relationship, in which the major role can be given to the effect of uncertainty on the structure of the financial market.

To make a brief summary of our results, we underline several major points for the case of Turkey in the 20-year period of financial liberalization:

1   Given the uncertainty on price stability, depositor myopia influences both the liability side of the balance sheet of the banking sector and the interest rate spread in the financial market.
2   The interest rate spread and credit ratio have a bi-directional causal relationship implying a feedback mechanism.
3   Credit creation precedes production, implying that cycles are instead driven by the supply side of the credit market. This result implies that:
4   Given that the credit conditions drive the growth of the economy, the budget constraint of the public sector improves in a way that leads to a decline in the default risk and thus facilitates borrowing in the longer term.

For further research, we may suggest different extensions of our results. A possible extension of this work would be to conduct similar analyses for other economies, particularly small open economies or countries under fiscal dominance. The case of Greece would be an interesting exercise to see whether such a feedback mechanism between uncertainty and the financial market is in play regarding the recent fiscal imbalances. A panel data analysis instead of a time-series approach should also be considered.

Notes

1   This research has been realized with financial support from the Galatasaray University Scientific Research Fund (project number: 11.103.004).
2   The twin crises of 1994 and 2001 are examples of such episodes where maturity and currency mismatches inside the banking sector amplified the severity of the liquidity crisis. In a recent study, Karabulut *et al.* (2010) investigated the determinants of the currency crises in Turkey and concluded that the share of short-term debt in GDP and the ratio of credit to deposit were the determinants of these crises.
3   See Kara and Öğünç (2008) for more discussion.
4   Tirole (2002) argues that short-term debt might be an optimal response to systemic or macroeconomic risks.
5   Since there is no information on the maturity of the credits, we cannot directly argue concerning the shortening of credit maturity.
6   See TCMB (2008) for further discussion.
7   The low savings rate is a controversial issue for the Turkish case, due to two decades of chronic high inflation. Van Rijckeghem and Üçer (2008) discuss how the saving–credit relation in Turkey is strongly linked to cycle effects.
8   Recently, new econometric techniques have been developed to address the non-stationarity problem. For example, while Maximum entropy bootstrap (Meboot; see Vinod 2004) can be used with non-stationary data, autoregressive distributed lag (ARDL) models (Pesaran *et al.* 2001) are designed for dealing with the variables that are integrated of different orders.
9   Since the literature is very rich on the subject, we do not discuss the methodological issues in detail. See, for example, Hamilton (1994) and Hayashi (2000) for a detailed time-series analysis.
10   We do not report the stationary test results to conserve space. All unreported results are available from the authors upon request.

References

Bencivenga, V. R. and Smith, B. D. (1991). "Financial intermediation and endogenous growth", *Review of Economic Studies*, 58(2): 195–209.

Bussière, M., Fratzscher, M. and Koeniger, W. (2006). "Uncertainty and debt-maturity in emerging markets", *Topics in Macroeconomics*, 6(1): 1–28.

Calomiris, C. and Kahn, C. (1991). "The role of demandable debt in structuring optimal banking arrangements", *American Economic Review*, 81(3): 497–513.

Chang, R. and Velasco, A. (2000). "Liquidity crises in emerging markets: Theory and policy", in B. Bernanke and J. Rotemberg (Eds), *NBER Macroeconomics Annual 1999*. Cambridge, MA: The MIT Press, pp. 11–78.

Diamond, D. W. (1984). "Financial intermediation and delegated monitoring", *Review of Economic Studies*, 51(3): 393–414.

Diamond, D. W. and Dybvig, P. H. (1983). "Bank runs, deposit insurance, and liquidity", *The Journal of Political Economy*, 91(3): 401–419.

Diamond, D. W. and Rajan, R. G. (2012). "Illiquid banks, financial stability, and interest rate policy", *Journal of Political Economy*, 120(3): 552–591.

Diamond, D. W. and He, Z. (2014). "A theory of debt maturity: The long and short of debt overhang", *Journal of Finance*, 69(2): 719–762.

Dickey, D. A. and Fuller, W. A. (1981). "Likelihood ratio statistics for autoregressive processes", *Econometrica*, 49(4): 1057–1072.

Engle, R. F. and Granger, C. W. J. (1987). "Cointegration and error correction: Representation, estimation, and testing", *Econometrica*, 55(2): 251–276.

Flannery, M. (1994). "Debt maturity and the deadweight cost of leverage: Optimally financing banking", *American Economic Review*, 84(1): 320–331.

Gatev, E. and Strahan, P. E. (2006). "Banks' advantage at supplying liquidity: Theory and evidence from the commercial paper market", *The Journal of Finance*, 61(2): 867–892.

Granger, C. W. J. (1969). "Investigation of causal relations by econometric models and cross-spectral methods", *Econometrica*, 37(3): 424–438.

Granger, C. W. J. (1988). "Some recent developments in a concept of causality", *Journal of Econometrics*, 39(1): 199–211.

Granger, C. W. J. and Newbold, P. (1974). "Spurious regressions in econometrics", *Journal of Econometrics*, 2: 111–120.

Hamilton, J. D. (1994). *Time Series Analysis*. Princeton, NJ: Princeton University Press.

Hayashi, F. (2000). *Econometrics*. Princeton, NJ: Princeton University Press.

Jeanne, O. and Guscina, A. (2006). "Government debt in emerging market countries: A new data set", IMF Working Paper WP/06/98.

Johansen, S. (1991). "Estimation and hypothesis testing of cointegration vectors in Gaussian vector autoregressive models", *Econometrica*, 59(6): 1551–1580.

Johansen, S. and Juselius, K. (1990). "Maximum likelihood estimation and inference on cointegration – with applications to the demand for money", *Oxford Bulletin of Economics and Statistics*, 52(2): 169–210.

Kara, H. and Öğünç, F. (2008). "Inflation targeting and exchange rate pass-through: The Turkish experience", *Emerging Markets Finance and Trade*, 44(6): 52–66.

Karabulut, G., Bilgin, M. H. and Danisoglu, A. C. (2010). "Determinants of currency crises in Turkey: Some empirical evidence", *Emerging Markets Finance and Trade*, 46: 51–58.

Kashyap, A. K., Rajan, R. A. and Stein, J. C. (2002). "Banks as liquidity providers: An explanation for the co-existence of lending and deposit-taking", *The Journal of Finance*, 57(1): 33–74.

Kaufmann, D., Kraay, A. and Mastruzzi, M. (2009). "Governance matters VIII: Aggregate and individual governance indicators, 1996–2008", World Bank Policy Research Working Paper No. 4978. Washington, DC: World Bank.

Kwiatkowski, D., Phillips, P. C. B., Schmidt, P. and Shin, Y. (1992). "Testing the null hypothesis of stationarity against the alternative of a unit root", *Journal of Econometrics*, 54(1–3): 159–178.

Levine, R., Loayza, N. and Beck, T. (2000). "Financial intermediation and growth: Causality and causes", *Journal of Monetary Economics*, 46(1): 31–77.

Lutkepohl, H. (1982). "Non-causality due to omitted variables", *Journal of Econometrics*, 19(2–3): 367–378.

Pesaran, M. H., Shin Y. C. and Smith, R. (2001). "Bound testing approaches to the analysis of level relationships", *Journal of Applied Econometrics*, 16(3): 289–326.

TCMB (Türkiye Cumhuriyet Merkez Bankasi/Central Bank of the Republic of Turkey) (2008). *Finansal İstikrar Raporu*, Kasım [November] 7: 1–76.

Tirole, J. (2002). *Financial Crises, Liquidity, and the International Monetary System.* Princeton, NJ: Princeton University Press.

Van Rijckeghem, C. and Üçer, M. (2008). "The evolution and determinants of the Turkish private saving rate: What lessons for policy?", paper presented at the TÜSIAD-Koç University Economic Research Forum Conference on Micro-Macro Perspectives on Private Savings in Turkey, 11 June 2008.

Vinod, H. D. (2004). "Ranking mutual funds using unconventional utility theory and stochastic dominance", *Journal of Empirical Finance*, 11(3): 353–377.

World Bank (2015). World Development Indicators. Available at: http://data.worldbank.org/products/wdi.

10 Dollarization and financial development

The experience of Latin American countries

Eugenia Correa and Alicia Girón

Introduction[1]

Dollarization in the 1970s and 1980s, banking crises in the 1980s and 1990s, and the Global Financial Crisis in the first decade of this century have all changed the main parameters of financial competition in the largest Latin American countries (LAc). Financial structures have changed as well, meaning that the financing relationships between banks and domestic firms have too. In addition, market-orientated policies have deeply changed economies, including the role of public credit, the ownership of public and domestic firms, and also the foreign financing of the local affiliates of global firms. It has not been an abrupt change. It has taken time and has adapted to changing political conditions.

The objective of this chapter is to study the main trends in the transformation of financial systems in Latin America in recent decades. It proposes an analysis following three historical stages of great changes: first, the growth of credit from foreign banks and the subsequent "debt crisis"; second, the high levels of foreign credit through bonds and the public debt "bonds crisis"; third, the growth of foreign credit to private firms and the expansion of global institutional investors. This chapter sustains the argument that the local currency–dollar rivalry created dollarization, as monetary policy or as a market trend, which has had direct consequences for the profitability of local firms.

Dollarization has taken different forms: full currency substitution, as in Ecuador, El Salvador or Panama; the denomination of bank deposits and loans in US dollars, which is the most common measure of dollarization; indexing or emission of financial instruments, such as *Tesobonos* in Mexico (1994), or Brazilian public bonds denominated in dollars; external credit to the public and private sectors. The International Monetary Fund (IMF) defines dollarization as "Co-circulation—also commonly known as dollarization—that results when a foreign currency, often the U.S. dollar, used as a means of payment and store of value in parallel with the national currency" (IMF 2010: 57). This chapter takes a wide definition of dollarization. However, what is crucial for its development is the credit expansion in US dollars and competition with local currency credit.

The dollarization of economies has been partly a response to the conditions of investment financing. A traditional problem of the local financial system is that it has served only in the financing of "goods in transit", as Minsky (1991 [1977]) explained. In the years following World War II, stable growth was possible because of public external debt, along with stable exchange rates and interest rates. However, since the 1970s, dollarization has been the response of liberalization and a condition of financial deregulation. Since then, the process of *pesificación*, or return to the peso, has been partial and temporary when applied. This monetary rivalry has been building a dual monetary circuit, with partial support from the international reserves of central banks, but with significant limitations when the credit cycle becomes unfavourable for exporting firms.

We begin this chapter with a short description of the first wave of credit growth in the dollar, produced by financial opening and credit expansion in the form of syndicated loans from large foreign banks. The chapter supports the idea that the financial crisis in the 1980s originated from financial liberalization and not because of financial repression as one could argue through the analyses of McKinnon (1973) and Shaw (1973). Later, we analyse the second wave of credit expansion, via bonds and securitization, which started in the 1990s, but which extended into the first decades of the current century. The third part studies the two waves of banking crisis and the emergence of global banks' subsidiaries as a result of the weaknesses of domestic banks. The last section shows that the dollarization process – analysed as currency and credit competition – is built through foreign debt and its many liabilities and returns, but also through the growing market for profits in foreign currencies. Minsky's (1991 [1977]) proposal to study local banking systems as institutions which create money for financing "goods in transit", warns about the double monetary circuit, and it is precisely this circuit that dictates the investments and profits of foreign and local firms (Parguez 2010; Vidal and Marshall 2013).

Financial opening and crisis: the first wave of foreign private credit

In the 1970s and until 1981 the LAc were net recipients of loan capital from transnational banks aiming to expand. The rapid growth of domestic and international credit banks in developed countries (between 1970 and 1981) managed to place in Latin America funds worth about US$200 billion (Girón 1995). Those credits were increasingly given with short maturity and adjustable interest rates. The rise of interest rates at the end of the 1970s increased refinancing of the principal and also overdue interest. In just four years, the external debt of Latin America (1978–1981) almost doubled, precisely as a result of rising interest rates. In some countries, growth in total external debt was even greater because of the degree of exposure to private creditors and the concentration of maturities. Such was the case for Argentina, Chile and Uruguay, and to a lesser extent, Mexico, Colombia, Ecuador, Brazil and Venezuela.

However, starting in 1981, creditors stopped the refinancing. The scheme of accepting further debt for payment in order to avoid the suspension of payments reached its limit with the Mexican crisis in 1982. In several LAcs, especially those with the highest debts, the suspension of payments began months later. This was mainly due to creditors staggering the maturities of the credits unpaid on their balance sheets through refinancing. The intention was to manage balance sheets in order to decrease the pressure for more reserves against bad loans, depending on the regulations in force in each country (Correa 1992).

The external debt – contracted in the 1970s – changed the financial systems and the conditions of banking competition. In addition, the largest banks started participating in international financial markets, and also in the syndicate loans lent to their own governments through the Euromarket.

With the suspension of payments from debtor governments, and the dollarization of their domestic balance sheets, the largest banks from Argentina, Brazil and Mexico confronted great market stress and bankruptcies. Besides the rapid growth of external bank loans since the 1970s, domestic financial systems had been undergoing radical changes. With the collapse of the gold-dollar standard, banks rapidly faced new competition in an increasingly international market. In addition, these credit flows also competed with local activities, meaning that lending and deposit rates and deposit instruments were adapted to this financial liberalization. From the 1970s, one could note some crucial liberalization reforms:

1   Authorization to create foreign currency deposits (Argentina, Colombia, Costa Rica, Chile, Peru, Uruguay and Venezuela).
2   Issuance of government debt, making way for public financing in the open market. Its prevalence in the 1980s changed monetary policy (Argentina, Brazil, Chile, Mexico, Peru and Uruguay).
3   Liberalization of interest rates and its connection to international financial market trends (Argentina, Brazil, Chile, Mexico, Uruguay and Venezuela).
4   Establishment and/or growth of foreign non-bank financial companies: leasing, factoring, mutual funds, insurance companies, etc. (Argentina, Brazil, Chile, Mexico, Uruguay and Venezuela).

The debt crisis implied devaluations of local currencies and created banking crises in Argentina, Peru, Chile, Colombia, Uruguay and Mexico. These crises, together with the stabilization and adjustment programmes of the IMF, imposed major changes on financial systems in two forms: first, in the particular forms of bailout designs; and second, in the design of the new competitive environment. Therefore, the 1980s gave rise to structural changes in LAc economies:

1   the growth of state involvement in the financial sector, as a lender of last resort to rescue companies and banks (Argentina, Bolivia, Chile, Mexico, Uruguay and Venezuela);
2   the laying of the foundations for the privatization process and the placement of domestic companies' stock in local stock markets (Argentina, Chile, Mexico).
3   the exchange of debt for shares in companies and foreign investment through the purchase of discounted debt (Argentina, Brazil, Chile, Mexico).

4   multiplication of instruments, sophisticated financial services for large treas-
    uries requiring diversification of their portfolios and assets looking for higher
    returns and lower risks.

Moreover, the constant pressure to reduce the fiscal deficit (the first point of the
Washington Consensus) meant the closure of public funding for development
banks which in Latin America had an important place in the overall financial
system. Development banks played a major role in financing the imported composition of public investment, intermediating funds in foreign currency for private
companies' investments. As Minsky (1991 [1977]) points out, domestic banks only
have the conditions of "financing transit-goods". Changes in the amount and composition of funding have had important consequences for policy and economic
structures in all LAcs. The significant dollarization of the 1970s was reversed in
the 1980s, due to declining external credit. However, the increasing pressure to
liquidate loan commitments in dollars kept the LA economies in the dollar credit
creation circuit (Parguez 2010).

Capital inflows: bonds markets and foreign direct investment (FDI)

The flow of funds into Latin America and its largest economies was modified
again in the 1990s due to financial deregulation in the US market. The decline in
interest rates and the expansion of public spending undertaken by Latin American
authorities to face a new episode of over-indebtedness was accompanied by a new
wave of financial innovation. This also spread to emerging markets. Indeed, it was
precisely in those years that this situation was created.

The high performance of various financial instruments, including securities
from different latitudes, remained one of the pillars of profitability achieved in US
dollars by banks and US funds. This model of financial business reached a temporary limit because of financial crises in Southeast Asia, Russia and Brazil in the
late 1990s (Kregel 1998a, 1998b, 2000; Correa 2013).

Capital inflows to LAcs in the 1990s came from new portfolio strategies in
international financial markets of non-bank financial firms, particularly as a result
of financial deregulation. Institutional investors channelled their investments into
some LA countries to take advantage of at least three conditions: the attractive
returns on government securities, at least in Argentina, Brazil and Mexico; local
firms' initial public offerings, especially in Mexico, Chile, Argentina, Brazil and
Venezuela; the interest of domestic financial firms in associating with investment
banks in order to participate in the lucrative business of securitization, issuance
and placement of bonds and interest rate arbitrage.

Thus, the (public and private) debt in securities grew from 3.4 per cent of the
GDP in 1994 to 17.4 per cent ten years later. The high speed of issuance and
the profitability of investments in Latin American securities found an early limit
in the Mexican crisis of 1994–1995. Even though it was the greatest financial
crisis in the history of Mexico, the large volume of portfolio inflows continued.

Table 10.1 Latin American countries: foreign portfolio investment net inflows
(billion US$)

	Total Portfolio	Debt Securities
1980s	0.4	−0.15
1990s	367.2	281.4
2000s	176.0	80.4
2010–2014	639.2	468.4

Source: Cepal (2016).

It again faced a second and remarkable limit with the crises in Brazil and Argentina of 1998–1999 and 2001–2002 respectively. The third wave of foreign portfolio inflows started with the great financial crisis of 2007, and was driven by the high interest rates on public debt in local currencies, as seen in Table 10.1.

Portfolio investment reached its first high point in 1993, when net foreign portfolio investment reached US$80 billion, its second peak in 2007 with US$80 billion, and its third peak in 2010 with US$144 billion (Cepal 2016). However, the level of profitability it reached was not sustainable. The outflow of dividends and interest payments required the entry of new and increased flows, or a substitution of investors who would accept another level of profitability.

The profitability of Latin American financial markets has depended on both the interest rate spreads with mature markets – and even with other emerging markets – and the exchange rate behaviour, as well as the size and liquidity achieved by the domestic markets. The reform of pension systems was explicitly targeted at improving these last two (Correa 2015).

One of the forces that gave a new boost to the bond market and the placements from institutional investors was the wave of privatizations in the second half of the 1990s. Mainly it was this process of privatization that explains the dynamic FDI to Latin America in those years. This was especially the case in Brazil, Chile, Argentina and Mexico. From 1997 to 2001, FDI flows into LAcs reached almost US$375 billion and the profits remitted amounted to US$93.3 billion, representing almost 25 per cent of the former figure.

This stage of privatizations distinctively influenced the largest banks and non-bank financial institutions, which had been weakened or broken by banking crises in preceding years. This was the case for Mexico, Argentina, Chile, Venezuela, Peru, and to a lesser extent, Brazil. Thus, while foreign banks in the region handled 20 per cent of the total assets of banks in 1994, this figure rose to more than 40 per cent by 2009. In the most recent years, this number has been estimated at around 30 per cent (World Bank 2015a).

Also highlighted in these years was the privatization of the pension funds, especially in Argentina, Bolivia, Chile, Colombia, Mexico and Peru. Systems of intergenerational solidarity had been formed within Latin American countries so that the contributions of active workers funded the retirement of others. With privatization, pension funds were formed, receiving contributions from active workers, while retired workers continued to receive their income from public budgets. While policies allowing a balanced budget continued, this meant significant reductions in other areas of social spending. In countries with a compulsory private system (Mexico, Chile, Colombia, Peru, among others) pension funds account for nearly 20 per cent of GDP in recent years (International Federation of Pension Funds Administrators 2014). Foreign banks, mainly from Spain and the United States, manage an important part of these pension funds.

The following and remarkable stage of FDI extended growth ran from 2007 to 2014, in which US$1.3 trillion accumulated, along with a transfer of profits of more than US$870 billion, or 67 per cent of FDI.

Thus, in this period, the presence of US dollars in LA economies grew; either with the expansion of global investment portfolios into local securities markets, or through FDI, and even with the well-known foreign debt flows. But the outflows linked to those inflows also grew, as shown in Table 10.2.

Dollarization in the three largest economies increased, even with different financial systems. For example, in Argentina, a Currency Board operated in the 1990s, the Argentine peso was fixed to the US dollar, and the money supply depended on foreign exchange earnings. In Mexico, the largest banks came to be owned by global banks, managing more than 80 per cent of the total banking assets. In Brazil, even with high inflation in the 1990s, bank assets in foreign banks grew to more than 40 per cent of total assets. There are three different processes of dollarization of domestic credit, as discussed below, which continued to develop over the following decades.

The new economic growth cycle started in 2003–2004 and began a period of increasing domestic funding, linked to the rise in prices of raw materials. The decline in international interest rates with the great crisis likewise served to decrease the cost of refinancing debt. As in the 1990s, this new cycle of growth included a significant wave of foreign portfolio investments, but this time in debt securities and mainly in local currencies.

For example, Mexico had between 2005 and 2014 a net foreign equity investment of US$13.8 billion and Brazil more than US$60 billion. In the same years, accumulated foreign investment in debt markets went to US$287.2 billion

Table 10.2 Latin American countries: capital inflows and outflows (billion US$)

	Capital Inflows: FDI, Portfolio; Loans	Outflows: Rents of Investments and Debt (–)
1990–1994	269.9	224.9
1995–1999	455.7	339.9
2000–2004	252.1	388.7
2005–2009	831.2	683.5
2010–2014	1903.7	997.7

Source: Cepal (2016).

Table 10.3 Outstanding external debt of private sector (billion US$)

	Argentina	Brazil	Mexico	LAc
2000	25.9	112.6	50.5	183.4
2005	26.3	69.5	32.7	134.9
2010	31.1	184.9	52.5	309.1
2014	50.0	320.2	98.1	559.6

Source: World Bank (2015b).

and US$160 billion respectively. Most of the securities in debt markets are government bonds (Cepal 2016).

This trend came with an important increase in the foreign debt contracted by the private sector, which has doubled in Mexico and Argentina in the last 15 years, while in Brazil it has increased by more than 180 per cent, as shown in Table 10.3.

However, the World Bank statistics offer little help in observing the phenomenon of the dollarization of domestic credit as a result of falling prices of commodities for export, such as raw materials and oil; or the decline in FDI inflows starting in 2014.

The process of dollarization, which entails monetary and credit rivalry, was constructed during three decades (1970s, 1980s and 1990s) hand-in-hand with the model of neo-colonial exploitation of raw materials and energy sources and workers (as a large reservoir for employment in *maquiladoras* [foreign-owned factories] or migration). In the early years of this century, the model was consolidated with changes in natural resource ownership and extraction contracts for the global corporations that are dominant in each sector. These trends are clearly illustrated in areas such as mining, agricultural production, oil and energy, among others (Sánchez-Albavera and Lardé 2006; Correa *et al.* 2009; IAASTD 2009; Zubizarreta 2013).

In turn, the three largest countries have taken different courses in their production patterns. The approach of Mexico, for example, is most related to the expansion of global corporations in the automotive and energy sectors, and to high migration; for Brazil, to the exploitation of natural resources on a large scale in addition to a diversified industrial base widely supported by public funds; and then there is Argentina's trajectory, with an agro-industrial and automotive base, of both domestic and foreign ownership.

However, those three economies, with all their differences, have shown in recent years the economic problems generated by an economic model mainly based on the export of primary goods or the *maquiladora*-type industrial processes that do not strengthen local production chains. The cycle of financial transformations, focused on the growing participation of banks and global corporations, again reached new limits. But as will be shown in the following section, new areas of expansion for asset securitization, based on high-growth economic activities, were still available.

Banking crisis and global banks' subsidiaries

The domestic banking systems of the largest Latin American economies were languishing because of successive banking crises (Ffrench-Davis 2001). Public credit was decreasing too, mainly because of fiscal balance policies that were preventing public banks from accessing Central Bank credit, forcing these to finance themselves at market rates.

The new financial competition in the region's markets, caused by the opening to foreign credit on a large scale and the liberalization of capital markets, created a constant confrontation between different yield structures, interest rates, margins and other important banking and credit prices. The weakening of some domestic banks became banking crises with successive episodes of varying magnitude.

The first wave of banking crises in the early 1980s was linked to the sudden advance of financial liberalization in the late 1970s, which directly created a huge volume of credit liabilities in foreign currencies for local governments. In a few years, domestic banks faced bankruptcy, triggered by currency mismatches and the insolvency of their own governments. Domestic banks were creditors (within banking syndicates) of their own governments which were in default. Banking crises were then observed in Argentina (1980 and 1989), Bolivia (1986), Chile (1981), Colombia (1982), Mexico (1982) and Peru (1983), among others (Lindgren *et al.* 1996; Cepal 2000). As governments and banks stopped having voluntary access to the international markets, their obvious bankruptcy occurred. The role of the lender of last resort in US dollars, like the IMF or US Treasury, and the financial crisis lasted almost throughout the entire decade.

Banking crises in the 1990s were more closely linked to domestic macro-economic conditions that were responding to the changing expectations of profit-ability in more open and global markets. These crises occurred in Argentina (1995), Bolivia (1994), Brazil (1994), Ecuador (1995) and Mexico (1994), among others. This second wave of banking crises witnessed massive bank failures, various forms of government assistance, and high fiscal costs. This wave was seen also in Asia, Africa, Central and Eastern Europe. In several of these economies, the crisis prompted a process of growing foreign control of the financial system. According to IMF figures, in Central Europe, for example, foreign control increased from 8 per cent in 1994 to over 56 per cent in 1999. In Latin America, excluding Brazil and Mexico, it rose from 13 per cent to 45 per cent.

This change in ownership of the most important financial firms was not limited to deposit banks. It also included insurance companies and a range of non-bank financial intermediaries that were part of investment banks and brokerages (Mathieson and Roldós 2001). Among banks, the rapid positioning of the two big Spanish banks, Banco Bilbao Vizacaya Argentaria (BBVA) and Banco Santander Central Hispano (BSCH), and of US Citigroup stand out.

The significant growth of global bank subsidiaries in some of the largest economies in Latin America has so far faced obstacles in both Argentina and Brazil. In the first case, the crisis of 2002–2003 and the financial policies that followed have reduced the share of these banks in local assets which had accounted

Table 10.4 The 50 largest banks in Latin America by ownership[a] (%)

	Domestic Private	Foreign	Public
Argentina	0	0	100
Brazil	45.5	27.3	27.3
Mexico	20	80	0

Source: América Economía (2015).

Note: a The 50 largest Latin American banks from the ranking by assets.

for more than 50 per cent of total assets before the Currency Board crisis. In the second case, it was slowed by the financial policies of leftist governments which strengthened public banks, as shown in Table 10.4, using data from *América Economía* (2015).

Several analyses have been written about the origins of the banking crisis. For example, there are those that attribute them to national behaviour, which is a difficult position to sustain when crises have occurred massively worldwide in recent years. Other explanations are based on the idea that the financial systems in emerging markets are fragile and external shocks can quickly turn into a banking crisis, particularly due to destabilizing macroeconomic policies, including hyper-inflation, large devaluations, nationalizations, and everything that undermines the confidence of investors. In particular, systems with inadequate accounting standards, with unreliable judicial–legal frameworks, relatively small intermediaries, short-term liabilities, little financial depth, and poor development of non-bank financial institutions are seen as vulnerable (Rojas-Suárez and Weisbrod 1997).

Financial reforms in the 1990s led to ownership changes in many important financial institutions. However, the proposed benefits for society were not achieved, including a decline in funding costs, greater availability of financing for local businesses investment, better options for returns for savers and a decline in poverty (World Bank 2002).

In addition, a number of the 30 largest banks have partial foreign ownership with the most notable exceptions so far being the largest Brazilian banks. The banks that expanded most in the region have been the Spanish BBVA and BSCH (Vilariño 2001; Ferreiro and Rodríguez 2004), having the largest branch networks and participating in the administration of pension funds; and the US and UK banks, like Citibank, Goldman Sachs, JP Morgan Chase and HSBC.

The criticisms regarding the prevalent financing conditions in the region at the beginning of this century, caused by the policies of openness and financial deregulation, manifested themselves politically and at the national level in Latin American countries. After tough elections, a group of countries had new governments that put aside policies recommended by the IMF and even abandoned its economic and financial supervision, especially those countries that could settle all loans with the IMF.

In turn, the idea that the processes of liberalization and financial openness had led to economic and financial instabilities, banking crises, slowing or no economic growth, rising poverty, etc., was confirmed (Girón *et al.* 2005; Claessens *et al.* 2014).

The IMF kept repeating that liberalization and opening had positive impacts on growth, although it accepted that the empirical evidence in this regard was weak. In any case, liberalization was accepted as a cause of instability when macro-economic policies have been inconsistent, and particularly when institutional requirements and financial supervision were inadequate. The processes of liberal-ization and opening up have worsened income distribution, levels of poverty and the conditions of education and health in developing countries (Demirgüç-Kunt and Detragiache 1998; Claessens *et al.* 2014).

The argument sustained here is that financial liberalization and deregulation have created conditions that weakened financial systems. Domestic banks have not been able to expand their offshore activities at the pace that their economies required. This is especially true under conditions of massive capital outflows, or high and sustained returns on capital in domestic markets, and for those domestic capitals that are internationalizing. Again, Brazil has been the only large country to conserve the domestic ownership of its private banks.

During the first 15 years of the twenty-first century, two major trends in the financial systems can be identified. First, financial systems were being restruc-tured in order to limit the supply of local currency funding, in addition to articu-lated infrastructure development and the working capital of big business. Also, mortgage and consumer credit segments were growing. In great contrast to what was happening in developed economies, bank lending to the private sector in the region has remained at consistently low levels, as seen in Table 10.5.

It may be noted that lending to the private sector in Argentina and Mexico remains below 30 per cent of GDP, whereas Brazil's lending, although showing increases in the last ten years, has been based largely on public bank lending. These public banks in many other LA countries have been participating in only a few activities and have generally decreased their share of domestic credit.

In addition, domestic financial systems are very fragile in the face of massive capital outflows or inflows. In the LAc crises, the common denominator of large capital inflows can be identified in the run-up to a crisis, and has also been identified to preclude subsequent outflows (Ffrench-Davis and Ocampo 2001). The waves of massive capital inflows and outflows occur through bank loans,

Table 10.5 Credit to private sector (local and foreign) (% of GDP)

	Argentina	Brazil	Mexico
1990	15.5	30.0	16.3
1995	19.7	32.6	25.2
2000	23.2	28.7	11.4
2005	9.6	31.0	16.2
2010	11.6	52.8	24.3
2014	14.4	69.1	31.4

Source: World Bank (2015a).

portfolio allocations in stocks or bonds, or FDI as well. Financial systems, even though they become more liquid and deeper than in the past, remain very vulnerable and defaults can arise because of currency mismatching or the massive increase of non-performing loans. A large wave of capital outflows can create a systemic bankruptcy for both the domestic banks and the subsidiaries of global banks. This is true as long as the governments do not take the decision to regulate these capital outflows.

The net capital inflows to Latin American countries, according to World Bank data, were positive during some years in the 1990s, mainly because of FDI inflows, which were explained by the large-scale privatizations in Brazil, Argentina and Mexico. But from the great crisis in 2007 onwards, those inflows have had high growth, primarily in portfolio placements and FDI, and especially in Brazil and Mexico. The trend of capital inflows (which include loans, portfolio allocations and FDI) and income outflows (which include payments of interest, dividends and profits) changed after the great crisis. There were years of large amounts of inflows to local financial markets attracted by higher interest rates, especially in the government bonds in the deep and strong markets of Brazil and also Mexico (see Tables 10.5 and 10.6).

Since late 2014, FDI and portfolio allocations started to decline, linked to the overall cycle of lower economic growth. Just as Brazil was the largest recipient of capital inflows, now it is the country with the worst recession in the last three years. In fact, none of the largest economies have the conditions to find and develop growing sources of foreign currency flows at the rate at which interest payments on its liabilities require. This becomes especially evident in times of drastic changes in export prices and/or increased demand for dividends and pro-cyclical repatriated profits.

These two major trends in the financial systems have as a common feature the direct link to the way the double monetary circuit has been working: highly

Table 10.6 Latin American countries: capital inflows and outflows (billion US$)

	Capital Inflows	Outflows: Rents of Investments and Debt (–)
2001	70.9	77.4
2005	97.7	105.3
2006	117.6	131.2
2007	268.9	152.9
2008	168.7	159.5
2009	178.8	135.3
2010	400.5	195.6
2011	376.4	221.5
2012	359.1	198.4
2013	377.4	193.1
2014	399.8	189.2

Source: Cepal (2016).

Table 10.7 Foreign credit to private sector* (% of total)

	Argentina	Brazil	Mexico
1995	15.3	3.7	26.9
2000	18.7	14.4	33.4
2005	33.3	18.8	26.7
2007	22.6	10.3	19.7
2008	17.8	8.2	19.0
2009	14.9	9.7	20.6
2010	13.1	9.6	21.7
2011	10.8	9.4	21.7
2012	9.2	11.0	25.1
2013	7.9	13.3	28.2

Source: World Bank (2015a).

Note: *Foreign credit to private sector as percentage of the total credit (local and external) to private sector.

constrained financing in domestic currency coupled with a great expansion of credit in foreign currency.

An indirect indicator of this process is the external credit to the private sector in its relation to domestic credit. During 1995–2003 and 2008–2014, the external credit in relation to the domestic credit in Argentina, Brazil and Mexico was becoming increasingly important, as may be observed in Table 10.7.

In the last five decades, many Latin American countries have seen their financial structures change significantly. These countries have moved from the model that Minsky called "financing of transit-goods" – which was generously funded by public credit (Lichtensztejn 1984) – towards a model based on global banks, securitization and high returns on public bonds. All these changes have not modified the main trends of dollarization, but rather evolved with them.

Dollarization, investment and profits in the "new financial architecture"

The international financial architecture has been one of the recurrent themes that arises every time international financial crises spring up, such as the ones in Asia, Russia and Brazil in the 1990s. Roughly at the time of these crises, several important reports were issued. These include the US Congress Meltzer Report (2000), or the Group of 22 Report (1998) – the association that was created in Washington in April 1998 and presented its Report together with the meeting of the IMF and World Bank in October of the same year. The Goldstein Report (Goldstein *et al.* 1999) and that of the UN Conference on Trade and Development (UNCTAD 2001) were also significant. Relevant books and articles were also written, such as that of Eichengreen (1999).

The great crisis of 2007 once again increased the production of financial architecture reports, such as the Stiglitz Report organized by the United Nations (2009), or the UNCTAD Report (2015). Another important outcome was the creation of the Financial Stability Board (FSB), a multi-institutional organization composed of the finance ministers and Central Bank governors of the G20 countries, the IMF, the World Bank, the Organisation for Economic Co-operation and Development (OECD) and the Bank for International Settlements (BIS). Until February 2016, the Governor of the Bank of England chaired this organization and it was the most important body advancing reforms for the global financial market. It has produced policies, standards of supervision and regulation for the financial sector.

Successive financial crises were making the need for reforms ever more evident. The majority of these reports point to the need for reforming the Bretton Woods institutions, but also for formal mechanisms to negotiate international debt, regulate international capital flows, and stabilize the persistent currency volatility among major industrial countries. The great crisis represented new challenges such as systemic risk and "too big to fail" banks, banks' subsidiary regulation, regulation of financial innovation and credit rating agencies, and even reforms of regulatory institutions.

Meanwhile, the focus of the Financial Stability Board (2015) on the international financial architecture is different, especially in terms of the financial sector in developing economies, with financial problems like portfolio flow volatility, foreign currency over-indebtedness, higher interest rates for financing in local currency, and high risk ratings, among others.

Building global financial governance is under way in legislation (Dodd-Frank Act 2010) led by financial consortia to stabilize financial markets and continue global expansion. An important element of this process is the participating governments' adoption of common legal frameworks or resolution processes in the case of the bankruptcy of financial institutions. These procedures allow for the legalization of bailouts wherever the subsidiaries of the global financial institutions are located. Also, they allow for the separation of profitable segments from the larger entity upon bankruptcy.

Thus, the reconstruction of the international financial architecture, more like financial governance driven by the market, has not affected the main structural characteristics of the double monetary circuit and the dollarization trends in Latin American countries. This double monetary circuit, along with liberalization and deregulation, mean an ongoing need of US dollars for lenders of last resort. This role has been played either by the US Federal Reserve or the IMF, with conditions placed over macro policies and financial system regulation.

This feature of the financial system has developed to such an extent that the IMF continues a programme of assessment of financial systems (IMF 2001). This programme includes a range of actions to promote financial deepening and to harmonize regulatory frameworks. It states that

> the areas of improvement have included reforming financial law (law of the central bank and banking supervision), conducted in line with international best practices, [to] strengthen risk management in the insurance sector, modernize payment systems to collect and monitor indicators of financial

sector vulnerability, intervene and resolve problems of troubled financial institutions.

(IMF 2001: 19)

However, neither the double supervision (domestic and IMF) nor the regulations concerning capitalization, good practice, fraud control, money laundering, risk management, modernization of systems, etc. have been able to contain the effects of dollarization on the balances of the banking sector or regional economies as a whole.

Quantifications and comparable information on the level of dollarization of LA economies are hard to come by and difficult to elaborate on one's own. However, for example, in Chile, 22 per cent of total banking assets are in foreign currency; in Peru, the dollarization ratio of liquidity is 27 per cent; and for Latin America as a whole, the World Bank gives 27 per cent. However, these figures leave out many off-balance-sheet operations as well as important segments of the economy that are dollarized.

As has been seen with the large-scale development of global banks, institutional investors and securitization in local markets, dollarization is also a strong force of economic structural change. The dollarization of profits encouraged not only growing public and private indebtedness, but also privatizations, mergers and acquisitions. Domestic firms and investors as well as foreign banks and firms do measure profitability in foreign currency. It is not pure desire, but pure economic rationality.

Moreover, as the subsidiaries of foreign banks have shown in Argentina, Brazil and Mexico, they have no special interest in expanding and deepening domestic markets. They wish to take advantage of a position that guarantees a return above that achieved in their countries of origin. They cannot face the currency mismatching against their profits or dividends at the expense of shareholders. Losses due to exchange rate adjustment can be passed on to insurance deposits or any other mechanism of government support or to depositors' savings.

To the extent that income from commodities exports started to fall in 2014, it is inevitable that the dynamics of dollarization will thrust upon regional economies new episodes of financial fragility and the devaluation of local currencies. Even with foreign banks having more than 30 per cent of the market, and stalling the most acute consequences of this fragility, governments are left in a position with less to do. This is due to the fact that these banks respond to the business strategies of their parent banks and public credit is restricted by austerity policies.

With the dollarization of profits, the features outlined by Minsky concerning Latin American financial systems as entities "financing transit-goods" now have new meanings.

Note

1 This chapter is a result of the DGAPA–UNAM research project Competencia Financiera Global y Regional: Modelos de Financiamiento Post-Crisis. The authors are grateful to Jesús Sosa for his support and to Fernanda Vidal for his Spanish to English translation of the chapter.

References

América Economía (2015). "Ránking 250 mayores bancos de América Latina". Available at: http://rankings.americaeconomia.com/mejores-bancos-2014/ranking-250-mayores bancos-de-america-latina/ (accessed 7 November 2015).

Cepal (2000). *Crisis Bancarias: Causas, Costos, Duración, Efectos y Opciones de Política.* Santiago de Chile: United Nations. Available at: www.cepal.org/es/publicaciones/ 7512-crisis-bancarias-causas-costos-duracion-efectos-y-opciones-de-politica (accessed 8 November 2015).

Cepal (2016). Cepalstat Database. United Nations Economic Commission for Latin America and the Caribbean. Available at: http://estadisticas.cepal.org/cepalstat/WEB_ CEPALSTAT/Portada.asp (accessed 9 January 2016).

Claessens, S., Köse, A., Laeven, L. and Valencia, F. (Eds) (2014). *Financial Crises: Causes, Consequences, and Policy Responses.* Washington, DC: IMF.

Correa, E. (1992). *Los Mercados Financieros y la Crisis en América Latina.* México; IIEc–UNAM.

Correa, E. (2013). "Modelo de negocios financieros y reforma regulatoria en la crisis financiera global", in G. Vidal, A. Guillén and J. Déniz (Eds), *América Latina: ¿Cómo Construir el Desarrollo hoy?* Madrid: Fondo de Cultura Económica, pp. 133–156.

Correa, E. (2015). "Budgetary impact of social security privatization: Women doubly unprotected", *International Journal of Political Economy*, 44(4): 260–276.

Correa, E., Déniz, J. and Palazuelos, A. (2009). *América Latina y Desarrollo Económico.* Madrid: Akal.

Demirgüç-Kunt, A. and Detragiache, E. (1998). "Financial liberalization and financial fragility", IMF Working Paper WP/98/83.

Dodd-Frank Act (2010). Dodd-Frank Wall Street Reform and Consumer Protection Act. Available at: www.sec.gov/about/laws/wallstreetreform-cpa.pdf (accessed 6 September 2015).

Eichengreen, B. (1999). *Towards a New International Financial Architecture: A Practical Post-Asia agenda.* Washington, DC; Peterson Institute Press.

Ferreiro, J. and Rodríguez, C. (2004). "Sistema financiero Español y su expansión hacia América Latina", in E. Correa and A. Girón (Eds), *Economía Financiera Contemporánea.* Mexico City: Miguel Ángel Porrúa, pp. 211–233.

Ffrench-Davis, R. (Ed.) (2001). *Crisis Financieras en Países "Exitosos".* Santiago de Chile: Cepal and McGraw Hill.

Ffrench-Davis, R. and Ocampo, A. (2001). "Globalización de la volatilidad financiera: Desafíos para las economías emergentes", in R. Ffrench-Davis (Ed.), *Crisis Financieras en Países "Exitosos".* Santiago de Chile: Cepal and McGraw Hill, pp. 1–44.

Financial Stability Board (2015). *Second FSB Annual Report.* Available at: www.fsb.org/ wp-content/uploads/FSB-2nd-Annual-report.pdf (accessed 2 February 2016).

Girón, A. (1995). *Fin de Siglo y Deuda Externa: Historia sin Fin.* [*The End of the Century and External Debt: A Story without End.*] México: Cambio XXI and IIEc–UNAM.

Girón, A., Correa, A. and Chapoy, A. (2005). *Consecuencias Financieras de la Globalización.* Mexico City: Miguel Ángel Porrúa.

Goldstein, M., Hills, C. and Peterson, P. (1999). *Report of an Independent Task Force Sponsored by the Council on Foreign Relations.* Washington, DC: Institute for International Economics.

Group of 22 (1998). *Summary of the Reports on the International Financial Architecture.* IMF: Washington, DC. Available at: www.imf.org/external/np/g22/ (accessed 8 August 2015).

IAASTD (International Assessment of Agricultural Knowledge, Science and Technology for Development) (2009). *Agriculture at the Crossroads. Vol III, Latin America and the Caribbean.* Washington, DC: Island Press. Available at: www.unep.org/dewa/agassessment/reports/subglobal/Agriculture_at_a_Crossroads_Volume_III_Latin_America_and_the_Caribbean_Subglobal_Report.pdf (accessed 6 November 2015).

IMF (2001). *Report of the Managing Director to the International Monetary and Financial Committee: The Fund's Crisis Prevention Initiatives.* Washington, DC: IMF. Available at: www.imf.org/external/np/omd/2001/111401.htm (accessed 10 December 2015).

IMF (2010). "Dollarization declines in Latin America", *Finance and Development*, 47(1): 57. Available at : www.imf.org/external/pubs/ft/fandd/2010/03/dataspot.htm (accessed 8 February 2016).

International Federation of Pension Funds Administrators (2014). *Executive Statistical Report.* Santiago de Chile: FIAP. Available at: www.fiapinternacional.org/wp-content/uploads/2016/01/informe_ejecutivo_estadistico_no_35__datos_a_dic__2014_-1.pdf (accessed 3 January 2016).

Kregel, J. (1998a). "Yes, 'it' did happen again", The Levy Economics Institute of Bard College Working Paper No. 234, April, Annandale-on-Hudson, New York.

Kregel, J. (1998b). "East Asia is not Mexico", The Levy Economics Institute of Bard College Working Paper No. 235, May, Annandale-on-Hudson, New York.

Kregel, J. (2000). "The Brazilian crisis", The Levy Economics Institute of Bard College Working Paper No. 294, February, Annandale-on-Hudson, New York.

Lichtensztejn, S. (1984). "Una aproximación metodológica al estudio del capital financiero en América Latina", *Revista Economía Teoría y Práctica*, 2, México, Universidad Autónoma Metropolitana. Also published by *Ola Financiera*, January–April 2009: 137–186.

Lindgren, C.-J., Garcia, G. G. and Saal, M. I. (1996). *Bank Soundness and Macroeconomic Policy.* Washington, DC: IMF. Available at: www.imf.org/external/pubs/cat/longres.aspx?sk=1538 (accessed 18 November 2015).

McKinnon, R. (1973). *Money & Capital in Economic Development.* Washington, DC: Brookings Institution.

Mathieson, D. and Roldós, J. (2001). "The role of foreign banks in emerging markets", paper presented at the World Bank, IMF and Brookings Institution 3rd Annual Financial Markets and Development Conference, 19–21 April, New York. Available at: www1.worldbank.org/finance/assets/images/Role_of_Foreign_Banks_in_Emerging_Markets__body.pdf (accessed 12 October 2015).

Meltzer, A. (2000). *International Financial Institutions Reform: Report of the International Financial Institutions Advisory Commission, March 2000.* Available at: www.eldis.org/go/home&id=28196&type=Document#.VyGgRsrQVFU (accessed 5 February 2016).

Minsky, H. (1991 [1977]). "La banca central y el comportamiento de una economía", in L. Bendesky (Ed.), *El papel de la banca central en la actualidad.* Mexico City: CEMLA México, pp. 174–198.

Parguez, A. (2010). "El doble circuito monetario depredador: Los costos de la plena integración al sistema financiero y productivo multinacional", *Ola Financiera*, 6, May–August: 1–33.

Rojas-Suárez, L. and Weisbrod, S. (1997). "Las crisis bancarias en América Latina: Experiencias y temas", in R. Hausmann and L. Rojas-Suárez (Eds), *Las Crisis Bancarias en América Latina.* Tlalpan, Mexico: Fondo de Cultura Económica, pp. 1–24.

Sánchez-Albavera, F. and Lardé, J. (2006). *Minería y Competitividad Internacional de América Latina.* Serie Recursos Naturales e Infraestructura, No. 109. Santiago de Chile: Cepal.

Shaw, E. (1973). *Financial Deepening in Economic Development*. New York: Oxford University Press.UNCTAD (2001). *Trade and Development Report*. New York and Geneva: United Nations. Available at : http://unctad.org/en/Docs/tdr2001_en.pdf (accessed 8 February 2016).

UNCTAD (2015). *Trade and Development Report*. New York and Geneva: United Nations. Available at http://unctad.org/en/PublicationsLibrary/tdr2015_en.pdf (accessed 8 February 2016).

United Nations (2009). *Report of the Commission of Experts of the President of the United Nations General Assembly on Reform of the International Monetary and Financial System*. Available at: www.un.org/ga/econcrisissummit/docs/FinalReport_CoE.pdf (accessed 4 February 2016).

Vidal, G. and Marshall, W. (2013). "Financial flows and Mexico, the dollarization he e market, and for LA the WB gives 27%bank, Goldman Sachs isis and reached a al markets atracted ncial 's disintegrated spaces of production", in L. P. Rochon and M. Seccareccia (Eds), *Monetary Economics of Production*. Northampton, MA: Edward Elgar Publishing, pp. 160–178.

Vilariño, A. (2001). "La presencia de los bancos españoles en la economía mexicana", *Información Comercial Española*, 795: 101–112.

World Bank (2002). *World Development Report*. Washington, DC: World Bank. Available at: https://openknowledge.worldbank.org/bitstream/handle/10986/5984/WDR%20 2002%20-%20English.pdf?sequence=1&isAllowed=y (accessed 5 August 2015).

World Bank (2015a). Global Financial Development Database. Washington, DC: World Bank. Available at: http://data.worldbank.org/data-catalog/global-financial-development (accessed 5 August 2015).

World Bank (2015b). *International Debt Statistics 2015*. Washington, DC: World Bank. Available at: http://data.worldbank.org/sites/default/files/ids2015.pdf (accessed 5 August 2015).

Zubizarreta, J. H., de la Fuente Lavín, M., De Vicente Arias, A. and Koldo Irurzun Ugalde, K. I. (Eds) (2013). *Empresas Transnacionales en América Latina. Análisis y Propuestas del Movimiento Social y Sindical*. Universidad del País Vasco. Available at: http:// publicaciones.hegoa.ehu.es/assets/pdfs/294/Empresas_transncionales_en_America_ Latina.pdf?1372929459 (accessed on 5 February 2016).

11 Financialization in Brazil

A paper tiger, with atomic teeth?

Pierre Salama

Introduction[1]

Can we consider that there is a happy financialization in Brazil? In a world where the rise of finance has been accompanied by increasing income inequalities, a reduction in job security, a strong disaffiliation and real wages stagnation, Brazil is a singular case. On the one hand, finance is developing, credit is rising, international reserves are climbing; and on the other hand, poverty is in decline, income inequality has fallen slightly, income is rising, the ratio of formal/informal employment is improving, unemployment is down and idle production capacity remains low. Is financialization a "paper tiger", as China once, in the 1960s, branded the United States? Or inversely, does this Brazilian singularity hide an underground disintegration process? Does it mask real threats to employment and income? Continuing the metaphor suggested by the debate between China and the Union of Soviet Socialist Republics (USSR) surrounding the United States, if financialization is a paper tiger, does it have atomic teeth – in other words, in the long term, does financialization result in grave consequences for the level of employment and income? To date, deindustrialization is approaching the point of no return in Brazil, imports have risen dramatically, especially for medium- and high-technology sectors. Brazil's external vulnerability is rising and its dependence on the export of raw materials is becoming ever more perilous; growth has slowed down and already the rise in income has become modest. Is the rise of financialization the principal reason for Brazil's deindustrialization and new forms of vulnerability? What are then the main roots of the process of financialization and the boom in raw material exports throughout the 2000s?

After defining what is meant by financialization and deindustrialization, and highlighting the particularity of the Brazilian path, this chapter seeks to explain why income and employment rose in Brazil while in other countries they were in decline. We analyse the limits of this model and show how the "paper tiger" that is financialization can prove to be dangerous for employment and income.

Finance, financialization, deindustrialization, employment, income . . . the Brazilian specificities

What does financialization mean?

To avoid the confusion caused by the vagueness of various terms, such as finance, financialization and deindustrialization, it is necessary to define the concepts used within this chapter. Financialization is the threshold from which the more lucrative financial sector develops at the expense of the real sector. Finance seems to become less dependent on the real economy. The relationship between finance and labour becomes complex and an object of obsession. Complex because of the existing relationship between the development of finance and labour conditions (wages, employment and types of employment), a relationship that is not only apparent during a crisis. An object of obsession because finance and labour appear to operate in two completely different domains: money appears to empower itself, and like the miracle of loaves and fishes, to produce new money from itself, without any relationship to labour and working conditions. In the context of commercial and financial globalization, these relationships, which go beyond the context, are difficult to decipher.

Contrary to numerous studies, this chapter focuses on the dividends paid rather than on interest payments. The net interest received by the financial system is important and explains, in part, the financialization process. However, as this study focuses on the effects of financialization on the manufacturing sector, it seems that financialization with regard to dividends is more important than the effect of high interest rates. The ideal would be to analyse the distribution of dividends in the manufacturing sector to see if there is a link between this distribution and deindustrialization. However, there is a lack of data in this area that prevents us from undertaking such an analysis. Data is available on the payment of dividends by sector (finance, raw materials, industry in general), but not for the manufacturing sector. Specifically, we do not have any data on the ratio of profits allocated to dividends. Brazilian law obliges companies to pay at least 25 per cent of their profits to shareholders and we know that with financialization this has increased significantly, without being able to measure it more precisely. We will therefore be led to use proxy variables, and more often, to proceed through deductive logic.

The vagueness of the terms used is even more apparent when it comes to "industry". This can be considered as including the processing industry, the extractive industry, the water industry, and even civil construction. The processing industry is sometimes described as manufacturing and the extractive sectors, or finally, as solely the processing-transformation industry. Examining deindustrialization, and its relationship with financialization and its effect on labour, we will use the third definition, the processing industry. Indeed, deindustrialization does not affect industry in general, but the processing industry.

Finance and financialization

Finance, like Janus, has two faces, one "virtuous", the other "vicious". The development of financial activities is not, by nature, parasitic. In general, enterprises take action without complete and perfect information and within a macroeco-nomic environment that they cannot control. The complexity of production today increases the uncertainty surrounding the profitability of projects. Covering these new risks leads to the development of equally complex financial products. This is the result of the complexification of the production system. Financial complex-ity increases drastically with financial liberalization (generalized deregulation of financial markets). This has a cost, but it is supposed to be outweighed by the benefits.[2] The development of finance and the rise in sophisticated financial prod-ucts allow the development of capital, as the capital cycle can only function if the financial system allows productive capital to be valued. The development of the increasingly sophisticated industrial sector requires the development of a more than proportional financial sector. The development of finance, from this point of view, is virtuous.

Financial activities are also parasitic and predatory. With financial globalization and market liberalization, the vicious nature of finance tends to dominate the virtuous nature. Finance therefore tends to transform into financialization.

Finance, and its bias towards financialization, is measured at the macroeco-nomic level by the weight of financial assets in the Gross Domestic Product (GDP); and at the microeconomic level by the search for shareholder value. The move-ment towards financialization occurs when the development of these activities conforms to:

- a philosophy of shareholder value and of the increase in the power of share-holders. The importance of shareholder value is manifested by the impor-tance given to high profitability, and tends to favour short-term projects and the payment of high dividends;
- the appeal of new financial products[3] for their own sakes, rather than with the objective of reducing the risk of real activity financing.

The shareholder view of business has quite rapidly imposed itself over the last two decades. The relationship between managers and shareholders has changed. The primary objective of a company is increasingly to boost the value of its shares and to increase the payment of dividends.[4]

On a global scale, according to the Henderson Group,[5] the total amount of divi-dends paid reached US$1,030 billion in 2013. This represents a 43 per cent rise from 2009 to 2013, with an average yearly growth of 9.4 per cent over these five years, well above the average world GDP growth.[6] Emerging economies have gone from paying 10 per cent (in 2009) to 14 per cent (in 2013) of total dividends paid in the world.[7] The BRIC (Brazil, Russia, India, China) countries have con-tributed more than half of dividend payments in emerging economies. In Brazil, the distribution of dividends (in all sectors) reached US$9.9 billion in 2009, US$16.1 billion (+62.1 per cent) in 2010 and US$20.9 billion (+30.2 per cent) in 2011. From 2012, the value of dividends paid fell to US$16.7 billion (–20.1 per cent) and US$13.1 billion (–21.6 per cent) in 2013, following the drop in value on the stock exchange. In 2011, 60 per cent of dividends paid to Brazilian shareholders came from ten companies. Two in particular stand out: Vale (16 per cent) and Pétrobras (8.5 per cent).

Even though the available data are not disaggregated, it is interesting to compare the net inflow of foreign direct investment (FDI) to Brazil with the outflow of capital through dividends paid and the repatriation of profits. Between January 2011 and January 2012, the FDI inflows reached US$69.1 billion and the payment of dividends and repatriation of profits reached US$37.3 billion. As the stock of foreign capital increases, the ratio of FDI flows to dividends paid to shareholders falls, and the payment of dividends rises quicker than capital inflows (FDI). These capital outflows have become considerable and explain in large part the negative balance of the Brazilian current account (–US$80 billion in 2013). They largely outweigh the outflows to service foreign debt.

Capital outflows for the payment of dividends and the repatriation of profits have a negative effect on the balance of the current account. After being in surplus from 2003 to 2006, the current account balance deteriorated progressively to reach –US$81.3 billion in 2013 (3.6 per cent of GDP), a drop of nearly US$100 billion in 2014 from its peak of US$14 billion in 2005. The amount paid in dividends and profit repatriations over the last years explains, in large part, this deficit. The extent of this deficit of the current account requires ever-increasing capital inflows for the equilibrium of the balance of payments. The sustainability of the Brazilian model depends increasingly on these inflows: foreign direct investments (FDI; US$64 billion in 2013) and portfolio investments (US$25.5 billion in 2013) have increasing difficulty in compensating for the growing deficits of the current account. The rise in dividends paid is to the detriment of reinvestment and in favour of short-term choices at the expense of long-term strategies.

Financialization is different depending on the country and the level of development in the financial sector. In industrialized countries, it affects the assets and liabilities of non-financial companies. In the emerging economies of Latin America, sophisticated "toxic" financial products remain scarce: only large companies (playing on exchange rate expectations) and banks, sometimes, used them over the last years, and even then in a relatively small measure. Therefore, *in these countries, financialization essentially relates to the interest on loans and the payment of dividends. It is therefore the constraints imposed on companies by the financial system (high profit level, high distribution of dividends, high remuneration of lent capital) that characterize financialization rather than the abuse of toxic products.* According to the calculations of Bruno (2008, 2012), the proportion of total profits reinvested has dropped significantly.

Early deindustrialization

Beyond a certain level of development, it is normal to observe a fall in the relative importance of the industrial sector in GDP, with a rise in the importance of the service industry without necessarily a process of deindustrialization. Deindustrialization generally relates to a reduction in the absolute added value of industry and/or a reduction in the relative weight of the nation's industry in total global industry. For example, deindustrialization is observed in most advanced economies following numerous firms offshoring some activities and the geographic rupture of the value chain. In Latin America, and particularly in Brazil, deindustrialization occurred earlier than in most advanced economies, which raises the notion of "early deindustrialization". Indeed, deindustrialization is considered to be early when the per capita revenue in the country is less than half that of advanced countries when they began their deindustrialization process.

Apart from the success of a few sectors, such as the aeronautical industry, the automotive industry, the oil industry, etc., the deindustrialization process in Brazil developed in the 2000s. Contrary to advanced economies, deindustrialization in Brazil did not occur due to the massive offshoring of activities, but as a result of the partial destruction of the industrial structure. This resulted in the loss of competiveness of Brazilian industry and the inadequacy of infrastructure (railroads, ports and airports, roads), even access to electricity. In some studies, industry consists of the processing industry, civil construction, the extractive industries, and the production and distribution of water, gas and electricity. In others, only two components are considered: the processing industry and the extractive industries (even if they do not have the same weight in the economy. For instance, the share of extractive industries in GDP was 1 per cent, while the share of the processing industry was 15.1 per cent in 2011 in Brazil). In the following study, we mainly consider the processing industry.

The relative weight of the processing industry in GDP is falling. The Brazilian example is emblematic. According to the Organisation for Economic Co-operation and Development (OECD 2013), the weight of the Brazilian processing industry in the global processing industry (in added value) was 1.8 per cent in 2005 and 1.7 per cent in 2011. According to the same source, the Chinese processing industry made up 9.9 per cent and 16.9 per cent in 2005 and 2011 respectively, while India's weight was 1.6 per cent and 2.1 per cent. The weight of the Brazilian processing industry has dropped slightly, while it has risen sharply in China and slightly in India.

In Brazil, the rise in household demand (due to the increase in real wages, the growth of employment and the increased availability of credit for consumption) did result in an imports increase instead of a rise in national industrial production. The Instituto de Estudos para o Desenvolvimento Industrial (IEDI) reported in 2015:

> In the first nine months of 2015, the manufacturing industry saw its production fall 9.2%, with the month of September contributing with a 12.5% drop compared to the same month of 2014. Such variations led to an 8.2% decrease in 12 months.
>
> (IEDI 2015: Letter No. 707, 27 November: para. 1)

This tendency is also documented by de Paula *et al.* (2013) who state that compared with their level of 2003 (the base year, 100 points), the index of industrial production rose to 130 in 2013, while the imports index went to more than 220. The rise in imports of manufactured products is also due to the increased demand from firms since the intermediary products, semi-finished products and capital goods are not produced locally because of their high degree of technical sophistication; or they are produced locally, but at a higher cost than the international competition. The appreciation of the local currency favours these imports as their price in local currency falls. This exchange rate advantage for import-dependent firms leads to increased margins.

The import penetration coefficient in the processing industry increased twofold between 2005 and 2013. This is representative of an "inverse import substitution" process, whereby an increasing portion of added value is not produced locally. National production can therefore no longer satisfy the increased demand from households and the needs of intermediary products and capital goods. This was mainly due to a lack of investment (16 per cent of GDP in 2014 and 18.4 per cent in 2013) and a lack of flexibility in the productive structure. Exporters of industrial products are disadvantaged by an appreciation of the exchange rate, but also by the lack of past investment and a low level of research funding (less than 1 per cent of GDP, concentrated in only a few firms). The productive structure has proven to be less and less capable of responding to the evolution of global demand for industrial products. Exports have fallen to a greater or lesser degree based on their level of technology. The trade balance for industrial products is increasingly negative. More accurately, exports of manufactured products (processing industry) have fallen in relative terms, from 53 per cent of exports (in value) in 2005 to 35 per cent in 2012, to the benefit of the primary exports of agricultural and mining products. The trade balance of the processing industry became negative from 2008. This deficit grew between 2008 and 2013, notably due to high-, medium-high- and medium-low-technology products. Only low-technology products remain in a positive trade balance, as seen in Figure 11.1.[8]

However, since 2001, the overall trade balance has been positive, reaching US$46.5 billion in 2006 due to the growing exports of primary products. This has been reducing since then, however, and by 2013, it had fallen to only US$2.5 billion, almost 20 times less than in 2006.

The surplus of the trade balance is therefore increasingly low and no longer sufficient to compensate for the deficit of the services sector. The deficit of the current account is, in fact, growing. The external and internal deficits (current account and budget deficits) plus the possible attraction of other financial centres reinforce the volatility of portfolio investment and increase the difficulty of "balancing" the balance of payments. Therefore, external constraints reappear and, with them, the risk of "pendular growth" with all the negative consequences on the level of employment and real wages.

The Brazilian distinctive features

One of the peculiar facts about the Brazilian economy is its low unemployment despite the growing labour force. Formal employment has increased in all sectors, weakly in industry, strongly in retail, very strongly in services. Formal employment has been growing quicker than informal employment since 2012.[9] However, the effects of "de-qualification" can be observed. Unskilled workers had a 27 per cent unemployment rate in 1970 compared to 5 per cent in 2010, with a marked reduction over the entire period. Unskilled labour is becoming rare as a consequence

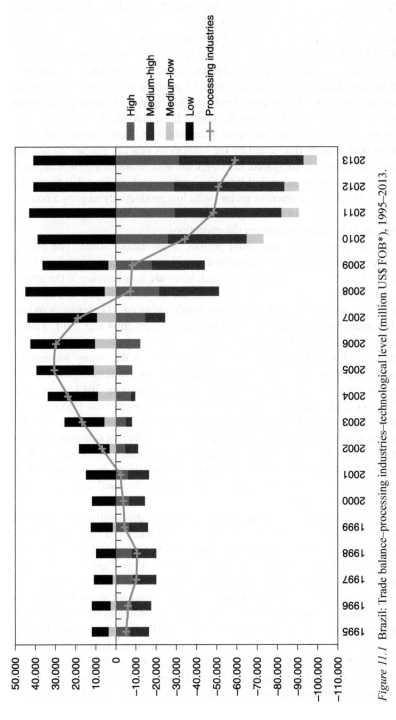

Figure 11.1 Brazil: Trade balance–processing industries–technological level (million US$ FOB*), 1995–2013.

Source: Secex (Secretariat of Foreign Trade)/ALICE (System of Analysis of Foreign Trade Information).Our own formulation based on the taxonomy of OECD/Standatabase.

Note: * Free on Board.

of increased education and the high demand for this type of employment. According to Pochmann (2013), using data from the Instituto Brasileiro de Geografia e Estatística (IBGE), individuals attending school until the age of nine suffered an increased unemployment rate (from 21.5 per cent to 33.9 per cent over the period from 1970 to 2010). This increase has been stable except for an exceptional increase in 2000 (to 40.6 per cent). Those who attended school until the age of 12 also suffered an increased unemployment rate (from 3.5 per cent to 41.5 per cent over the same period). It can therefore be considered that there is an ever bigger gap between entrepreneurs' demand for labour and the supply from individuals who do not find employment corresponding to their level of qualification. This is confirmed when the level of qualification (measured by the number of years in education) and the productivity of labour are compared. In 2009, there was no observable link between the two variables, except in capital-intensive sectors such as the oil industry, IT services, etc. In contrast, numerous sectors with low productivity employ a considerable number of employees who have attended education until the age of 11 or 12; agriculture and civil construction are the exceptions.

Two factors explain the substantial growth in the labour force. The first is linked to the fertility rate, which despite a significant reduction, remained relatively high 15 (and more) years ago. These children are now arriving in the labour market. The second is related to the rise in female workers. Despite this increase in the labour force, the unemployment rate continues to fall. Therefore, a reduction in the unemployment rate can be observed between 2004 and 2014. This is not observable in advanced economies, especially in European countries.

Another peculiar fact about the Brazilian economy is the strong increase of real income followed by a significant slowdown in its evolution. Real income increase has been slowing since 2011, becoming negative in 2013. According to the OECD (2013), real wages in Brazil in US dollars went from US$4.35 (per hour) in 2000 to US$8.44 in 2006 and US$11.65 in 2011. This increase is partly due to a significant increase in the minimum wage;[10] partly to a substantial difference, in all sectors, between the supply of skilled labour and firms' demand, which is more positioned towards non-skilled labour; and finally, to an increase in real income (partly due to the strong appreciation of the national currency – the real – in relation to the dollar).

Contrary to what is observed in advanced economies, the functional distribution of income is improving in favour of employees. The weight of wages in GDP is increasing in Brazil, unlike in advanced economies. According to Bruno (2012), it went from 40.2 per cent of the added value in 2004 to 43 per cent in 2010. More surprisingly, the Gini coefficient,[11] while remaining at a high level, has fallen. The personal distribution of income has improved, to the detriment of the four best-off deciles of the population and the richest 1 per cent. According to the data provided by the Instituto Brasileiro de Geografia e Estatística (IBGE),[12] in 1996, the income of the richest 1 per cent was above that of the poorest 50 per cent (13.5 per cent versus 13 per cent of the total income of the population), and in 2013, it had inverted to 12.9 per cent and 18.5 per cent respectively. The portion of income going to the richest decile also fell over the same period, from 34.4 per cent to 29.1 per cent.

Less significant than in Brazil, income inequality in advanced economies is not reducing. Over the last 20 years, an increase in the portion of overall income going to the richest 1 per cent, 0.1 per cent – and even more so the 0.01 per cent – can be observed, to the detriment of the rest of the population. The growth in inequality is even more pronounced when the income of the richest 0.1 per cent and 0.01 per cent is measured. Even though Brazilian data on the richest 0.1 per cent and 0.01 per cent are (bizarrely) not available, it can be surmised that they are also increasing, based on studies by Capgemini (2013) on the number of billionaires in Brazil.

The connection between finance, deindustrialization and labour

The connection between finance and labour varies depending on the country. In Brazil, this connection is different from that seen in Anglo-Saxon countries such as the United Kingdom, the United States, etc., and in European countries, such as Germany, France, etc. This section will particularly focus on the Anglo-Saxon countries. Even though the importance of credit is not comparable between Brazil and the Anglo-Saxon countries, certain aspects of financialization are comparable: up until the start of the 2008 financial crisis in the Anglo-Saxon countries, and until recently in Brazil, financialization has been accompanied by a low unemployment rate, a high growth of consumer credit, deindustrialization and a trade balance deficit for manufactured goods. However, the differences remain important: in Anglo-Saxon countries, in the best-case scenario, real income has stagnated, while in Brazil it is rising.

Financialization in advanced Anglo-Saxon countries

The added value produced can be separated into income (wages), profits and taxes on production. The profits can be divided into reinvested profits, distribution of dividends, interest payments on debt and taxes on profits. The demand for share-holder value represents an increase in the portion of profits used for the payment of dividends. Also, for the portion of profits reinvested to remain stable, total profits in the added value must rise with a reduction of the share of wages. This evolution explains, in large part, the increase in inequality between profits and wages observed in advanced economies. The functional distribution of revenue has therefore been to the benefit of capital and to the detriment of labour. If the share of wages in the added value does not decrease any more (as was the case in advanced economies during the 2000s), or even increases (as in Brazil), the relative increase in the profits distributed through dividends then results in a decrease of the reinvestment of profits.

The stagnation of real (average) wages (and even a small increase), even with the effects of redistribution (progressive taxation, social payments) should lead to weak household demand, especially from low-income households. This weakness of demand should have negative effects on firms producing intermediary goods and capital goods and result in a drop of firms' profitability. Taking into account the rising weight of dividends paid and this reduction in profitability, investment should drop and then stagnate. However, this was not seen in Anglo-Saxon countries prior to 2008.

Even if income does not increase, or only slightly, it remains "too high" compared to emerging economies if the difference in productivity between Anglo-Saxon and emerging countries is not compensated by the wage differences, at a given exchange rate. The production of some goods, especially those requiring a significant labour force, can become less and less profitable. It is also the production of these goods that will be the first to be relocated to a country with lower wage costs. These goods increasingly correspond to segments of line production and the production will therefore be divided between numerous countries. The international division of labour is moving towards a fragmentation of the value chain. This enables multinationals, directly (through subsidiaries) or indirectly (through outsourcing), to maximize their returns, allowing them to generate sufficient profits to meet shareholders' expectations.

In Anglo-Saxon countries, until the start of the 2007–2008 crisis, the negative effects of a moderate rise of income on demand[13] were compensated for, for a time, by the increase in credit. Household demand, instead of stagnating, continued to grow due to the rise in credit granted to households. The growth in household demand and the resulting increase in demand for intermediary and capital goods led to an increase in production, but also to a considerable increase in imports. As the wage level remained depressed, employment could rise and the risk of an increase in unemployment was lowered. In such a process, numerous virtuous circles appear as:

- stagnant wages, high growth in credit, increase in household demand, improvement in profitability, increase in dividends distributed;
- increase in credit, creation of complex financial products allowing for a high level of speculation;
- importance of shareholders and the strong growth of dividend payments;
- increased profits of financial institutions; and finally
- - global rupture of the value chain following relocation of some industries and reallocation of profits to shareholders' dividends.

Is financialization the cause of deindustrialization in Brazil?

Financialization has roughly the same effects in emerging countries as in advanced economies. The amount of dividends paid hinders investment in the manufacturing sector, and the amount of interest paid occurs to the detriment of the reinvestment of profits. This process makes the rise of the rate of investment difficult and prevents a higher and durable growth. The investment rate in the Brazilian economy was relatively volatile and low, with a peak of 19.5 per cent of GDP in 2010 (a year of high growth), and a low of 15.3 per cent in 2003. The gap between domestic saving and the investment rate has risen considerably since 2008, revealing an increasingly consumerist behaviour especially from shareholders:[14]

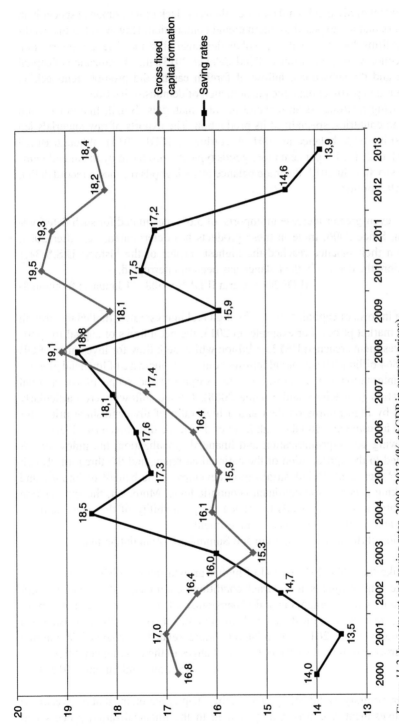

Figure 11.2 Investment and saving rates, 2000–2013 (% of GDP in current prices).

Source: IBGE. Our own interpretation, from the National Account, three-monthly index.

The extent of dividends paid partly explains the lack of investment, especially in the sectors that are exposed to international competition. However, the financialization of firms does not, by itself, explain deindustrialization. The re-primarization of the economy (see, for instance, Trindade *et al*. 2015), the liberalization of capital markets and the subsequent inflow of foreign capital did promote rent-seeking behaviour and partly explain the phenomenon of deindustrialization.

Following a strong Asian demand for raw materials, Brazil, like other Latin American countries, specialized its production. The exports of raw materials led to a positive trade balance in 2001. According to IEDI (2014), although Brazil exported, in 2013, 1.3 per cent more goods typically produced by the manufacturing industry than in 2012, the trade balance of such goods reached a record deficit of US$59.7 billion:

> The even-greater increase in imports, of 5.6%, accounted for such deterioration. Since 2006, trade in these products has deteriorated, i.e., after 2005, when their balance reached the highest surplus of the history: U.S.$ 31.1 billion, the decline in the balance has been uninterrupted.
> (IEDI 2014: Carta IEDI No. 608, 24 January: footnote 8)

Massive inflows of capital, attracted by high real interest rates, fuelled the growth in stock market prices. For example, in 2013, the net inflows of capital for portfolio investments reached US$25.5 billion while the inflow for investment (FDI) was US$64 billion. These capital inflows point to the increase of financial globalization; international financialization then surpassed the scope of commercial globalization (see Kliass and Salama 2008). Capital inflows were particularly attracted by high returns on debt and a high ratio of dividend/share price (for portfolio investments) and the high level of dividends distributed (for FDI).

Following the re-primarization and financial globalization, the inflow of US dollars led to the appreciation of the national currency, and the threat of "Dutch disease"[15] increased. Deindustrialization develops to the benefit of imports and rent-seeking becomes the dominant economic logic. Moreover, the appreciation of the national currency tends to reduce the profitability of the manufacturing industry and results in low levels of investment.

In an insightful analysis, Serrano and Summa (2012) maintain that:

> Unlike the 2004–2010 period of higher growth rates, which was caused by large improvements in external conditions combined with a modest shift towards a more pragmatic and expansionist set of domestic economic policies, we argue that the drastic reduction in the rate of growth of the Brazilian economy since 2011 was relatively more related to changes in internal macroeconomic policy rather than in changes to the external conditions.
> (Serrano and Summa 2012: 166)

However, contrary to this interpretation, this chapter maintains that the weakness of the investment rate was mainly related to the financialization process and the appreciation of the domestic currency. Only an industrial policy at a national level and a monetary policy aiming to sterilize the inflow of foreign capital and maintaining a depressed exchange rate are capable of slowing down the deindustrialization process.

The limits of "happy" financialization: disillusioned days to come

It is worth noting that the increase in real wages and the reduction of the unemployment rate cannot be explained by financialization. On the contrary, financialization tends to slow the increase in wages, to increase the unemployment rate and to develop the flexibility of labour. Aside from the strong flexibility, characterized by a high turnover and an increased precariousness of employment, no negative effects are observed, at least until 2013. This is why "happy" is used with a question mark in the first line of this chapter .

Financialization in Brazil resulted in a modest investment rate and high flexibility in the workforce. Political decisions regarding the indexation of the minimum wage and the labour market explain the rise in wages and the high employment rate. The functioning of the labour market depends on the supply of and demand for labour. Labour is increasingly qualified due to the lengthening of education. Demand for employment has not followed this trend, a consequence of the effects of financialization towards a regressive specialization in the international division of labour. The link between financialization and the functioning of the labour market has to be identified through the effects of financialization on the productive structure of the country. As financialization, along with the re-primarization of the economy, contributes to the deindustrialization, the increased household and firms' demand for manufactured goods is satisfied by an increase in imports. This is made possible, first, by the trade balance surplus (a consequence of the re-primarization and, therefore, of the increase in the price and volume of raw materials traded); and second, by the inflow of capital once the period of commercial surpluses has elapsed. Let me now examine those relations.

Deindustrialization affects the composition of industry and, as a result, the demand for labour

The high- and medium-technology sectors are, in general, the least resistant to international competition (see Figure 11.3 and Figure 11.4).[16] The low-technology sectors have resisted more effectively, but without high prospects for the future. On the one hand, exports of low-technology goods are not very dynamic, due to the reasons already mentioned, and on the other hand, the countries where wages are lowest are competitive "threats" to the continuation of local production.

Therefore, how to explain the rise of wages and employment in the economy as a whole? Numerous factors can be used to deal with this paradox. For example, for the minimum wage, the indexation mechanisms to past inflation and to the GDP growth rate result in a considerable and rapid increase in the minimum wage. Parallel to this, the supply of and demand for labour evolve under the

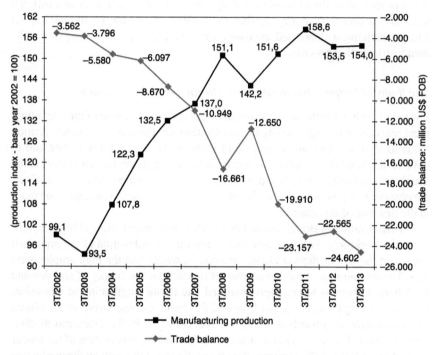

Figure 11.3 High-technology manufacturing production and related trade balance, 2002–2013.

Source: IBGE – Monthly industrial research newsletter. Our own interpretation based on the taxonomy of OECD/Standatabase.

scissors effect. Labour is increasingly qualified, due to an extension in the time spent in education. However, the demand for labour is lower for two reasons: first, the the manufacturing sector is reducing in relative importance. Second, the relative weight of low-technology sectors has increased while that of high- and medium-technology sectors has declined. Firms using relatively unsophisticated techniques tend to favour low-skilled or unskilled labour. Also, it seems that the services and commercial sectors that are naturally protected from international competition absorb more and more unskilled labour. A process of disaffiliation and downgrading[17] then emerges from this increasing differential between supply and demand. Qualified workers are unable to find sufficient employment at the level of their qualifications. Rocha (2013) documents how employment, depending on the level of education, rises rapidly for those who have attended 11 or more years of education, and slightly less so for those who have been in education for 8–10 years. However, these jobs do not always correspond to the level of qualification, as shown by Pochmann (2013).

A comprehensive study by Lopez-Calva and Rocha (2012) documents how a qualified worker, whose employment does not correspond to their level of

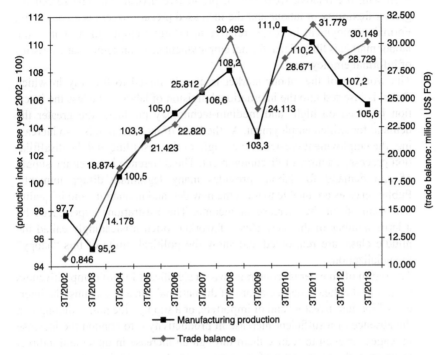

Figure 11.4 Low-technology manufacturing production and related trade balance, 2002–2013.

Source: IBGE – Monthly industrial research newsletter. Our own interpretation based on the taxonomy of OECD/Standatabase.

qualification, receives a wage superior to the wage she/he would have received with a lower education level. Individuals who have spent more time in education earn more than those who have spent less time in education, but the gap reduced between 1997 and 2009, except for the highest earners. The ratio of the income of individuals having spent 15 or more years in education over the income of individuals having spent 12 to 14 years in education tends to rise in favour of the former. This is the same evolution for those having 12 years of education compared to those with between 8 and 11 years of education.

Disillusioned days to come?

Three factors transform a "happy" financialization into an "unhappy" financialization.

1   A greater flexibility of labour can create conflicts between rent-seeking profits and profits for investment, to the extent that total profits can grow sufficiently to allow for an increase in the relative portion destined to the financial profits

even with the relative weakness of productive investment. The search for greater flexibility of labour and the increased precariousness is a *constraint*. Formal employment increases relative to informal employment, but as the labour market is liberalized, formal employment takes on some characteristics of informal employment.

2   The working of the labour market is closely linked to the way in which Brazil is inserted into the international division of labour. The less the insertion is based on high- and medium-technology products, the greater the demand for skilled employment. As the level of qualification is also increasing, the employment created is the origin of the deskilling and the disaffiliation process, a source of discontentment. The difference between the supply of and demand for labour provides many legitimate disappointments. Public services are unable to meet the new demand in quantity and in quality that stems from the increase in income. The frustrations experienced by a large number of this new class of worker, often misleadingly called the middle class, are reinforced and show the political limits of this "happy" financialization.

3   The return of an external constraint with a significant loss of competitiveness should lead either to depreciations of the national currency, against the interests of foreign investors and of importers, or a supply-side policy aiming – in the absence of a sufficient increase in productivity – to contain the increase in wages, or even to reduce them through an increase in direct and indirect taxation and the transfer of employer social contributions towards new forms of taxation. This policy, if it is chosen, would result in the slowdown of economic activity and an increase in unemployment.

Financialization and re-primarization, by producing new vulnerabilities, show the economic weaknesses of such a model. Therefore, financialization can be considered a paper tiger, with atomic teeth.

Notes

1   The author wishes to thank Julien Vercueil for his valuable comments on a first draft of this chapter. This chapter was presented at the conference organized by the UNICAMP and UGT (trade union) in São Paulo in May 2014 in its Portuguese version. A previous version of this chapter was published on 23 May 2014 in *Les Possibles*, 3, Spring 2014, an online review published by Attac France (available at: https://france.attac.org/nos-publications/les-possibles/numero-3-printemps-2014/debats/article/financiarisation-au-bresil-un). This chapter, comprising a longer version of that publication, has been translated from the French by Ronan Fox, a student in Master 2 (Master of Governance of International Organizations and Development) at the Grenoble Faculty of Economics.
2   In Marxist terms, the financier is "indirectly productive". The labour that finance deploys is not productive, but neither is it unproductive. Paid on the capital gain, it allows it to increase due to an improved rotation of capital. But the development of finance is not only to improve the valuing of capital; it is also the consequence of speculation. The predatory dimension of the capital gain is accentuated and indirectly productive labour becomes unproductive; that is to say, non-susceptible to the creation

of value. These two types of labour coexist. With financialization, unproductive labour dominates indirectly productive labour.

3 These products become toxic once they are not based on the ability to repay by the debtors to whom the loans were granted, but on the anticipation of the future value of their wealth. As long as the financial bubble continues, money seems to produce money, but when it bursts, the resulting liquidity crisis precipitates the economic crisis.

4 In 2012, in France, non-financial companies distributed a record 8.9 per cent of their gross profits. This is more surprising given that their gross operating surplus (what is left to pay taxes, interest, the amortization of previous investments and dividends) fell sharply in 2011. The payment of dividends continued to rise despite falling profitability. Consequently, investments have become an adjustment variable. Two examples from current affairs reveal the increasing importance of shareholders. The first is the example of French telecommunications giant, Orange, which specialized in new technologies that require massive investments to maintain market share and to resist competition which is particularly strong in this sector. In 2012, Orange distributed dividends superior to its profits (€2 billion versus €0.8 billion), handicapping its ability to invest sufficiently (see *Le Monde*, 28 May 2013). The second example is that of Airbus (formerly EADS). According to a new manager of the group, the company had become a "normal company" seeking the best return on investment and the satisfaction of its shareholders. The objective was to obtain, by 2015, an operational margin of 10 per cent and to redistribute 30–40 per cent of net profits to shareholders. This led the main financial newspaper in France, *Les Echos*, to write (2 January 2014, author's translation): "the objectives are in line with best practice within the sector. But [they] would never have allowed EADS to engage in programmes as risky as the A380, A400M, NH90 and even A350XWB".

5 Henderson Global Investors (2014): Henderson Dividend Index (www.henderson. com/henderson) for all data above.

6 In general, the rise in dividends distributed was particularly high in high-tech industries (aerospace, defence, construction, engineering, electronic equipment, transport, according to the Henderson Group's classification). However, it is the financial sector that contributes the most to dividends (24 per cent). Industry, excluding telecommunications and high-technology products (that is to say, according to Henderson, fixed and mobile telecommunications; and for high-technology products, hardware and electronics, semi-conductors, software and related services) distributed in 2009, US$57.6 billion; and in 2013, US$74.3 billion. In 2013, industry paid less than telecommunications (US$81.8 billion), a bit more than high-technology products (US$62.7 billion) and a lot less than the financial sector (US$217.6 billion).

7 The financial sector, in emerging economies, contributes more to the payment of dividends than in advanced countries: 32 per cent in 2013, more than the oil, gas and energy sector (26.2 per cent) and the mining sector (10.9 per cent). Having risen rapidly during the boom in raw materials prices, it has declined slightly with the reversal in this tendency.

8 Source: "Comércio exterior de bens da indústria de transformação: Exportando menos, importando bem mais", Carta IEDI No. 608, 24 January 2014. Available at: www.iedi. org.br/cartas/carta_iedi_n_608.html (accessed 31 January 2014).

9 Informal employment has decreasingly been the result of old-style production relations such as authoritarianism – paternalism. It is increasingly a way to bypass the payment of social contributions. The increased weight of formal employment compared to informal employment does not indicate increased employment stability. As in advanced countries, part-time employment has developed and the flexibility of employment has increased (for a detailed study of unemployment, see Demazière *et al.* [2013]). A twofold process has emerged with the liberalization of the labour market: less informal employment, more formal but precarious employment.

10 The minimum wage increases depending on inflation and the past growth of GDP. More precisely, the average growth in GDP in t–2 and t–1 (2 years and 1 year before time t) and the inflation rate in t–1 are indexed to the increase of the minimum wage. The more volatile the GDP, the more the uncoupling of the minimum wage with GDP in time t is, in one or the other direction.

11 However, it is necessary to complete the Gini coefficient with other indicators. The Gini coefficient, before social transfers (*bolsa família* [social welfare programme], disability benefits and *especially* pensions) was 0.631 in 1998, and it was 0.598 after social transfers. These two coefficients were significantly reduced in 2010, while remaining high: the pre-transfer Gini was 0.598 and it was 0.543 after transfers, according to the Instituto Brasileiro de Geografia e Estatística (IBGE), national accounts, data and tables, various years, available at: www.ibge.gov.br/english/ (accessed 31 January 2014).

12 Instituto Brasileiro de Geografia e Estatística (IBGE), national accounts, data and tables, various years, available at: www.ibge.gov.br/english/ (accessed 31 January 2014).

13 However, it allows for certain goods, including those where certain segments of production have been relocated, to be sold at relatively low prices, lower than if they had been produced locally. It therefore has an anti-inflationary effect which can benefit households, particularly for new electronic goods.

14 Source: Instituto Brasileiro de Geografia e Estatística (IBGE), data available at: www.ibge.gov.br/home/presidencia/noticias/imprensa/ppts/0000001656040213201404552 7778631.pdf (accessed 31 January 2014).

15 While the prices of rent-seeking export products increase, their export creates a surplus of foreign currency inflows. If the local currency is not stabilized through sterilization measures, it will appreciate. This appreciation modifies the relative prices between tradeable and non-tradeable goods. The export price of non-rent-seeking goods suffers from this appreciation while the price of imported goods tends to fall, further reducing the competitiveness of the sectors producing tradeable goods. Therefore, the export of the non-rent-seeking goods falls as imports increase. Non-tradeable goods benefit from these changes in relative prices. Naturally protected against external competition, these goods become the object of speculation. Savings are increasingly directed towards, for example, real estate, rather than towards productive investment. This movement in relative prices favours deindustrialization. However, in the case of Brazil, the appreciation of the domestic currency cannot be attributed to the re-primarization of the economy. While Brazil does export more and more raw materials at an increased price, these exports loosen the external constraint on growth. Even though the trade balance becomes positive, the current account is not. It also seems difficult to attribute the effects of deindustrialization solely to a "Dutch disease", if this is associated with the country's specialization in raw materials. Fundamentally, it is capital inflows that explain the appreciation. It is therefore necessary to have a wide interpretation that does not limit it to the inflow of foreign currency due to the export of raw materials. The total inflow of foreign currency favours industrialization, while the appreciation of the domestic currency due to the effects of these inflows is not counteracted by adequate monetary policy.

16 Source: "A indústria de transformação por intensidade tecnológica: O retrocesso em curso", Carta IEDI No. 707, 27 November 2015. Available at: www.iedi.org.br/cartas/ carta_iedi_n_707.html (accessed 31 January 2016).

17 Upon leaving education, increasing numbers of young people are only able to find precarious employment, often part-time in sectors far removed from their areas of specialization, or employment that does not correspond to the level of their qualification, often just under the qualification corresponding to their number of years in education. However, from a certain threshold, the greater the number of years in education, the lower the probability of being disaffiliated, or even downgraded.

References

Bruno, M. (2008). "Régulation et croissance économique au Brésil après la libéralisation, un régime d'accumulation bloqué par la finance", *Revue de la régulation* [online]. Available at: http://regulation.revues.org/4103.

Bruno, M. (2012). "Regimen de crecimiento y accumulacion de capital en Brasil: Una caracterizacion del periodo 1995–2010", mimeo. Available at: http://cei.colmex.mx/Proyecto%20Bizberg%20Am%C3%A9rica%20Latina/Mesa%202%20Bruno.pdf.

Capgemini (2013). *World Wealth Report*. Paris: Capgemini and RBC Wealth Management & RBC Insurance, Royal Bank of Canada.

Demazière, D., Guimaraes, N. A., Hirata, H. and Sugita, K. (2013). *Etre chômeur à Paris, São Paulo, Tokyo*. Paris: Presses de Science Po.

de Paula, L. F., de Melo Modenesi, A. and de Castro Pire, M. C. (2013). "A tela do contágio das duas crises e as respostas da política econômica", in Associação Keynesiana Brasileira (Ed.), *A Economia Brasileira na Encruzilhada*, p. 74. Available at: www.akb.org.

Instituto Brasileiro de Geografia e Estatística (IBGE). National accounts, data and tables, various years, available at : www.ibge.gov.br/english/ (accessed 31 January 2016).

Instituto de Estudos para o Desenvolvimento Industrial (IEDI) (various years). Various letters. Available at : http://www.iedi.org.br (accessed 14 December 2015).

Kliass, P. and Salama, P. (2008). "A globalização no Brasil: Responsável ou bode expiatório?", *Revista de Economia Política*, 28(3): 371–391.

Lopez-Calva, L. F. and Rocha, S. (2012). *Exiting Belindia? Lessons from the Recent Decline in Income Inequality in Brazil*. Washington, DC: World Bank-LAC.

OECD (2013). *Latin American Economic Outlook 2013. SME Policies for Structural Change*. Paris: OECD and the United Nations Economic Commission for Latin America and the Caribbean (UN-ECLAC).

Pochmann, M. (2013). *Subdesenvolvimento e Trabalho*. Campinas Universidade Estadual de Campinas, Instituto de Economia, Centro de Estudos Sindicais e do Trabalho, CESIT. São Paulo, Brazil: LTR, Editora Ltda.

Rocha, S. (2013). "Evolution des inégalités de revenus", mimeo. Document prepared for the BRICS Research Seminar Series, Maison des Sciences de l'Homme (MSH), Paris.

Serrano, F. and Summa, R. (2012). "A desacelareção rudimentar da economia brasileira desde 2011", *Oikos*, 11(2): 166–202.

Trindade, J. R., Cooney, P. and Pereira de Oliveira, W. (2015). "Industrial trajectory and economic development: Dilemma of the re-primarization of the Brazilian economy", *Review of Radical Political Economics*, first published on 4 August 2015. doi: 10.1177/0486613415591807.

12 National and supra-national financial regulatory architecture

Transformations of the Russian financial system in the post-Soviet period

Nadezhda N. Pokrovskaia

Introduction

The discussions on the role and functions of public regulation in the economic system directly or indirectly rest on the issues related to the conditions of production of public goods and related external effects. Those issues are usually linked to the political debate on the limits of state intrusion into the natural spontaneous evolution and growth of market economies, assumed to work in an efficient way under perfect free competition and profit-seeking private agents' decisions.

From the late 1970s onwards, liberalization and opening up of domestic markets to global trade and finance through world-wide business and financial flows gave strength to the assertion that economic development is inevitably related to the evolution of countries towards a liberal market economy. The Scandinavian models of a cooperative societal system and labour relations gave way to the unsustainable but profit-orientated Anglo-Saxon ultimate capitalism during its growth at the end of the twentieth century.

However, the financial crisis of 2007–2008 showed the necessity of reinforcing the regulation of the banking system and financial sector. The attempts to limit speculation with the Tobin tax or restraining bonuses for banking managers represent only separate measures and facets of a possible relevant regulation. Today, the "high-road competition" (Wright and Rogers 2015) needs not only individuals' and corporate hunger for innovative value creation with highest financial returns based on "creative destruction" (Sombart 1913), but also clear and sustainable rules of fair play with a multi-angle approach. The Russian experience may be a good example in such an analysis as the pursuit of a fragile balance between regulation and deregulation seems to be one of the particular characteristics of the evolution of the Russian economy during the last 25 years (1990–2015), a period of transition for the country from a highly planned economic regime to a market-based capitalist economy. An in-depth analysis of the Russian case as a process of condensed and accelerated building of an emergent market economy sheds light on the fluctuations between the total "wild" deregulation in the 1990s and the sharp re-regulation of the financial system since September 2013.

Eeconomic policy did indeed experience the deregulatory surge in the 1990s when the liberalization of the financial system and consumer prices affected the whole population. Weak governance in the private and public sectors led to a peculiar situation: on the one hand, economic relations were considerably de-monetized, giving place to barter exchanges and fuelling the lack of accounting and market experience. On the other hand, individuals' and authorities' naïve short-term financial decisions through "Ponzi borrower" behaviour (Minsky 1992) resulted in the collapse of the public debt in August 1998.

The deregulated model ended in January 2000, when Vladimir Putin's symbolic "vertical authority" replaced the total liberalization. The stabilization was per-ceived by people as a basic prerequisite to enhance real sector production with the aim of social and economic development. To date, "order and stability" represents one of the essential vital values for the Russian population[1] and one of the major reasons for the majority to support the government's economic policies.

The Russian financial system experienced a wave of speculation in February and December 2014, when the national currency crashed. After the Olympic Games of 2014, in March the ruble fell 15 per cent against the dual-currency (euro-US dollar) basket. At the end of 2014, between 1 November and 17 December, the rate of the ruble to the US dollar dropped down twice from 42 to 80 rubles. An immediate reaction ensued from the new *Mega-Regulator* (Central Bank): on the night of 17 December, the Russian Central Bank decided to raise the reference rate from 10 per cent up to 17 per cent, pointing to an efficient mechanism of withstanding speculative pressure through a centralized power of decisive vertical regulation.

The situation resulted in a feeling of stability and "an increase in confidence amongst Russian private sector firms".[2] The strengthening of the economy is related not only to the appropriate activity of the centralized mega-regulatory monetary and financial authority, but the Central Bank also played the role of a powerful actor for balancing the context for economic growth.

The Russian experience points to some possible financial regulation alterna-tives during crisis times within the peculiar institutional and socio-cultural context of a transition, and with specific results for regulation modelling.

The analysis of financial regulation mechanisms and macro-economic data in Russia during the last quarter of the 20th century reflects two tendencies:

1 an internal vertical regulation model with some positive results; and
2 a regionally geographically integrated national economy through various coor-dination bodies such as the Shanghai Cooperation Organisation, the Eurasian Economic Union (EAEU) and the BRICS group (Brazil, Russia, India, China, South Africa).

This chapter aims to analyse the pendulum of regulation preferences of the Russian social and economic model within the historical genesis of transitive chaos from the Soviet command planning towards the naïve liberal ideas. It then moves back to sustainable middle-term strategic policy choices, aiming at creating investment programmes and plans; from 2009, even long-term projects were discussed in the form of the national industrial policies outlined inthe strategic papers (i.e. the national Energy Strategy [Ministry of Energy of the Russian Federation 2010]), and in the tools of structural modernization of the economy (for instance, direct public financing for research and development [R&D]) and stimulation of private innovations with a tax incentives policy).

Deregulation of the financial system in the decentralized economy

The differentiated liberalization of industries

The attempts of the Russian government to follow the recommendations of liberal economists and the International Monetary Fund (IMF) provoked a deep economic and social downturn in the years from 1990 to 1998: the economic recession was reflected in the 44.2 per cent decrease of GDP between 1989 and 1998 (Figure 12.1a), while the fertility curve on the demographic "Slavic cross" slid down and the mortality curve leapt up (Figure 12.1b).

The market rule was first set up through the liberalization of consumer prices and financial deregulation and resulted in hyper-inflation and unpredictable changes to the legislative framework.[3] However, the industrial enterprises,

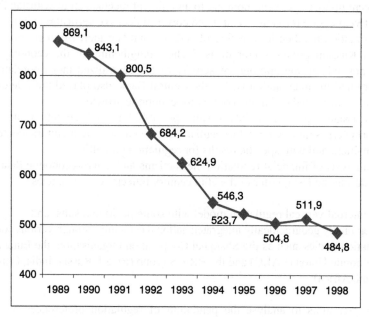

Figure 12.1a The transition dynamics towards the market economy in Russia, 1989–1999: loss of national GDP (billions of US$ 2005) as an economic indicator.

Source: World Bank at: http://databank.worldbank.org/data/home.aspx.

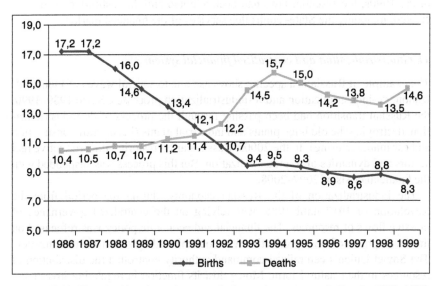

Figure 12.1b The transition dynamics towards the market economy in Russia, 1988–1999: the Slavic "cross" of demographic dynamics (deaths and births per 1,000 people).

Source: World Bank at: http://databank.worldbank.org/data/home.aspx.

especially large plants, were excluded from this process of liberal transition. As they were the major tax-payers in the regional or national budget, they conserved the "Soviet" rules of functioning for some years until the end of the 1990s.[4] The backroom negotiations with local or federal authorities provided large enterprises with advantageous specific conditions of activity. Strategic enterprises also got a specific position, according to the Presidential Decree of 2004 (N 1009).[5] And as late as November 2015, the list of 314 "mono-cities" ("mono-profile municipal units"), based on a constitutive local industrial employer, represents a particular aspect of the public economic policy (Government of Russian Federation 2014).

In the transition environment, people did not have any basic economic under-standing. Vasiliev (2005) documents how tens of millions of citizens were involved in over 1,000 financial pyramid schemes during 1993 and 1994 in Russia. The withdrawal of the State-guided social protection system and a distorted market chaos had a great impact on individuals and the new small companies. The prior-itization of financial gains over long-term productive engagements are typical of most financialized economies "that attempt to integrate into the global market" (Nesvetailova 2004: 999). Subsequent development of financial capital loses links with concrete territory (Soederberg 2002) or the value creation process. This led to speculation, payment problems, tax and wage arrears.

The financial regulation system changed fast and constantly without compulsory establishing rules, and the rules in force were often contradictory. By the middle of the 1990s, the essential laws had been adopted and the institutions had been created, including the State- controlled services of the financial market.

The industrialization and centralized financial system

The example of Russia is a specific showcase due to several waves of industrialization, de-industrialization and re-industrialization processes. Since 1989–1990, the Russian transition had been passing through the process of de-industrialization, destroying the old huge plants and industrial giants (i.e. aircraft construction and car manufacturing). In the 2000s, Russia started restoring the productive real sectors and dynamics of re-industrialization. But this process was suspended with the financial crisis of 2007–2008.

The industrialization of the Russian economy, during the period from the Revolution of 1917 until 1985, was relying on the centralized governance of massive flows of resources. The financial and economic policy was refocused on the development of mass-production with societal modernization and urbanization. The Soviet Union's centralized command authority controlled the distribution of resources in their natural form. Money lost its function in regulating investment flows among sectors. Decisions were taken on the basis of "industrial rationality" (Boltanski and Thévenot 2006 [1991]). But this framework is no longer appropriate for the information society and knowledge economy with its prompt changes and flexible management. One of the reasons for the "perestroika" was the fact that research work and R&D results were implemented very rarely and not correctly in mass-production. So the classical process of transfer from invention to innovation was blocked because of administrative barriers and slowness.

Liberal principles of individual decisions and profit-seeking interests could have unlocked the situation if they had been implemented consecutively from the small business to middle-sized enterprises. But in Russia, the privatizations of huge industrial giants were carried out in the form of sharing the "vouchers" among people who did not have any adequate idea of the market economy because they were educated in the 70-year period of the Soviet administrative command planning. Only after 15–20 years, by 2000–2010, did the population start to understand the meaning of such words as "shares", "joint stock", etc. The first courses in universities on the market economy were introduced from the 1990s, and the first professionals in financial regulation appeared after 1995.

The first catastrophic experiences resulted in the regulatory activity needed by industries and by individuals and showed that all industrialization processes require at a macro level centralized regulation mechanisms for financial flows.

Financial regulation in a transitive economy

The Soviet political economic model needed a structural modernization to eliminate the disproportion between strong regional economies based on the advanced industrial sectors and the weak consumer goods and services sector orientated to satisfy mass demand with an appropriate purchasing power.

The intrusion of individual consumer choice within the economic decision process and the apparition of market freedom and of profit-driven financial capital led to a special context of external dependence on exports for the domestic economy. In the face of such "new" constraints, the abundance of natural resources created the framework for the "resource curse" (Corden and Neary 1982; Sachs and Warner 2001), and rent-seeking strategies allowed economic decisions to focus on the extracting sector to the detriment of other industries (Auty 2001; Torvik 2002).Innovative growth based on the high-road practices of returns on investment in knowledge – instead of returns on investment in oil, gas or forests – needed an elaborated policy, but the Russian society in transition in the early 1990s had neither the competences nor the resources to produce a complex strategic vision with a differentiated regulation framework.

The transformation of centralized administrative planning into market liberal principles was coupled with deregulation such that:

1   The essence of normative changes was directed towards the so-called market's spontaneous self-regulation mechanisms according to individual interests.
2   Former regulatory norms (including old legal requirements and informal social and business practices, the inherited and reformed judiciary system and structure of arbitrage) were assumed to be inefficient.
3   The new legal system was simplified in order to deal with a more complex connections-based real economic system.

The emergence of new important players on the international scene (i.e. BRICS) is related to their fast growth in productivity. More efficient persons and organizations can also be the source of deregulation due to the higher autonomy of economic and social players in these economies. The collectivist social behaviour, assimilated in the community, was changed into more individualist behavioural patterns related to anonymous shareholders' strategies in the composition and the use of capital. At the same time, problems of deregulation were exacerbated by insufficient individual and professional financial literacy, and mistakes were made.

The macro-economic level of the first steps of emergent economies is characterized by the adaptation of resource utilization to a new type of economy, based on technologies and rational management and production processes, which is typical of industrialization dynamics. So, the internal imminent contradictions for the emergent markets are threefold:

1   resource-driven mass-production as a basis for the accumulation of assets to build the knowledge-driven innovative growth (the resource curse) and the volatile expansion of services and the banking sector. This is related to the high-tech dependency that is able to destroy the efficient regional economy (as Ornston [2014] demonstrated in the case of Finland);
2   individualistic behaviour in the sophisticated universe has to take account of the societal consequences, the socio-professional communities and industrial

clusters as an efficient means of transfer of knowledge and techniques (a collective ground for individual success);

3   entrepreneurial initiative and cultural background as the essential basis of creative innovation versus the inefficient and slow legal regulation of the heavy bureaucratic system (creativity and entrepreneurship as a complex subject of regulation).

These dilemmas offer opposing ways to assure economic growth in emergent markets within the context of global high-road competition.

Regulatory activity for liberalization of financial markets

Market principles are based on spontaneous coordination and freedom of choice that is orientated to the individual micro-level behaviour. Since the period from 1985 to 1991, the post-Soviet Russia has been building a new financial system from "ground zero". Attempts to introduce the liberal basics of deregulation into the financial system demonstrated their efficiency in the first period of capital accumulation (1991–2000) in Russia.

In the Soviet Union, from June 1990, the organizational form of the joint-stock company was introduced for enterprises with equity share capital. The same decree of 19 June (Council of Ministers of the USSR 1990) approved the creation and legal status of securities and then the primitive financial market was created.

At that moment, the laws were based on two essential sources – the Soviet legislation and the direct copying of some Western countries' laws chosen for the occasion. Regulation was perceived as an evil inherited from the Soviet period and the illusion of a panacea along with liberal market principles dominated society.

The first experience of spontaneous functioning resulted in the adoption of Law N 445-1 on Enterprises and Entrepreneurship in December 1990 (RSFSR 1990), and Law N 208-FZ on Joint Stock Companies in December 1995 (Government of the Russian Federation 1995), the latter still being in force nowadays. The securities were created to give everyone the possibility of sharing the capital of companies (Law N 445-1), but the competence to use them is still questionable – until very recently, people had no idea of the meaning of the words "bond" or "stock".

The specialized financial companies were regulated by the Federal Services which had a twofold function. But some important fields of financial flows, such as pension funds, insurance or brokerage activities at stock exchanges suffered from a lack of regulation.

At the same time, the deregulation permitted emergent countries to support low exchange rates that contributed to the rise of exports. The default of August 1998 provoked a decrease in industrial production for some months, but by the end of 1998, the ruble devaluation led to the recovery of the Russian productive sector, so the output losses were comparatively low (Perotti 2001: 16–17). Figure 12.2 represents the increase of the share of GDP produced by the national agricultural sector (7.3 per cent in 1999 against 5.6 per cent in 1998) and the decelerated

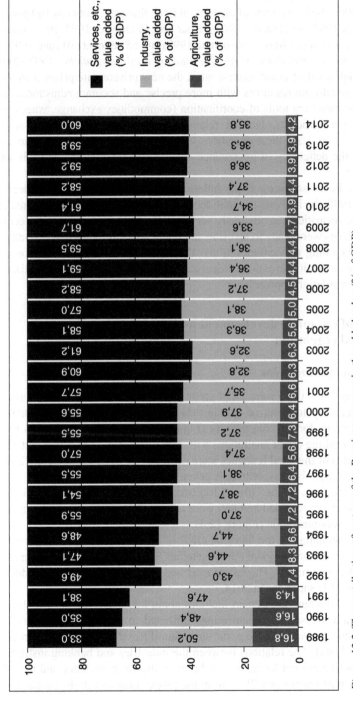

Figure 12.2 The contribution of sectors of the Russian economy in the added value (% of GDP).

Source: World Bank at: http://databank.worldbank.org/data/home.aspx.

reduction of added value by the industrial sector in 1999 and 2000 (37.2 per cent and 37.9 per cent respectively).

In the 1990s, the interest rate of the Central Bank fluctuated between 160 per cent (1 December 1995–9 February 1996), 21 per cent (6 October 1997–10 November 1997), 150 per cent (27 May 1998–4 June 1998) and 55 per cent (10 June 1999–23 January 2000) (Central Bank of Russia, *Banking Statistics Bulletin*, 1997–2001). With the high level of credit interest rates, the new private enterprises were constrained to re-allocate resources with more precise and accurate adjustments and through non-monetary tools of coordination (commodities exchange, wages paid with employer' products, familial relationship instead of competition among market agents, etc.). All these operations took place in the "market" economy, but because of the deficiency of governance mechanisms the non-market tools were unavoidable.

With the Ponzi schemes, hyper-inflation, and the default on State debt on 17 August 1998, the individual's confidence in the banking sector, and in financial markets and securities was obviously very low. By 1997, fewer than 5 per cent of Russian citizens were ready to invest in any financial instruments (except banking deposits) according to Vasiliev (2005). The necessity for stability of economic policy led to the evolution of the political economic regime from total liberalization to the tight regulation approach.

Stability of economic development and the level of financial regulation

The financial system review

On 1 January 2001, there were 2,124 credit organizations in the Russian financial system (according to Bank of Russia data) registered by the Central Bank or holding a licence for banking activity (Figure 12.3). Among them, 1,274 banks and 37 non-banking credit institutions with 3,793 branches were active, but 1,529 (40.3 per cent) of the local branches were departments of Sberbank, and 22 were foreign credit organizations with only seven local branches.

At the same time, on the Official Register, the banking licences of 806 credit organizations were repealed and 869 were taken off the list due to withdrawal of licence or to reorganization (Figure 12.4).

From the beginning of the financial crisis of 2007–2008 and during the whole period of its evolution, ten giant ("too big to fail") banking organizations were supported by the government. The last support was granted just after the introduction of the US and EU sanctions in 2014.

Nowadays, the banking system includes about 800 banks among which there are credit and investment organizations affiliated to strategic enterprises (e.g. Gazprombank), to industries (e.g. the agricultural Rosselkhozbank) or to regions (e.g. Lenoblbank). The relations between the industries and banking institutions are based not on market logic, but on the necessity for confidence and trust that the allocation of resources will occur at the proper time and in the proper place.

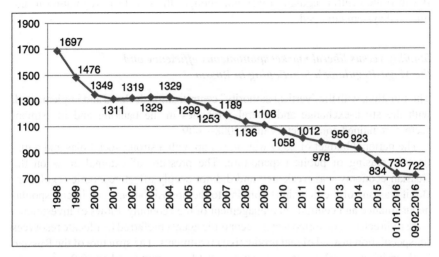

Figure 12.3 The number of active licensed banks and credit institutions in Russia, 1998–2016 (until February 2016).

Source: Central Bank of Russia, *Banking Statistics Bulletin,* issues 1998–2016.

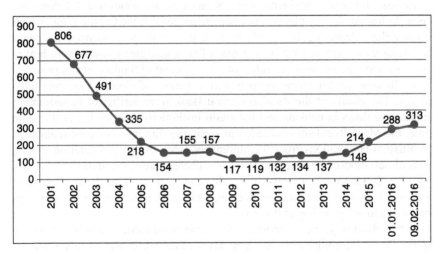

Figure 12.4 The number of annulments of licences and closures of active licensed banks and credit institutions in Russia, 1998–2016 (until February 2016).

Source: Central Bank of Russia, *Banking Statistics Bulletin,* issues 1998–2016.

Because the central regulation was not enough, the mid-level regulation in the financial system emerged.

Stability versus liberal market spontaneous efficiency and the Mega-Regulator's functioning in Russia

The situation, with the "vertical authority" centralization declared and implemented, with the stock-exchange and liberal principles in the banking and investment sectors, remained contradictory until 2008–2009.

The national budget of 2009 was drawn up with a strong social bias and a distinct increasing of public expenditure. The pressure of external crisis on the Russian economy was weakened and did not deeply affect economic regulation. But it was one of the first signs pointing to the opposition between liberal spontaneous finance and centralized management of the economy. Flows of investments were redirected in distorted ways – economic agents preferred to allocate resources for speculation instead of real productive investments. The structure of the Russian banking institutions' assets on 1 January 2014 was composed of 79.9 per cent in rubles and 20.1 per cent in foreign currencies; the investment in debt bonds was 82.1 per cent in rubles and 17.9 per cent in foreign currencies. On 1 January 2016, two years later, after the important speculation period, the evolution is considerable: already 36.8 per cent of securities and 43.1 per cent of debt instruments are in foreign currencies, the increase is 1.8 times for securities and 2.4 times for debts. In Russia, the key player, since September 2013, is the Central Bank, which became the "Mega-Regulator". There are a number of consequences, including bankruptcies for banks, for private pension funds, investment institutions, broker agencies, etc. The evolution of rules, of priorities and of fundamental approaches primarily concerned the tools and policy for targeting inflation with the "key rate" design. The efforts of the Russian Central Bank were inefficient in restraining speculative flows in banking and the credit institutions' market, but at the same time, the Mega-Regulator succeeded in separating the flows of debt repayment by Russian corporations from the currencies' stock exchange operations which were almost blocked by the extremely low exchange rate of the ruble (81.84 rubles for 1 US dollar 1 on 27 January 2016): this almost stopped the desire of Russian individuals or small companies as stock exchange players to move in any way – no one wants to sell or to buy at this rate.

In a cyclical way, the evolution of recentralization came to a new ring of the spiral. On 20 December 1991, the State Bank of the USSR was dissolved and all its assets, liabilities and property in the Russian Soviet Federative Socialist Republic (RSFSR) were transferred to the Central Bank of the RSFSR (Bank of Russia). After the global financial crisis of 2007–2008, all around the world, financial stability and regulation arose again as a common good/common concern in the economy. Financial system regulation was reinforced in the European Union. The discussions on the recentralization of the financial control and monitoring came to an end in Russia with the Law N 251-FZ of 23 July 2013 (Government of the Russian Federation 2013). According to this law, the Central

Bank took the Mega-Regulator role and a whole set of functions of control and supervision of financial markets and institutions. At the time of writing, 24 years on from 1991, the Russian Central Bank has changed its role and represents a structure with the deployed system of mechanisms and tools for regulation.

Knowledge economy and innovative growth: goal and reality

The new challenge of the global high-road competition concerns the competences to regulate creative and entrepreneurial activities, from R&D to its implementation into industrial technologies or products.

At the same period of the financial crisis, in November 2009, a strategic document – the *Energy Strategy* (Ministry of Energy of the Russian Federation (2010) – with the clear aim of modernizing the national economy appeared. The strong dependence of Russian GDP on the export of natural resources is obvious, as shown by the comparison of Figure 12.5 and Figure 12.6.

The pure financial regulation of innovative activity could not help with the problem of the dependency on natural resources. The analysis of the R&D activity of Russian companies demonstrated the inefficiency of the State regulation of knowledge production. In July 2014, the first well in the Russian Arctic was opened, and the boring was carried out with the transfer of knowledge from Norwegian professionals who in fact organized the sinking process. On 9 August 2014, the Russian oil giant Rosneft and the US ExxonMobil announced the start of drilling in the Kara Sea, at Russia's northernmost well Universitetskaya-1.[6]

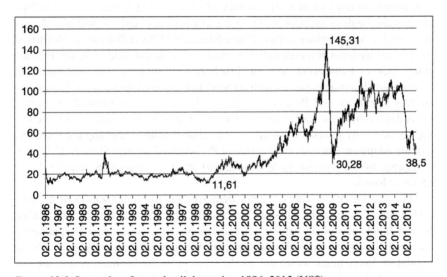

Figure 12.5 Spot prices for crude oil dynamics, 1986–2015 (US$).

Source: U.S. Department of Energy, Energy Information Administration (EIA) (www.eia.gov/dnav/pet/pet_pri_spt_s1_d.htm).

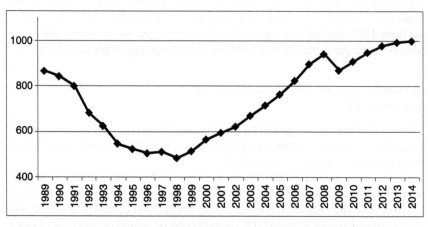

Figure 12.6 The GDP of the Russian Federation, 1989–2014 (constant billions of 2005 US$).

Source: World Bank at: http://databank.worldbank.org/data/home.aspx.

The drilling was carried out by ExxonMobil and North Atlantic Drilling specialists from Norway with the West Alpha oil rig which was designed and built by the Norwegian company. This case permits us to note that Russian technologies in the sector are deeply dependent on the foreign contribution that is still blocked by US and EU sanctions.

Attempts to implement a similar mix of state–market regulation to development in the fields of creation and transfer of knowledge did not succeed. Russia still took the leading place in direct State financing of R&D, but the tax incentives for private business research activities remain inefficient, due to heavy bureaucracy, lack of transparent rules of distribution of support, and weaknesses in technological competences as well as low qualifications in terms of human resources (Garanina and Pokrovskaia 2015). The recurrent reform of tax policy (intended to stimulate R&D), the reinforcing of institutional background (including the necessity to restore confidence to national science and applied research) and the adoption, since October 2015, of the renewed Energy Strategy (Ministry of Energy of the Russian Federation 2010) are all measures to help the R&D sector in Russia.

The example of the energy sector demonstrates the optimization of the real sector, functioning on the basis of market logic. The US and EU sanctions against Russia block access of national companies to both (i) foreign technologies, especially for energy-related equipment; (ii) Western financial markets. The State regulatory instruments which are partly efficient in the financial sector, are not implemented in the same way in the real sector, which needs a sophisticated categorization of supporting tools, supported subjects, and of the limits and rules; i.e. the transparency of criteria for getting any support.

The economic sanctions exposed the vulnerability of the Russian economic model, taking into account the tremendous part played by energy resources in the Russian national income: the oil and gas sector accounts for about 70 per cent of Russia's exports, 25 per cent of GDP and 50 per cent of budget revenues (Garanina and Pokrovskaia 2015). But, at the same time, they gave Russian national economic policy an exceptional opportunity, forcing Russian industrial enterprises to address Russian R&D companies, labs and university departments. The Russian research activity had become ruptured from its practical implementation, partly due to the complex bureaucratic controlling regime and the excessive documentation, special accounting systems, etc. needed to get financial support (i.e. introducing specific registers into the company's accounting system, in order to get the right to tax incentives in the form of charging the R&D activity's costs to the corporate profit tax), and the difficult and expensive intellectual property registration procedures (not easily accessible for individuals, researchers or engineers).

But due to the sanctions, there is a probability that the connections between the labs and the industrial plants will become closer, the tax legislation and Federal Taxation Service instructions could be revised, or a consultancy service could be offered by tax inspectors and the tax authorities for companies.

Since February–March 2014, the financial regulation system, even with the downfall of the ruble (which has been much softer than predicted) demonstrated successful goal-setting in controlling the national currency fluctuations, but especially in the realization of the policy of inflation targeting. Paradoxically, with the fall of the ruble exchange rate twice against the reserve currencies basket (US dollar and euro), inflation is supposed to remain within the limits of 11 per cent and 16 per cent, according to expectations for 2015–2016 (12.9 per cent in 2015, according to data from RosStat, the government statistics agency). Efforts to improve the regulation system are also embedded in the integration process of "emergent" economies through the Eurasian Economic Union (EAEU: Armenia, Belarus, Kazakhstan, Kyrgyzstan and Russia) and BRICS (Brazil, Russia, India, China and South Africa).

Supranational regional financial implications

The regional integration and extension of the EAEU, the successful opposition to the US and European Union sanctions, represent also a source of stabilization for the national economy.

The Chinese yuan and Russian ruble's low exchange rates reflect the export-orientated monetary policy, but this can result in not only an increase of GDP and a contribution to achieving the desired national income level, but also in the threat of the "middle income trap". According to Eichengreen *et al.* (2013: 4), "the regime changes – from autocracy to democracy – increase the likelihood of slowdowns". The involvement of the national currencies of BRICS countries in the mutual payments, the creation of common financial institutions and investment flows aim to help to cope with the global challenge of the "centre–periphery" relations that worsened after the 2008–2009 crisis.

Regarding the financial markets, the complex re-regulatory efforts are focused in the following directions:

1   use of the ruble (and other national currencies, including those of Asian countries, especially the yuan) in bilateral trade;
2   re-orientation of IPOs[7] and financial activities towards the market places of Singapore and Shanghai, etc.;
3   creation of a sophisticated policy of credit for project investment;
4   encouraging banks to grant credits to small-sized enterprises;
5   stimulating direct investments into infrastructure, especially transport and roads;
6   reforming and modernizing the Russian Academy of Sciences to support applied research and new technologies' improvement;
7   reforming the legislation and laws needed for international economic activities; e.g. transfer prices' control and taxation, "de-offshore" regulations; currency and gold reserve and funds' functioning towards economic growth stimulation.

The regional regulation among EAEU members (especially the three closest partners, Russia, Belarus and Kazakhstan) is still at the level of negotiations. By contrast, a significant institutional foundation has been built by the BRICS countries; the Asian Infrastructure Investment Bank (AIIB) has been created in Beijing (China) with India and Russia among the participants and the first agreements were signed in 2015.

Conclusion

The evolution of the Russian financial system represents an example of reforms with regard to the development of macro-economic policy, institutions and related regulatory mechanisms. The analysis of this evolution is helpful for the understanding of the optimal role and set of financial system regulation mechanisms, especially, for emergent countries which are threatened with the "middle-income trap" and face various challenges such as knowledge development, regional high-tech leadership and other challenges of the up-to-date global environment.

Profit-driven accumulation is efficient only when it is based on the rules of the game imposed by relevant and sustainable social institutions such as consistent property laws, well-framed monetary and financial markets, regulatory mechanisms and development policies in relation with the needs and the means of the domestic economic structure. The confidence in the stability of the monetary system, and the trust in the capacities of the State to oversee market operations and ensure regular legal infrastructures to strengthen "justice for all", are necessary to assure stability and the attractiveness of incentives to encourage people to undertake wealth-creating economic activities. But, at the same time, the State has to play its role of general coordinator to moderate the short- and long-term projects and interests according to the needs and constraints of society.

Notes

1 Stability as ideology provoked a specific effect of the fertility increase in 2002 that overcame the "Slavic cross" tendency of the birth rate in Russia from 1985 to 2001.
2 See Markit Russia Business Outlook, "Business confidence continues to steadily improve". Available at: www.markiteconomics.com/Survey/PressRelease.mvc/c72b33 b3d6e441ffa422ca1a25b215d4 (accessed 5 May 2016).

> Market Business Outlook Survey indicated an increase in confidence amongst Russian private sector firms, with sentiment strengthening further from last October's series low. In June 2015 a net balance of +24 percent of firms are anticipating growth of activity over the next 12 months, compared to +20 percent in February and October 2014's +10 percent.
>
> (Markit news release, 13 July 2015: para. 1)

3 Including the retroactive force of new laws; i.e. in July 1992, the new taxation rules were adopted with implementation from January 1992.
4 For example, GazProm started, with a delay of 12 years, from 2004 to implement the State Decree of 1992 on elimination of the social infrastructures from the corporate assets.
5 Decree N 1398-p (Government of Russian Federation 2014) changed the list – which was initially composed of 549 organizations (Presidential Decree N 1009, 4 August 2004) – by reducing it to 172 organisations on 14 October 2015.
6 Reported at the website of Rosneft: www.rosneft.com/news/pressrelease/09082014. html
7 Initial Public Offering, i.e. operation of first sale of stock of a private company to the public in financial markets that seek capital expansion.

References

Auty, R. M. (2001). "The political economy of resource-driven growth", *European Economic Review*, 45(4): 839–846.
Boltanski, L. and Thévenot, L. (2006 [1991]). *On Justification: Economies of Worth.* Princeton, NJ and Oxford: Princeton University Press. (English translation of *De la justification. Les économies de la grandeur*. Paris: Gallimard.)
Central Bank of Russia (1997). *Banking Statistics Bulletin*, issue 4.
Central Bank of Russia (1998). *Banking Statistics Bulletin*, 2–3(57–58). Available at: http://cbr.ru/publ/BBS/Bbs9802-3.pdf (accessed 5 May 2016).
Central Bank of Russia (2001). *Banking Statistics Bulletin*, 1(92). Available at: http://cbr. ru/publ/BBS/Bbs0101r.pdf (accessed 5 May 2016).
Central Bank of Russia (2016). *Banking Statistics Bulletin*, 160. Available at: http://cbr.ru/ analytics/bank_system/obs_1602.pdf (accessed 5 May 2016).
Corden, W. M. and Neary, J. P. (1982). "Booming sector and de-industrialisation in a small open economy", *The Economic Journal*, 92(368): 825–848.
Council of Ministers of the USSR (1990). Decree N 590 of 19 June. On Approval of the Joint-Stock Companies and Limited Liability Companies and of the Securities Act.
Eichengreen, B., Park, D. and Shin, K. (2013). "Growth slowdowns redux: New evidence on the middle-income trap", NBER Working Paper No. 18673.
Garanina, O. L. and Pokrovskaia, N. N. (2015). "Industrial policy design, innovations and quality of institutions: The case of Russia", in *International Conference "GSOM Emerging Markets Conference 2015: Business and Government Perspectives",*

Graduate School of Management of St Petersburg State University (October 15–17, 2015). St Petersburg: Graduate School of Management of St Petersburg State University, pp. 151–160.

Government of the Russian Federation (1995). Federal Law N 208-FZ of 26 December (edition as of 29 June 2015). On Joint Stock Companies.

Government of the Russian Federation (2013). Federal Law N 251-FZ of 23 July. On Amendments to Certain Legislative Acts of the Russian Federation in Connection with the Transfer to the Central Bank of the Russian Federation Powers to Regulate, Control and Supervise in the Financial Markets.

Government of the Russian Federation (2014). Decree N 1398-p of 29 July (last changes adopted on 24 November 2015). Approving the List of the Mono-Profile Single-Industry Municipal Entities of the Russian Federation (Mono-Cities).

Ministry of Energy of the Russian Federation (2010). *Energy Strategy of Russia for the Period Up to 2030*. Moscow: Institute of Energy Strategy. Available at: www.energystrategy.ru/ projects/docs/ES-2030_(Eng).pdf (accessed 5 May 2016).

Minsky, H. P. (1992). "The financial instability hypothesis", Working Paper No. 74, The Jerome Levy Economics Institute of Bard College, Annandale-on-Hudson, New York.

Nesvetailova, A. (2004). "Coping in the global financial system: The political economy of nonpayment in Russia", *Review of International Political Economy*, 11(5): 995–1021.

Ornston, D. (2014). "When the high road becomes the low road: The limits of high-technology competition in Finland", *Review of Policy Research*, 31(5): 454–477.

Perotti, E. (2001). "Lessons from the Russian meltdown: The economics of soft legal constraints", Working Paper No. 379, University of Amsterdam.

Presidential Decree (2004). Decree N 1009 of 4 August (last changes made 10 February 2016). On Approval of the List of Strategic Enterprises and Strategic Joint-Stock Companies.

RSFSR (1990). Law N 445-1 of 25 December. On Enterprises and Entrepreneurial Activity.

Sachs, J. D. and Warner, A. M. (2001). "The curse of natural resources", *European Economic Review*, 45(4–6): 827–838.

Soederberg, S. (2002). "On the contradictions of the New International Financial Architecture", *Third World Quarterly*, 23(4): 607–620.

Sombart, W. (1913). *Krieg und Kapitalismus*. München, Germany: Duncker & Humblot.

Torvik, R. (2002). "Natural resource rent seeking and welfare", *Journal of Development Economics*, 67(2): 455–470.

Vasiliev, D. (2005). "Capital market development in Russia". Available at: http://lnweb90.worldbank.org/eca/eca.nsf/Attachments/Vassiliev/$File/VassilievPaper.pdf (accessed 5 May 2016).

Wright, E. O. and Rogers, J. (2015). *American Society: How it Really Works*. New York and London: W.W. Norton & Company.

13 Minsky in Beijing

Shadow banking, credit expansion and debt accumulation in China

Yan Liang

Introduction

Since the Global Financial Crisis that erupted in 2008, China has undergone two salient developments in its financial landscape.[1] First, there has been a rapid and massive growth of the "shadow banking" sector that has played an increasingly weighty role in credit creation. And second, debt level, especially in the corporate sector, has risen significantly to reach an alarming level. The two changes have led some commentators to claim that China was soon to experience a "Minsky Moment", where a sudden unwinding of debt would trigger destructive debt deflation.

Indeed, things look bleak. China had one of the largest levels of growth of credit: 83 percentage points increase in credit as a percentage of Gross Domestic Product (GDP) during 2007 and 2014 (McKinsey & Co. 2015). This fast growth of credit helped China to weather one of the worst global recessions, but at a lasting, hefty cost. It puts China, especially the private corporate sector, deeply in debt. The total debt in China increased from US$7.4 trillion to US$28.2 trillion from 2007 to the second quarter of 2014 (McKinsey & Co. 2015). But a high level of debt in and of itself may not be indicative of financial fragility, as Minsky teaches. What is more important is to examine the level of debt obligations and the capacity to pay. This can be done by taking a balance sheet approach, through which the asset and liability structure of an economic unit will be revealed.

The rise in shadow banks played a critical role in expanding credit. Shadow banks, or non-bank financial institutions (NBFIs), encompass a variety of institutions and products in China, including bank off-balance-sheet wealth management products (WMPs), trust loans, entrusted loans, undiscounted bank acceptance, peer-to-peer (P2P) lending, leasing and finance companies, pawnshops, and so on (see Liang forthcoming). Wealth management products and trust loans are the two most important components of the shadow banks, given their sheer size and significant impacts. Due to the opaqueness of the sector, estimates of the size of the shadow bank sector range widely, from 14 to 70 per cent of GDP (Yao 2015). But it is unequivocal that shadow banks have grown rapidly. According to the China Banking Regulatory Committee (CBRC 2015), the assets of the shadow banks grew seven-fold, from 3.5 trillion yuan (US$556 billion) in 2008 to 25 trillion yuan in 2014 (US$4 trillion). The growth rate in assets peaked during 2012–2013 at 34 per cent and dropped to 10 per cent in 2014, mainly due to tighter regulations. In 2014, shadow banks accounted for around 18 per cent of the total social financing (TSF), a measure of broad credit flows in China.

The surge in shadow banking is driven by both structural and transitory factors. On the structural front, China's banking sector is dominated by state-owned commercial banks (SOCBs), which primarily lend to large state-owned enterprises (SOEs) and large private enterprises. This leaves many small and medium-sized private enterprises (SMEs) underfinanced. It was estimated that SMEs account for 97 per cent of registered industrial firms, 65 per cent of urban employment and 60 per cent of GDP and yet, they receive only 25 per cent of SOCBs' lending (Tsai 2015). These SMEs have to rely on internal funding or shadow banks for financing. On the other hand, due to the ceiling on deposit rates (which was just removed in October 2015), investors seek alternative venues to invest their savings. Wealth management products became an appealing alternative, because they are often distributed by formal banks (even if they are not issued by these banks) and considered as safe as bank deposits and yet they offer an average yield of 5.5 per cent, compared to the 1.75 per cent on one-year deposits. These provide the demand-side incentives for shadow banks. On the supply side, banks face stringent regulations in terms of capital and reserve requirements, loss reserves, loan-to-deposit ratio, lending rates, industrial exposures, etc. To evade regulations, banks are incentivized to move some of their operations off the balance sheet. The same regulatory arbitrage also creates a market niche, which allows trusts and other shadow institutions to grow without having to compete directly with the powerful banks.

In addition to the structural factors, the 2008 global financial crisis and the Chinese government's response to the crisis gave extra momentum for shadow banks. The Chinese government launched a US$586 stimulus plan in 2008, most of which was funded by credit. The monetary authorities also ordered banks to lend aggressively. Loans worth US$15 trillion – the size of the entire US commercial banking sector – were lent out in just five years (Keohane 2014). In anticipation of inflation and an overheated real estate market, the government ordered the banks to tighten credit in 2010. However, projects that had been initiated called for continuous financing, and banks scrambled to search for profitable business opportunities in the low-yield environment. Therefore, the expansion and contraction cycle of bank credit fuelled the growth of non-bank credit.

Certain institutional features of shadow banks render them a risky element to the financial system. But more importantly, the level and pattern of credit creation by these shadow banks significantly elevate financial fragility. From this perspective, this chapter aims to take a Minskian approach to examine the role of shadow banks in credit expansion and the implications thereof for financial stability. Minsky's incisive analysis of shadow banks (or what he called "fringe banks") and the endogenous process of financial fragility would shed great light on China's situation, even if Minsky's writings primarily focus on the United States.

The chapter is organized as follows. The second section provides a brief rundown of Minsky's key insights on financial fragility. The third section then uses the Minskian lens to examine the institutional risks of shadow banks. The fourth section underlines some institutional risks that stem from the development of shadow banking. The fifth section then develops the analysis by investigating the role of shadow banks in expanding credit and worsening the quality of credit, which aggravates the debt problem. The last section provides some concluding thoughts.

Minsky on shadow banks and financial fragility

Minsky denounced the mainstream financial market efficiency hypothesis and propounded the Financial Instability Hypothesis (FIH). Minsky[2] argued that a financially complex capitalist economy tends to develop financial instability over time. In particular, when economic units use debt financing to make a position, they are susceptible to various degrees of financial risk, which hinges upon the distinct income–debt relations. Minsky identified three financing positions; namely, hedge, speculative, and Ponzi finance. Hedge financing units are those that can meet all their debt payment obligations through cash flows from normal operations; speculative units can meet payment commitments on "income account", but not the principal of their liabilities, which require them to rollover their liabilities. And for Ponzi units, their cash flows are insufficient to pay either the principal or interest. They will need to resort to refinancing or selling assets to meet their debt obligations. Minsky (1992) wrote:

> It can be shown that if hedge financing dominates, then the economy may well be an equilibrium-seeking and – containing system. In contrast the greater the weight of speculative and Ponzi finance, the greater the likelihood that the economy is a deviation-amplifying system.
>
> (Minsky 1992: 7)

Moreover, over a long period of stability, the economy tends to move from a financial structure where hedge finance dominates to one where speculative and Ponzi finance become significant. And therefore, as the oft-cited Minsky catchphrase goes, "stability is destabilizing". There are multifaceted factors that contribute to the transformation; and these factors are endogenously created. For example, stability brews a sense of complacency and encourages imprudent risk taking. Stability and inflationary pressure prompt monetary tightening, which could push some speculative units into a Ponzi position.

Minsky long ago noted the rise of shadow banks and the implications thereof. As he (Minsky 2008 [1986]: 96) argued, the financial system became more speculative and "accelerate[d] the trend toward fragile finance" in the early 1960s. And one of the contributing factors is that "fringe banking institutions and practices – such as business lending by finance companies, the issue of commercial papers by corporations, REITs and nonmember commercial banks have grown relative to other elements in the financial system" (2008 [1986]: 96). Minsky (2008 [1986]: 231) observed that "Ponzi financing is quite often associated with fringe or fraudulent financial practices . . . Interest- and dividend-paying units that borrow to pay for investments and that accrue income engage in a variety of Ponzi financing." Following this line, Wray (2010) puts emphasis on the fact that unlike other economic agents, banks take positions in longer-term assets by issuing short-term liabilities. Therefore they have a much higher leverage ratio and a severe duration mismatch. In other words, banks by nature engage in speculative financing and rely on refinancing. This makes the central bank's lender of last resort facilities indispensable for the stability of the banking system. However, unlike traditional banks, shadow banks do not have direct access to the central bank's liquidity. This suggests that fringe banks are much riskier than traditional banks and yet they have a much lower capacity to bear risks. This makes shadow banks a highly destabilizing element to the financial system.

Worse still, fringe banks are tightly connected to traditional banks, so any problems in the former are likely to be transmitted to the latter. This is because fringe banks rely on traditional banks as their *de facto* lenders of last resort "through relations that are often formalized by lines of credit" (Minsky 2008 [1986]: 96). As Kregel (2010) interpreted Minsky's analysis:

> A consolidated balance-sheet for the financial system as a whole – every liability in the nonbank financial system, as well as the short-term liabilities of the nonbank nonfinancial system – are all ultimately dependent on the liquidity of the deposit liabilities of the banks. This means that a failure to meet a payment commitment by a financial institution will have an impact on all the others in the system.
>
> (Kregel 2010: 4)

To put it another way, the interconnectedness between shadow banks and traditional banks renders the latter vulnerable:

> [S]ome assets held by banks weaken when the losses and cash-flow shortfalls of the fringe institutions become apparent to the market. Consequently, the already weakened portfolios of some banks are made even weaker when these banks act as the proximate lender of last resort to fringe institutions.
>
> (Minsky 2008 [1986]: 99)

It becomes even more debilitating for traditional banks when they need to bail out fringe banks. This leads Minsky to conclude that:

> The potential for a domino effect, which can cause a serious disruption, is implicit in a hierarchical financial pattern. The introduction of additional layering in finance, together with the invention of new instruments designed to make credit available by tapping pools of liquidity, is evidence, beyond that revealed by the financial data itself, of the increased fragility of the system.
>
> (Minsky 2008 [1986]: 99)

Although Minsky's writings focus on advanced capitalist economies like the United States, his insights could shed great light on developing countries like China, to which we now turn.

Institutional risks of shadow banks

As mentioned above, Minsky holds that shadow banks have the tendency to take excessive risks, and that seems to reverberate with the situation in China. Shadow banks face stern competition from the state-owned and -controlled commercial banks that dominate the Chinese financial system. Therefore, shadow banks tend to adopt riskier business practices to gain a market niche and higher returns. However, shadow banks are much more loosely regulated and do not have the direct, explicit access to public backstops, which means that their capacity to bear risks is much weaker.

Take the trust companies, for example. Trusts are the largest NBFIs in China, and their asset under management (AUM) has tripled since 2010 to reach 14 trillion yuan at the end of 2014 (Yao 2015). Trusts face a very low capital requirement in China, which stood at a minuscule 300 million yuan as of 2010. Although the Measures for the Administration of Net Capital of Trust Companies passed by the China Banking Regulatory Commission (CBRC) in 2010 requires that trust companies maintain a ratio of no less than 40 per cent of net capital to net assets, the International Monetary Fund (IMF) (2014) data show that the trust AUM far exceeded their thin capital, producing a leverage ratio of 40 times for the top ten trusts. This means that a mere 3 per cent reduction in asset values could wipe out their entire capital. Trusts are also opaque: KPMG (2012) reports that only 29 registered trusts (out of 66) disclosed their net capital for regulatory reporting purposes, and only two publicly listed trusts reported their returns. Trust loans made up 11 per cent of TSF in 2013 (People's Bank of China 2015), but the loans were often given to industries that were either plagued by excess capacity or prohibited by the government, and hence declined by banks. Figure 13.1 shows the asset distribution of trusts, where fundamental industry (manufacturing, mining, etc.) and real estate accounted for 31 per cent of the total trust assets. It is well noted that the manufacturing and mining industries have suffered from severe excess capacity and the real estate sector is also saturated with inventory and undergoing downward price adjustments.

In addition to making loans, trusts cooperate with banks in many other areas, such as intermediating entrusted loans (where a client relends bank loans to a third party, using trusts as the intermediary). Trusts often use banks to market and distribute WMPs. Banks also sell loans to trusts that, in turn, package the loans into WMPs and sell them to investors. Finally, it is estimated that the majority of funding for trusts – as much as 70 per cent of it (Yao and Hu 2015) – comes from banks. These tight connections between trusts and banks suggest that if any problems occur in the trusts, they could be contagious and spread to banks.

Wealth management products are equally risky. These are essentially informal securitizations of bank loans and other assets by banks (off balance sheet) and

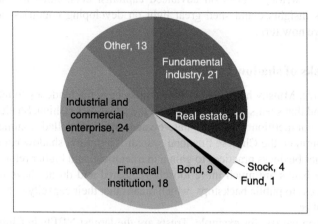

Figure 13.1 Trust asset distribution by sector (%).

Source: CEIC.

trusts. As of the third quarter of 2013, outstanding WMPs had reached 9.9 trillion yuan, or 18 per cent of GDP. First, the majority of the underlying assets of WMPs are bank loans. In particular, banks tend to securitize and sell off those loans that are considered risky and thus require higher-risk-weighted capital. Because the number of loans is limited, the diversification of risks is weak. Although the CBRC mandated that post-2010 WMPs must contain at least 30 per cent non-loan assets (mostly government, central bank and corporate bonds and various inter-bank obligations), there was little detail given on which particular bonds or instruments were included in a given product or the share thereof. It is estimated that 40–50 per cent of WMP assets find their ways to loan-type activities (Standard Chartered 2014). Second, although WMPs closely resemble collateral debt obli-gations (CDOs) in structure, there is no rating system, no tranching based on credit risk, and no secondary market where investors can transfer ownership of WMPs. Therefore, liquidity risk is excessive. Third, an increasingly large share of WMPs are short-term. In 2007, less than 10 per cent of WMPs were for under 90 days, and more than half were for a year or more. By the end of 2010, about 40 per cent were for under 90 days and less than 20 per cent were for a year or over. However, funds raised through WMPs are often invested in long-term projects, such as property development, which aggravates the maturity mismatch.

Fourth, banks and trusts adopt many problematic practices in producing and selling WMPs, of which the most prominent ones are asset pooling and "ever-greening". The former refers to the practice where banks pool money from various money market instruments, interbank notes, bonds, credit assets, etc., into an asset pool and issue WMPs based on this asset pool. This heightens liquidity and matu-rity mismatches and provides insufficient information on the risks and returns of the underlying assets. Ever-greening refers to the practice where banks sell new WMPs and use the funds to meet obligations of old WMPs. This has aptly been denounced as a Ponzi scheme by a senior banking executive (Reuters 2012). One recent example is telling. Tianjin Infrastructure Construction & Investment Group Co. Ltd., the city's biggest financing vehicle, took four billion loans at an interest rate above 10 per cent from trusts, including two billion from CITIC (China International Trust and Investment Corporation). Tianjin's main local government funding vehicle (LGFV) faces loan-servicing costs totalling 246 billion yuan between 2013 and 2019. But its investment has been generating negative returns for years. This kind of lending makes ever-greening a common practice for trusts. Although the CBRC banned the practice in 2010, the effectiveness of the ban is highly dubious, as trusts often pool funds from different WMPs. So it is not clear what the sources and uses of the WMP funds are. Finally, banks often act alone to originate, distribute, and provide custody and management of WMPs; this puts them in a vulnerable position and puts their reputation in danger should one or a few WMPs default.

All the above echoes Minsky's characterization of shadow banks. Due to profit-driven motives and lax regulations, shadow banks adopt risky practices, "notably for the amount of leverage they can use, the size of their liquidity buffers and the type of lending and investing they can do" (McCulley 2009). And yet, without public backstops, shadow banks are incapable of weathering major difficulties. Defaults of individual WMPs and closures of trusts have started to emerge, but a system-wide debacle has not yet occurred, thanks partly to bailouts by banks. One prominent case is the default of the "Credit Equals Gold #1" WMP in 2014. "Credit Equals Gold #1" was a WMP produced by the China Credit Trust Company and marketed by the Industrial and Commercial Bank of China (ICBC). Issued in 2010, the product raised around 3 billion yuan for Shanxi Zhenfu Energy Group, a mining company based in Shanxi province. The WMP promised to pay 10 per cent annual return and had a maturity of three years. However, Shanxi Zhenfu Energy Group ran into some legal problems and its mining operations were suspended. As a result, it was not able to repay the trust WMP upon maturity. Enraged investors demanded that ICBC should repay the WMP, but ICBC declined initially, asserting that it was only responsible for marketing the product. Eventually, under the increasing pressure from investors and the media exposure, ICBC set up a bailout and paid back the principal in full (Perry and Welterwitz 2015). Bailouts effectively stave off widespread defaults of WMPs, and yet they exacerbate the moral-hazard problem and promote excess demand for and supply of WMPs.

Shadow banks, credit expansion and systemic risks

The rapid growth of shadow lending contributes to excessive expansion of credit and degrading quality of credit, both of which elevate systemic risks. As mentioned above, credit expanded by 83 percentage points in just seven years, which led some observers to put China in the league of crisis-wrecked countries like Greece, Ireland, and Portugal (McKinsey & Co. 2015). China's debt-to-GDP ratio now reached 217 per cent (if the financial sector debt was included, the ratio would have increased to 281 per cent). What is more problematic than the credit expansion and

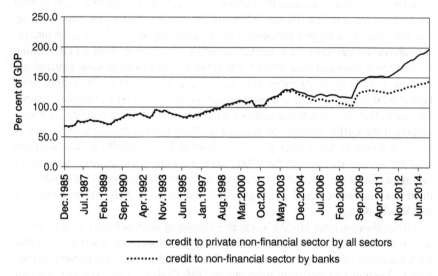

Figure 13.2 Credit to private non-financial sector by all sectors and credit to private non-financial sector by banks.

Source: BIS (2015).

rising level of debt is the declining quality of debt. Much of this credit expansion and declining quality of debt can be attributed to the shadow banks.

Figure 13.2 compares credit extended to the non-financial private sector by all sectors and credit extended to the non-financial private sector by banks. It clearly shows the divergence between the two sources of credit since 2008, and this divergence reflects shadow lending. Between 2007 and mid-2014, bank lending grew at an annual rate of 18 per cent, while shadow lending doubled that rate. Figure 13.3 demonstrates that trust loans have grown drastically while the growth of bank loans has decelerated. Other forms of shadow lending, such as bank acceptance bills and entrusted loans, despite their decelerating growth, still registered a higher growth rate than bank loans. It is evident that without shadow banks, credit would not have expanded at such a fast pace. This is especially the case after 2010, when formal banks were ordered to tighten lending. As a result of the vast credit expansion, the total debt in China increased from US$7.4 trillion to US$28.2 trillion between 2007 and the second quarter of 2014 (McKinsey & Co. 2015).

The sector that receives the largest credit flows and hence is most indebted is the corporate sector, as illustrated by Figure 13.4. The corporate sector debt has grown from 72 per cent of GDP to 125 per cent in just seven years. However, the increase in indebtedness is coupled with a declining profitability. This is highly disconcerting because, as Minsky (1976) puts it:

> The behavior of the economy is affected by the relation between cash payment commitments on existing debts and anticipated cash receipts. The

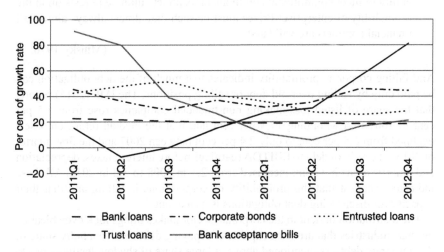

Figure 13.3 Annual growth rate of bank loans and selective shadow lending.

Source: IMF (2014).

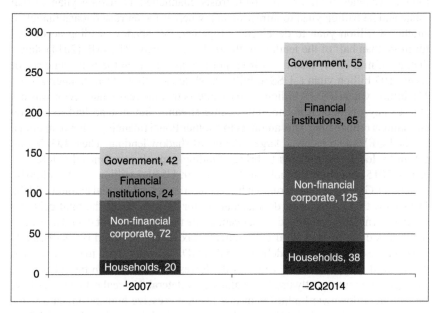

Figure 13.4 Debt-to-GDP ratio by sectors, 2007 and mid-2014.

Source: McKinsey & Co. (2015).

ability to meet commitments on financial contracts ultimately rests upon the profitability of enterprise: Prices must be such that almost always almost all financial contracts are validated.

(Minsky 1976: 3)

And falling corporate profitability indicates that much of the debt obligation can be paid only by rolling over old debt or selling positions. The IMF (2014) reports that the share of listed loss-making non-financial companies rose from 5.5 per cent in 2007 to a whopping 17.3 per cent and that the median return on assets declined from 6.5 per cent to only 2.4 per cent between 2007 and the first quarter of 2013. The ratio of debt to EBITDA (earnings before interest, taxes, depreciation and amortization) in China increased from 2.1 in 2008 to 3.2 in 2012. All these indicators suggest that the profitability of corporations is falling and that their capacity for discharging debt obligations is weakening.

The distribution of debt in the corporate sector makes things look even bleaker, because industries that are least capable of repaying debt receive a hefty share of the corporate debt. As mentioned above, a large share of shadow lending goes to industries that have excess capacity and/or are deemed unprofitable or are prohibited by the government, since those industries have no other ways of getting credit but from the shadow banks. Two such sectors are real estate and local government funding vehicles (LGFVs). In 2014, trusts channelled 11 trillion yuan to real estate and 23 trillion yuan to infrastructure, whereas the entrusted loans funnelled another 8 trillion yuan to developers. Together, this shadow lending accounted for more than half of the lending to the real estate sector. The IMF (2014) shows that, as of mid-2014, cash flows from normal operations in the real estate sector were −103 billion yuan (−US$16 billion), while cash flows from financing were 116 billion yuan (US$18 billion). This suggests that the real estate sector was not able to pay off debt from normal income streams, but instead had to rely on continuous refinancing. This amounts to another Ponzi financing scheme in effect.

The LGFVs also received large amounts of shadow lending. These LGFVs are set up by local governments to bridge funding gaps. It is estimated (McKinsey & Co. 2015) that LGFVs took out loans worth US$1.7 trillion as of mid-2014. Through LGFVs, local government has accumulated a substantial amount of debt. Data show that government debt accounted for 55 per cent of the total debt, but local governments comprised 51 per cent of the total government debt. On the one hand, it is doubtful that local governments' tax revenues would rise sufficiently to cover the ever-expanding debt, given that GDP growth dipped to 6.9 per cent as of the third quarter of 2015, which is the lowest since 2009. On the other hand, local governments mostly use land values as collateral. Yet real estate prices have undergone a downward adjustment due to the excessive housing inventory and lower sales. At the end of 2014, new home prices had dropped by 3.1 and 4.2 per cent in tier 1 and tier 2 cities, respectively. This means that local governments may have to come up with extra collateral, or loans will be recalled. Finally, local governments invested mostly in infrastructure, such as railroads, highways and public housing. These projects, albeit socially beneficial, have a long gestation period to generate economic profits, or generate any profits at all, given that some of these projects are politically driven and not economically viable. The most infamous case is the "ghost city" of Ordos in the Kangbashi district of Inner Mongolia, where apartments were built and could shelter a million people, about four times the city's current population (*BBC News* 2012). In short, local governments have incurred debt that they simply seem unable to repay.

Despite the rising credit flows and debt level, credit is becoming less effective to drive real GDP growth. The credit intensity – the change in credit-per-unit increase in GDP – has increased significantly from 1.01 in the period 2004–2007 to 1.8 in the period 2010–2013 (IMF 2015a). Aside from the fact that much of the credit has gone to sectors/projects that contribute little to real economic growth, the increase in credit intensity is also attributable to the fact that much of the credit has not been used to promote investment (new capital formation), but for other purposes (IMF 2015a). One of the worst cases is where credit is used to pay for debt services. Because shadow banks accounted for an increasing share of credit and typically charged higher interest rates (see Table 13.1), it is not surprising that interest expenses grew at an annual rate of 27.8 per cent in China between 2007 and 2012 – the highest among all large emerging markets. According to the BIS (2015), the private non-financial-corporations'debt-service ratio increased from 13 per cent in 2008 to 20 per cent as of the first quarter of 2015 (see Figure 13.5).

Table 13.1 Selected interest rate on bank loans and shadow credit, 2013

Loan type	Average interest rate (%)	Average maturity (yr)
Bank loans: short term	4.6	1
Bank loans: medium/long term	7.2	8
Shadow credit: short term	6	1
Shadow credit: medium/long term	9	3

Source: Mackenzie (2013).

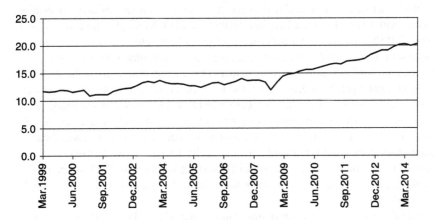

Figure 13.5 Debt servicing ratio of non-financial corporates.

Source: BIS (2015).

As a result of falling profitability and rising debt services, Chinese firms resort to borrowing to cover their debt obligations. The Beijing-based Hua Chuang Securities Co. estimated that 7.6 trillion yuan (US$1.2 trillion) credit, or 45 per cent of the new TSF, was used to make interest payments (Bloomberg News 2015). The use of credit to refinance existing debts creates pernicious debt snowballing without contributing to real economic activities.

In closing, shadow banks played an indispensable role in credit expansion and debt accumulation. But such debt accumulation has not been validated by real economic growth. Shadow banks' lending to industries/entities that are not capable of meeting debt obligations contributed to the declining quality of credit. The high costs of shadow bank credit, coupled with the declining corporate profits, make debt repayment increasingly difficult for the corporate sector. Although data paucity prevents a precise calculation, it is reasonable to suspect that many corporations may transform into speculative and Ponzi entities as they rely on continuous refinancing or collateral/asset price appreciation to discharge debt obligations. All these suggest an elevated level of financial fragility in China.

That said, it is unlikely that a debt deflation type of financial crisis will erupt in China in the very near future. There are several factors that help the Chinese financial system to avert a debt crisis. First, China's debt is predominantly domestically owned. Although Chinese corporations have been tapping cheap global credit – for example, non-bank corporations took out new foreign loans worth US$366.4 billion in 2013 – this accounted for only about a quarter of the US$1.45 trillion in new domestic loans lent by Chinese banks. Furthermore, China's US$960 billion worth of external debt represented only 9 per cent of GDP and 35 per cent of export and primary income revenues in 2014. And China has accumulated close to US$4 trillion foreign exchange reserves. This means that China has the capacity to honour its external debt and to stave off disorderly capital outflows that could trigger banking and currency crises. Second, the financial system is still dominated by state-controlled commercial banks; and although banks' asset quality has declined in recent years, the amount of non-performing loans (NPL) is still low and capital buffers are abundant. According to the IMF data (2015b), the NPL as a percentage of gross loans stood at 1.23 per cent for large state-owned banks, 1.12 per cent for joint-stock banks, 1.11 per cent for city banks and 1.87 per cent for rural banks. This means that even if the NPLs of shadow banks partly migrate to banks' balance sheets given their tight connections and contagion risks, the low base would provide much of the margins for cushioning. Furthermore, capital as a percentage of risk-weighted assets weighs in at 12.62 per cent, 10.05 per cent, and 10.62 per cent for state-owned banks, joint-stock banks and other banks, respectively. These are two to three times the capital requirements set by the Basel III finance reforms in 2009. It seems that banks have the capacity to weather financial difficulties should shadow banks go south.

Finally, the Chinese central government has the policy will and financial resources to write off bad debt and recapitalize banks. According to a Fung Global Institute's research report (Sheng *et al.* 2015), China's national balance sheet shows that the public sector had net assets of 87 trillion yuan. Not to mention that the central government is essentially a monopoly of the sovereign currency. This means that the central government could restructure local government debt as sovereign debt, write off bad loans on banks' books and recapitalize them, and even support the real estate market through land purchases, etc. All these drive home the conclusion that a full-blown debt crisis is unlikely to erupt in China in the near future. However, the heavy indebtedness may scar the corporate sector and put constraints on local governments over an extended period, as they struggle to meet debt obligations and trim investment and discretionary spending.

Conclusion

Based on a Minskian analysis, this chapter argues that the surge in shadow banks in China has contributed to massive credit expansion in China. Evidence suggests that shadow banks have caused elevated financial risks at both the institutional and systemic levels. This has prompted some commentators to call for the advent of China's "Minsky Moment", featuring a sharp plunge in asset price and debt deflation. However, an imminent financial crisis is unlikely to occur due to the financial prowess of the traditional banks and the central government. That said, shadow lending and debt build-up are not inconsequential. The debt burden may push private enterprises to hold back investment and production, further slowing down the economy and, in turn, exacerbating the debt burden. Therefore, policymakers must take shrewd and measured steps to regulate shadow banking, to carefully deleverage, to continue to rebalance the skewed demand structure, and to boost real economic growth. Minsky's prescient policy suggestion is valuable and worth noting:

> In a world of businessmen and financial intermediaries who aggressively seek profit, innovators will always outpace regulators; the authorities cannot prevent changes in the structure of portfolios from occurring. What they can do is keep the asset-equity ratio of banks within bounds by setting equity-absorption ratios for various types of assets. If the authorities constrain banks and are aware of the activities of fringe banks and other financial institutions, they are in a better position to attenuate the disruptive expansionary tendencies of our economy.
>
> (Minsky 2008 [1986]: 281)

Notes

1 This chapter is part of a project funded by the Institute for New Economic Thinking (Grant No. INO14-00012).
2 See Minsky (2008 [1986]), among other works.

References

Bank for International Settlements (BIS) (2015). *BIS Statistical Data*, 2015. Available at: www.bis.org/statistics/ (accessed on 20 December 2015).

BBC News (2012). "Ordos: The Biggest Ghost Town in China", 17 March 2012. Available at: www.bbc.com/news/magazine-17390729 (accessed on 2 May 2016).

Bloomberg News (2015). "China Has a $1.2 Trillion Ponzi Finance Problem", 19 November. Available at: www.bloomberg.com/news/articles/2015-11-19/china-has-a-1-2-trillion-ponzi-finance-problem-as-debt-piles-up (accessed on 21 November 2015).

China Banking Regulatory Commission (CBRC) (2015). *CBRC 2014 Annual Report*. Beijing: CBRC.

International Monetary Fund (2014). *Global Financial Stability Report*, April. Washington, DC: IMF.

International Monetary Fund (2015a). *Regional Economic Outlook*, May. Washington, DC: IMF.

International Monetary Fund (2015b). *Global Financial Stability Report*. Washington, DC: IMF.

Keohane, D. (2014). "China's Credit Spiral", *Financial Times FT Alphaville blog*, posted 3 January 2014. Available at: http://ftalphaville.ft.com/2014/01/03/1731392/chinas-credit-spiral/ (accessed on 6 June 2015).

KPMG (2012). *Mainland China Trust Survey*. Hong Kong: KPMG.

Kregel, J. (2010). "Minsky Moments and Minsky's Proposal for Regulation of an Unstable Financial System", presentation at the 19th Annual Hyman P. Minsky Conference on the State of the US and World Economies, Jerome Levy Economics Institute of Bard College, Annandale-on-Hudson, New York.

Liang, Y. (forthcoming). "Shadow Banks and Credit Driven Growth", *The Chinese Economy*.

McCulley, P. (2009). "The Shadow Banking System and Hyman Minsky's Economic Journey", Economic and Market Commentary, May 2009, Pimco. Available at: www.pimco.com/insights/economic-and-market-commentary/global-central-bank-focus/the-shadow-banking-system-and-hyman-minskys-economic-journey (accessed on 10 October 2015).

Mackenzie, K. (2013). "China's Debt Servicing Cost and Dat Minsky Moment", *Financial Times*, 4 June.

McKinsey & Co. (2015). *Debt and (Not Much) Deleveraging*, McKinsey Global Institute, February. Available at: www.mckinsey.com/global-themes/employment-and-growth/debt-and-not-much-deleveraging (accessed 13 March 2015).

Minsky, H. (1976). "Banking and a Fragile Financial Environment", paper prepared for the American Economic Association Meeting, Atlantic City, 16 September 1976.

Minsky, H. (1992). "Financial Instability Hypothesis", Jerome Levy Economics Institute of Bard College, Working Paper No. 74, Annandale-on-Hudson, New York.

Minsky, H. (2008 [1986]). *Stabilizing an Unstable Economy*. New York: McGraw Hill.

People's Bank of China (POBC) (2015). Survey and Statistics. Available at: www.pbc.gov.cn/eportal/fileDir/defaultCurSite/resource/cms/2015/07/2013s18.htm (accessed 14 January 2015).

Perry, E. and Welterwitz, F. (2015). "Wealth Management Products in China", *Bulletin*, Reserve Bank of Australia, June: 59–68.

Reuters (2012). "Bank of China Executive Warns of Shadow Banking Risk", article posted 12 October. Available at: www.reuters.com/article/us-china-banking-shadowloans-idUSBRE89B06D20121012 (accessed on 20 October 2012).

Sheng, A. Edelmann, C., Sheng, C. and Hu, J. (2015). *Bringing Light upon the Shadow: A Review of the Chinese Shadow Bank Sector.* Hong Kong: Fung Global Institute.

Standard Chartered (2014). "China: A Primer on Banks' Wealth Management", Standard Chartered Global Research, January 2014. Available at: https://research.standardchartered.

com/configuration/ROW%20Documents/China_%E2%80%93_A_primer_on_banks%
E2%80%99_wealth_management__07_01_14_06_18.pdf (accessed on 2 January 2015).

Tsai, K. S. (2015). "Financing Small and Medium Enterprises in China: Recent Trends
and Prospects beyond Shadow Banking", HKUST IEMS Working Paper No. 2015-24.
Available at: http://iems.ust.hk/wp-content/uploads/2015/05/IEMSWP2015-24.pdf
(accessed on 1 October 2015).

Wray, R. (2010). "What Should Banks Do? A Minskyan Analysis", Jerome Levy Economics
Institute of Bard College, Public Policy Brief No. 115, Annandale-on-Hudson, New
York.

Yao, W. (2015). "Shadow Banking with Chinese Characteristics", in A. Sheng and N. C.
Soon (Eds), *Bringing Shadow Banking into the Light: Opportunity for Financial Reform
in China*. Hong Kong: Asia Global Institute, University of Hong Kong, pp. 71–115.

Yao, W. and Hu, J. (2015). "Inherent Risks in Chinese Shadow Banking", in A. Sheng and
N. C. Soon (Eds), *Bringing Shadow Banking into the Light: Opportunity for Financial
Reform in China*. Hong Kong: Asia Global Institute, University of Hong Kong,
pp. 116–148.

Index

For further Rights, Sales and Information please contact our
representative GmbH International ...
Verlag GmbH: Kaulbachstraße 34, 80531 München, Germany